To Barry

5 Keys for Successful
Relationship

PURIFICATION
PRACTICE

1. FAITH

2. TRUTH.

3. WILL

4. HUMILITY

5. LOVE

Love
Joo Lian. Center.
x

PURIFICATION
PRACTICE

Wise & Holy Approach To Wholeness

*Blessed are the pure in heart, for they will see God.
(Matt. 5: 8)*

Spirit, Soul, and Body

JOO LIAN CARTER

To order additional copies of this book, contact:
Xlibris Corporation
0-800-644-6988
www.xlibrispublishing.co.uk
Orders@xlibrispublishing.co.uk
302983

Contents

Dedication

$\mathscr{I}$ would like to dedicate this book to serving the living God and His Son Jesus and the spread of His divine truths to serve humanity. To Ronald Carter and my two sons, Stephen Carter and Daniel Carter, who stood by me and made sacrifices through love as I spend my time away from them in solitude to write as I set out my journey of transformation.

Also to the budding spirituality of the universe and the rising genius network of energy and divine light that flows through eternal life. The truth for each man is in his own soul and spirit and discovering his own God-given destiny, believing that God has a life-changing purpose for every one of us. And so it came at last, and my time of being lead by light and seeing the light I must go forward and shine to the world.

This is respectfully dedicated by Joo Lian Carter, the author of Purification Practice, the wise and holy approach to wholeness.

Acknowledgement

I would like to express my gratitude and give my love and compassion to everyone just being alive in the universe that has inspired and supported me in their own unique way with love and made it possible for me to work and write this book. It is not an easy task, but it is a mystical challenge which I have accepted most of all through the Word of God, showering on me with love, inspiration, knowledge, truth, and wisdom that transform me to connect to my true nature or spirit in faith and obedience to God. Things happened in sacred three because I was woken at 3 a.m. for three mornings to read the book of Revelation, which was delivered to me at the door step. By the 17th December 2009 at 7 a.m., I had just finished reading this book of Revelation feeling tired and just before I settled down to sleep, I had a spiritual encounter with Jesus Christ who revealed Himself to me in a glorious bright figure. At that holy moment, I was overwhelmed with tears and peace at the same time and then I confessed and accepted Jesus into my heart and life as my saviour and Lord, who is also the key to my destiny. It was from that holy moment I became a born-again Christian, my life was renewed with purpose and felt inspired to write this book, which I believe God used me in writing it through Christ. 'When Christ, Who is our life, appears [in your heart], then you also will appear with Him in glory' (Col. 3: 4).

'It is the Spirit who gives life; the flesh profits nothing. The words that I speak to you are spirit, and they are life-giving.'
(John 6: 63)

And it shall come to pass afterward, that I will pour out my spirit upon all mankind; and your sons and your daughters shall prophesy, your old men shall dream dreams, your young men shall see visions.'
(Joel 2: 28)

My greatest pleasure, honour, privilege and aim of producing this book is to create realization and awareness so that a large number of individuals may shift into realization and become aware of themselves, to seek understanding of what they are, and who they are and live life within their own unique purpose from their true self, living in the Word of God. From that, they can connect to all the qualities and attributes of the spirit for a brighter everlasting life.

In the process of writing this book, many a time, I felt stuck with words which affected my motivation to continue my writing, every day, I pray to God for inspiration and truth to guide me with thoughts to accomplish my aims. Then the Lord showed me pages of tiny scripts rolling before my eyes, which I could not read, but the big word God on the top of the page and a lion on the top left side of the page. I acknowledged that the scripts were not clear enough to read, then I was lead to the Bible that made me realise what God was showing me. My intuitive self told me to confer my writing with the Holy Bible. Then, out of the blue, someone brought me a Holy Bible just to confirm my spiritual encounter that I had discovered reality and truth from the Word of God as the key. So do not be surprised to read many Bible quotes in this book of wise and holy approach to wholeness through step-by-step of the purification practice. All the Bible quotes in this book are from King James Bible. I write from the desire to seek the truth and God as well as from my own life experiences of forty years serving in the health care environment and from spiritual inspiration and knowledge from the Word of God. I paint those qualities that we may not possess but hope to inspire. As a Virgo star sign, my distinctive characteristic thriving to be perfect drives me to be analytical and continuously seeking for truth and perfection particularly serving the Lord and learning from each other to evolve our souls through purification practice. As in anything in life, it is the endurance of practice that leads to perfection. Jesus said, 'Enter through the narrow gate, for wide is the gate and broad is the way that leads to destruction, and there are many who go in that way. Because narrow is the gate and compressed is the way that leads to life, and there are few who find it.' (Matt. 7: 13-14).

My reward is not in the selling but in the purity of intention and serving that goes into my writing. The recognition of the value of my creative work and realization of possibilities for humanity beyond the circumstances enable me to fulfil my higher purpose of life. Perhaps it is better as it is in that I have discovered the key in the process of my work instead of at the beginning. I did not write the book to prove the proposition, but in writing this book, the truth has become apparent to me as I take my spiritual journey attuning and believing my consciousness towards the light of my soul and divine will at heart. Through my experience and inspired from that higher and finer creative energy vibration searching into the truth it has become clearer to me, until now I wonder that I did not understand long ago, that it has not always been apparent to all human beings. Surely, the revelation is the beginning of all knowledge, wisdom, truth, and righteousness in hope, faith, holiness, and being obedient to God living by His words.

This book is not just about healing the bodies. But most important and eternal is touching souls and rise to our highest potential self or spirit and being able to conceive the invisible possibilities and relationship with the universe and God. We choose to meet people, to learn lessons, and to evolve our souls because everything we do resonate around our souls and our spirit determined the life we live on the earth plane for a purpose that shapes our destiny. It is essential to have quality relationship first within ourselves and then with God and others to learn lessons to evolve our souls and spirit because happiness depends on our spiritual maturity, soul growth, faith, and holiness. My writing is the greatest contribution that I can make expressing my experience that I have evolved through searching, learning, and discovering personal, universal, and eternal truth, which is the eternal part of my spirit.

The Invisible World

I know of an invisible world
To which I wish to go
As my spirit flutters to be free
Through my brow, I hope to see

I look up to the stars
To mount the starlight afar
For I see on all around
There is one to be found

I am that which as the Creator made
I am here to live my fate
To bear me safe through Divine beam
Jesus saved me from my sin

He created us, the moon and the sun
We live to evolve and have fun
Because I can trust His love
To brighter everlasting world above

Joo Lian Carter

Knowing Your True Self, Values, Purposes and Destiny

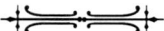

We are a combination of mind, body, soul and spirit that we cannot dismiss the interrelation and influence of anyone from the other. We are all brotherhood of man universally. Where awakening the soul successfully is enabling it to have a greater mastery over the body, in enabling it to realize its true purpose and to begin expressing itself in the natural law that it should.

Ultimately, the purpose of our journey is to restore ourselves to these universal truth, cosmic consciousness, and 'wholeness'

> *A man will always be ordinary until he is aware that he is asleep and wake up through his consciousness to know his true-self to fulfil his transcendent life purpose to evolve his soul-spirit.*
>
> *(Joo Lian Carter)*

Do we wonder where we are from, how we manifested, what we really are, and why we are here and where do we go after life on earth?

From the ray of creation, soul (essence) descends from the starry galaxy and passing through the sun and then the planetary zone enters the earth through our parents who create the environment for the reception of this soul that comes from the divine spark (spirit). Now we are all here in this dark planet, so low down in the ray of creation because each one of us has some unique qualities to become conscious of and because from the work point of view, we have something very special and very important to view our true self to begin to shine from within to fulfil our life purposes and prepare ourselves for when we leave here because there is life after life.

Everything in the physical is a reflection of the spirit but not in the form you recognize it.
To be an 'altar' of hope and pureness, seek God's grace and obey Him in holiness to inherit His nature.

(Joo Lian Carter)

Wise and Holy Approach to Wholeness

Blessed are the pure in heart, for they will see God.

(Matt. 5: 8)

*S*ometimes, the lessons and experiences that you have build in your life, somehow lacking meaning and fulfilment, you become deeply concerned and start searching for something on a far deeper and fulfilling level, till your true heart's desire may be found. This journey is not easy but effort is required to clear the false or superficial personality by consciously learning lessons, which may be a more effective way of discovering and understanding deeper meaning of compelling vision towards an important goal. Spiritual activity can improve mental, physical, emotional, and spiritual health to become whole. The key to reach the higher form of activity and to find God is to truly create an intimate relationship with God through pray or meditate in faith and obedience, focusing solely on your inner self during your spiritual journey. Each aspect of your life is connected with other aspects of your life, and the truth is your awakened life is the spirit in you. We show real love towards God when we truly worship and obey Him, leading to love those around us when we zealously obey and keep God's commandments, which is simply an expression of love.

Sin is the transgression of the law.

(1 John 3: 4)

There is still hope of purity from the changing grace available for us. We still have the chance to attain salvation, to be cleansed, and to be forgiven until we are purified with the knowledge of the truth.

'I will ask the Father, and he will give you another comforter [helper], so that he may remain with you forever; who is the Spirit of truth, which the world cannot accept, because it neither sees him, nor knows him. But you know him because he dwells with you [now], and shall be in you [soon]. I will not leave you comfortless like orphans; I will come to you' (John 14: 16-18).

The holiness of God cares for individuals like you and me. He recognises and understands our weaknesses, our sorrows, and our loneliness. Therefore, He will come back to us as spirit of truth, the Holy Spirit, for our continual holiness receiving the holiness and the godliness that the spirits impart on us. The Holy Spirit is an expression of His love, the care and his commitment. The provision of the Holy Spirit is a demonstration of Jesus' utmost concern for those who trust and respond to him.

In this present life, we are saved by grace through faith, the hope of being taught and led by the holiness of God, seeing Him, hearing Him, being delivered from sin, being cleansed, purified, perfected, brought to holiness, and then union with God, entering the kingdom through Jesus Christ.

> Behold, I stand at the door, and knock. If any man hears my voice and opens the door, I will come in to him, and will sup with him, and he with me.
>
> (Rev. 3: 20).

Jesus Christ pleading anonymously with you to open your heart and believe this to be true and to repent from sin and changing your life to holiness to receive his wisdom and Holy Spirit in response to your obedience. 'Seek first the kingdom of God, and His righteousness; and all these things will be added to you' (Matt. 6: 33). This is supposed to be the highest priority of your life more than your efforts to provide food, drink, and clothing. Stop spending your efforts on seeking things and worrying about tomorrow, instead change your mindset and attitude. Just seek God and His righteousness to be the highest priority of your life and then you will be blessed to prosper.

'Not everyone who says to me, "Lord, Lord", will enter into the kingdom of heaven; but he who does the will of my Father who is in heaven' (Matt. 7: 21). Through contentment, honour God, do what He wants you to do because you are not moving in God's timing, you lose your anointing favour and you are yourself to be blamed. Do not wait for all conditions to be favourable. Whatever God asks you to do, it is for your best interest and life saving. You may sacrifice, but it is not enough, you have to be obedient as well. You move according to God's will not yours and being flexible for Him to work on you and be blessed. 'If you confess with your mouth that Jesus is Lord, and believe in your heart that God raised him from the dead, you have been saved' (Rom. 10: 9).

For thousands of years, the mysterious universe has always been mankind quest for the truth to guide us to the right path to take in our lives. Trust God for the truth, learn how to seek Him first for who He is and not what He can do for you. You seek his face and not his hands, then He will reveal the truth to you and you will find that his hands is a lot more open for you and to guide you in your life. For your Father knows the things you need, even before you ask him. (Matt. 6: 8). Turn to Him with all your heart and soul, open your heart and mind, pray and cry out to Him, study the Bible and do what God says. He is somebody who knows everything about you and still accepts you totally the way you are and still love you like your own father.

'The natural man cannot receive the things of the spirit of God for they are foolishness to him; neither can he know them because they are spiritually discerned' (1 Cor. 2: 14). A natural man cannot believe or understand the mysteries of God. It is impossible for a natural man to become a spiritual man by reading, Bible study, seminary training, praying for understanding, or listening to other natural men talk; such only increases his fleshly knowledge, which must die to be replaced by wisdom and power from the Holy Spirit in the name of Jesus Christ. A natural man is only changed into a spiritual man by the teachings and changing grace of the spirit of God through revelation and power. Of course, God only reveals the mysteries to spiritual men but every individual is unique and has that potential within. The natural man cannot conceive the things of God and cannot perceive the depth of sin. This is why awakening to the spirit self in a natural man is essential in order to accept the things of God and to understand the concept of God's grace and the technology of salvation through faith. The natural man must be taught by revelation in that man's heart is the power of the Holy Spirit, words must be heard, and visions must be seen with clear understanding received in a man's heart.

Put on the full spiritual armour of God and fill with the Holy Spirit. Take your spiritual weapons and engage in spiritual warfare. Aim to be personally responsible and respond to God because you cannot afford to be spiritually lazy or not aware of your spiritual self. He made each one of us in His own image or nature. God's dream is part of our dreams to fulfil. The power of His Holy Spirit is our miracle worker that drives us in our lives through Jesus. When you are spiritually mature, God will challenge you with responsibility with His gift according to His will, if you are faithful according to his gift, then it becomes active within your spirit to carry out His will. God will not forsake us because He created us out of His love and light.

Discover your origin, find yourself love again, revive your roots, and be yourself. Resist the power of darkness, be wise, you can still be the guiding light of civilization. The key to your sacred self is to spend the quality, quiet time connecting with your true self in the presence of God. Make a decision to be good to people everywhere you go, this requires self-control, self-discipline, obedience, and submission to God, but remains resistant to the enemy. Stay in control in your emotion, stay in power, and put your trust in God, your obedience to him allow you to feel and act righteously.' Submit yourselves, then, to God. Resist the devil, and he will flee from you' (James 4: 7). The power to resist is in submitting. Get into a deeper attitude of being an important and a good person to live in an obedient lifestyle. It is vital you have discipline and self-control because to be obedient, you cannot do what you want to do all the time.

Every day of my life, I have to discipline my mind and my emotions. Every time somebody aggregates me, I have to discipline my thoughts, my words, and my action that I owe to myself and others. It is a constant mind-boggling task until I became accustomed to my changed attitude. Don't be weak or afraid because God is with you. Enjoy every moment of your life in God's presence and talk to Him whenever and wherever in your prayer or personal intimate counsellor. Submit yourself to God and allow Him to bless you, to work through you to give you that power to defend you from your enemy, to be somebody that He is going to be proud of. Get in line with God and be obedient to him because you love Him and Jesus. Anything that he wants you to do is for your best interest to save you a lifetime of agony and pain. Instead, soak in the presence of His peace and meditate on his word where you cannot attain in this world. 'And whatever you do in word or deed, do all in the name of the Lord Jesus, giving thanks to God the Father through him' (Col. 3: 17). A personal time with God is the most valuable time spent in true life. It is through your spiritual self that we make connection with Him in reality to feel His presence to have a valuable and true relationship. Many are going through a path of spiritual unfoldment without knowing it and still finding a path that genuinely enables us to understand life, to free ourselves from the bondage of the emotions and become independent from within as you walk the path of deep understanding of the inner mysteries of love and light in service to God through His words and the law of nature. To enter into a deep understanding of the power of God-life within, in wholeness to independently control our own life in a confusing world we live in now.

To have value in life and serve its real purpose, one requires spiritual qualities, progressing into the fullness of eternal life of here and now and after life. They are spiritual skill, spiritual purpose, and spiritual maturity. The mind coasts along in a precarious way in a steady progression until it reaches maturity. The spirit starts with steady steps and certainty. Its gains are not lost, but eternal. Values in life are spiritual skills, by resorting to them, one move from the mind to the spirit. If the whole life were easy with no pain, no struggle, no difficulties to conquer, and no obstacles to overcome, then there will be no recognition, no development, or no evolution. 'Do not labour for food that perishes but (instead labour) for the food that endures to everlasting life, which the Son of man shall give to you; for God the Father has authorized and certified him with his seal' (John 6: 27). Physical and material success does not give us true everlasting value. What truly matters is fulfilling the deepest need of a human heart, and most profound life purpose is to be loyal to the highest of our own spiritual natures, never to deny our own truth, to be faithful to ourselves, to obey our conscience, and by being reconciled to God and live His will through Jesus. Because we are dependent on the revelation of the spirit of God, it is vital that we attain our spiritual being to understand the connection with Him. He reveals to us the truth in the scriptures the natural mind cannot understand. If you have been blessed in the realm of Jesus Christ, you will know him and what is in him is in you in that glorious inheritance, you will understand the truth in the Word of God. Once you have received the Holy Spirit, it is always through Christ, you in Him, that you will never walk alone in your spiritual journey. So the culmination of grace is brought to you at the end, the revealing of Christ within you. The Kingdom, union with Christ and God, and the completion of salvation are brought to you by the grace of God, Jesus Christ, in his second appearance in the hearts of purified believers. We will see Jesus in his second coming in Glory bringing our salvation. 'To have Christ return to establish his kingdom in our hearts and rule us, for everyone who has this hope in himself, purifies him, just as he is pure' (1 John 3: 2-3).

'But now in Christ Jesus you who once were far off are made near by the blood of Christ' (Eph. 2: 13). The most precious thing in our lives is the relationship with one another and with God in Jesus Christ who unite us by His blood. The best place to be in is being in the heart of God's love and dwell in Jesus, filled with the Holy Spirit. 'As the Father has loved me, so have I loved you; therefore abide in my love' (John 15: 9). We must be spiritually conscious and realise how powerless we are against the divine power of God. The need to prepare with faith and hope spiritually for that time, Christ return is even more crucial now than ever in history. Therefore, we individuals need to be spiritually awake, alert, and spiritually clothed to face reality. From where you have been to where you are, and where you will be tomorrow, for everyday of your life, let prayer and meditation on the living God's word to lead your journey.

Prayer or meditation is more than just thinking about it. To reflect on a verse or an idea in the mind, to utter, to confess, in order to be successful we need to meditate on the word of God not to reflect but to confess the word of God and keep it on His lips. Follow that, you will succeed in everything you do that is something that every believer will appropriate divine provision and deliverance. All the promises of God can be appropriated through faith by His grace, without faith and grace, it is impossible to please Him. When we allow our spirit to express it and to radiate, it loses all things like fear and doubt because the spirit dwells in an atmosphere of confidence. The soul that needs healing is due to man's ignorance of his true relationship with himself and God. The light of the soul or the life force is a flame in the depths of our conscious love or consciousness that can never be extinguished, and it can be fanned into all consuming fire of power and mastery. If we will renew our mind, change the vibration of our energy field, and lift up our consciousness to behold the grandeur and majesty of our soul and spirit while still physically on the earth, we can enter to a higher spiritual dimension to be lived in. It's only a matter of time for our imaginary concept, the change of things will come to pass because things must move or decay and transition takes place in a blink. 'Wake up and be watchful, and strengthen the things that remain, which are ready to die; for I have not found your works perfect before God.' (Rev. 3: 2). Start living a peaceful and fear free life filled with unlimited possibilities to prosper. A withdrawal from the world for a period of solitude to seek God can be helpful to see the world more clearly as it is from the summit of your own mountain.

'Remember, therefore, what you have received and heard and hold fast and repent.' (Rev. 3: 2-3). We must embrace solitude to find that silent voice from within that will reveal to us in truth before we can achieve serenity in beatitude.

'He who overcomes, the same will be clothed in white raiment; and I will not blot his name out of the book of life' (Rev. 3: 5). 'Behold, I am coming quickly; Hold fast to what you have, so that no man takes your crown' (Rev. 3: 11).

As we are made in the likeness of God, we are potentially holy with hope to sanctify and honour all things that are of God. As individuals, you continue to expand in your demonstration and realisation process of purification, possessing holiness in your thoughts, feelings, and actions, hence, mature your spiritual life. In holiness, you feel blessed, and everyone around you in a conscious sense is affected by your blessing too. Because we are all one with each other and one with God, everything in infinity literally lies within you on many levels through telepathy. When you own your holiness, this creates a much greater Christ vibration in your aura and energy fields to bless everyone you contact and all the people you are connected with personally. Your holy consciousness is held within your aura and is felt even if you never say a word and even in your sleep. When you own your holiness, this means you are also seeing the holiness in others regardless of their level of development, for if you are not seeing it in them, then you do not truly own it within yourself. Never forget what you see in the world is really what you are thinking in yourself.

Glorious Creation

Through the fall of light and called forth the dark
We pray to God who has given us that spark
Since we exist only by virtue thought
And His will from the source, God
His glorious light in his emanation
He dissolves His own being capable of creation
He is without beginning and without end
Cosmos will continue the eternal defense
His unending love for us He has bound
It is up to us to love that was found
He absorbs darkness and purifies by the ethereal radiance
Until all darkness is enclosed to gain brilliance
We must search our inner self for that wisdom
and inspiration
We must reject all false assertion and wiring conclusion
In search of the truth for our soul's evolution
Until the veil is lifted from the divine reflection
God's light is always upon us shining from the
lamp stand
As long as we live, we will thrive to understand
Darkness cannot extinguish radiance of pure light
But can only contaminate and obscure life
By the power of God's will and determination
We materialized in the world thriving for perfection.

Joo Lian Carter

We Are Born to Be Free, to Be Born again for a Pure Purpose

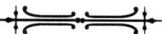

Jesus said, 'You shall love the Lord your God with all your heart, with all your soul, and with your entire mind.' (Matt. 22: 37)

*G*od created us for a purpose. Jesus came for a purpose and what is your purpose?

'To him who overcomes, I will grant to sit with me in my throne, even as I also overcame, and have sat with my Father in his throne' (Rev. 3: 21).

God and Jesus wanted to show and give us a good life and a place in heaven.

God's law, the Bible, reveals the spiritual dimension in the physical sense to govern human conduct, to make aware God's truth, and His plan for a glorious purpose for those who will accept His grace and love to enjoy the peace of true love.

I in them, and you in me, that they may be made perfect in one; and that the world may know that you have sent me, and have loved them, as you have loved me (John 17: 23). Father, I will that they also, whom you have given me, be with me where I am; that they may behold my glory, which you have given me; for you loved me before the foundation of the world' (John 17: 24).

We are beings created from God's impression, therefore, we are the chip off God, the infinite Holy Spirit, in that true form, we are all connected universally and is one. 'God is not far from every one of us. From in him we live and move our being' (Acts 17: 27-28). Because we are in the lower physical dimension sharing the same space as the higher spiritual dimension, we are not aware of this, but with our spiritual union with God and Christ consciousness we walk on earth by the light of God. The only difference is each individual has been given a mind to will freely in the flesh and also the spirit power to drive us in life to live righteously and abundantly, depending on individual's spiritual strengths and maturity to serve our purpose. The only way to salvation is by crucifying your selfish, sinful nature on the inward cross of self-denial. The problem is the material demand and the pull of the external force prevent people from thinking deeply about the purpose of their lives or understand the higher purpose for which they were created. If you are willing to seek that understanding, knowledge, and wisdom of truth, you are one dimension ahead if you are willing to humble yourself to think deeply about what you are and your true purpose. 'You present your bodies a living sacrifice, holy, acceptable to God, which is your spiritual service and worship' (Rom. 12: 1).

Each individual receives the spirit given to him or her by God according to the willingness of his or her heart. If you pay attention and obey, it results in union with God and then your heart will see and feel the power He wishes to make you like Him. We need to practice purification before we can truly worship. 'Which worship God in the spirit, and rejoice in Christ Jesus, and have no confidence in the flesh' (Phil. 3: 3).

It is for sure that no one can feel lost if you abide with the Word of God; you will come back with the testimony. What God wants to give us in our lives is His Word in our spirits.

The body is the temple where the sacred spirit dwells. Ignorance and superstition is the bondage of human mind and body. When the spiritual life matures in its expression, the divine spirit within emerges to the surface where one realises its potential to rise up to the fullness of oneness with the Holy Spirit to bask in the sunlight of spiritual truth. Everything that God does, he does with His word, His creative material and plan. 'Now to Him, who is able to do exceedingly abundantly above all that we ask or think, according to the powers in us' ((Eph. 3: 20)

'In the beginning was the Word, and the Word was with God, and the Word was God. The same was in the beginning with God. All things were made by him; and there was nothing made without him' (John 1: 1-3).

Therefore, if we get whole of the word of God, we can do the same.

Sometimes we are faced with challenges and questions, and the question why are there so many people suffering and in pain? That's why there are many who think if there is a God, why does He let people suffer? What is on His mind and what does He want from us and what does He want us to do? God does not have a problem with us; it is we who have problem with God with the mentality he gave us that we chose in our own free will to live our own way. Then we cannot blame God when we are suffering. He even sends His only son to suffer and show us the way to save us from the wrong that we chose to do.

'I know that, whatever God does, it shall be forever; nothing can be added to it, or anything taken from it; and God does it so that men should fear before him' (Eccles. 3: 14).

'And God saw everything that he had made, and behold, it was very good' (Gen. 1: 31).

It is our mentality that creates the brokenness in our human relationship with one another and spiritual relationship with God.

'In Christ Jesus you are being built together to become dwelling in which God lives by His Spirit' ((Eph. 2: 22). Very often we communicate through our minds and not through heartfelt abiding respect for each other. The failure to communicate effectively with commitment, giving attention and showing empathetic concerns and trust is one of the primary causes for broken relationship with us, to others, and with God.

We can effect changes in our personal lives through God's Word and think in His way and pray with faith to transform and enhance our personal relationship with Him. Through prayer, we can be intimate with our Father in a very special way to make a lot happen through the spirit in prayer. Sometimes having to make a decision what to do without having the knowledge to do so can be daunting. Because of that pressure, sometimes we need to decide something, and if we are not careful, we get pulled into the direction which is not really what God wants you to do. Having faith in God's will and his word to lead us to the right path is the key to the truth and reality. 'So I say to you, ask and it will be given to you; seek and you will find; knock and it will be open to you; for everyone who asks receives and he who seeks finds and to him who knocks it will be opened' (Luke 11: 9-10). 'I love those who love me, and those who seek me diligently will find me.' (Prov. 8: 17). God always give us the next step to lead us to the right path to serve his will and for your purpose to reach your destiny. If we pray to God for the strength that we need, the thoughts to guide us, his hands to sustain us, and His blessing upon us, together we will reach our destiny.

'And do not be conformed to this world; but be transformed by the renewing of your mind, that you may prove what is the good, acceptable, and perfect will of God' (Rom. 12: 2).

If you don't like what you see and how you feel, change the way of your thinking and mature your spiritual life until you are full, then you are not in need of anything in this world to make you whole. Success is not about how old you are and how much you have it is the condition of your spirit. God says to Abraham; 'for all the land that you see I will give to you and to your descendants forever' (Gen. 13: 15). The question is what can you see? What you can see with your spiritual eye is all yours. It is through changing your way of thinking and transforming to live the Word of God that you will live in truth and fulfil your purpose. When we live in two worlds, and we stand in direct conflict with each other, we cannot escape the pull of the world. Who has the greatest pull on you, your flesh or your spirit? I have to face that question every day of my life. It would be wise to withdraw from the world to seek the heavenly Kingdom of God and His righteousness as our highest priority in life. We need to have the courage to obey the word of God and what He wants not what we want. We cannot be a healthy believer unless we receive from the Holy Spirit.

Do we choose, what we want in our own will in flesh or allow the Holy Spirit to lead us to the truth and reality?

'Epaphras, a servant of Christ who is one of you, salutes you, always striving fervently for you in prayers that you may stand perfect and complete in all the will of God' (Col. 4: 12).

For anyone who wants to know what they were created for, what their purpose for, any who want to know that they are forgiven, or to have a second chance from the beginning, Jesus is our rainbow bridge. 'If you remain in my word, you are really my disciples and you will know the truth and the truth will set you free.' (John 8: 31-32).

We must be born again into Christ consciousness that simplicity and sanctity and cultivate an awareness of our spiritual needs, and Jesus will show us the secret sins in our hearts and with our obedience to his commands, he will free us from our sins, one at a time and lead us to freedom from our sins, the truth and reality until finally we are pure and fit for union with him in the Kingdom of God.

In order to receive the indwelling Christ in your life, you must receive the Holy Spirit and feel the power of spirit before you can have the power and will to do the work. You will know Christ because he dwells in you to transform you to change your life to realise your highest potential in Christ and you in him. 'The Lord is near to those who have a broken heart, and saves such as have a contrite spirit' (Ps. 34: 18).

'For then there will be great tribulation, such as has not been from the beginning of the world until now, no, and never will be' (Matt. 24: 21).

The body, the soul, and the spirit are one; for they are most intimately bonded and when one suffers the other sympathizes and sents a wishing well to provide its needs. (Joo Lian Carter)

My Life Journey

In my journey, I hope to go far
With my spirit, I shine like a star
In my mind, I think of possibilities
In my life, I take personal responsibilities

With my tears, I cleansed like rain
In my sorrow, I bear the pain
With my happiness, I share with gratitude
In my peace, I stay in solitude

In my world, I do my best to obey Thee
With my faith I ask for Your Grace to be
In my thoughts, I search for your wisdom
In my heart, I purify my emotions

In my prayer, you are my counsellor
In my dreams, you show me all the wonders
Every day I choose your word to walk my path
I surrender to you my Lord, with all my soul and
with all my heart.

Joo Lian Carter

My Life Programs and Aims

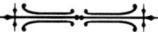

Start by being true to ourselves so that we perceive what is missing in order to sanctify from within and reach out for that finer vibration of upliftment rather than struggling to get what we want from without. (Joo Lian Carter)

'Now to Him, who is able to do exceedingly abundantly above all that we ask or think, according to the powers in us' (Eph. 3: 20).

'You will show me the path of life; in your presence is fullness of joy at your right hand is pleasures forevermore' (Ps. 16: 11).

Until I have defined my own aims for myself, I will not be able to begin to do anything. It is not possible to do anything without having an aim for a specific purpose.

My aim in writing this book is to help and inspire people with knowledge and understanding. I hope the creativity of this book can bring therapeutic healing effect and reality during their conscious transformation spiritually, mentally, physically, and emotionally.

My life programs and plans

First, how do I see myself?

I am awakening to my spirit self and on my journey of spiritual transformation starting from the valley of realisation, scaling the mountain. My spiritual transformation has led me to be aware of my higher self to think from my heart, open doors to change, to understand, and to identify what I am exploring in the invisible world of God, seeking

His truth, and His word is the truth and the way. Like a compass, the Bible always points to us the right direction in our journey of discovery, it shows us the world, our purpose in it, painted by our passions, our struggles, and our beliefs, and the journey brings us face-to-face with ourselves, our relationships, and our God. Through faith and knowing my true purpose, I activate my God-given vision, and driven by my true passion into the invisible world of reality, using my imagination, and supernatural powers to manifest things, which seems impossible, possible.

To spend the rest of my life caring, healing, and inspiring people to regain back their powers from experiences that drain the life force from their body, soul, and sprit. This is one of the reasons for writing this book to honour one another with inspiration from the divine will and the desire to be of service to others and have faith in God to serve His purpose.

Discovering my true identity

Who and what am I, what is my purpose here, my value and my destiny?

To find out what I am, I focus on identifying my substance, that is, my body which occupies space, my mind which thinks, and my spirit that gives me life, together it forms a single unique individual, that is what I am.

I am body, mind, soul and spirit, that make up the duality-in-unity of the two worlds. Yet we cannot comprehend until we reach maturity of our whole divine being, like a luminous pearl revealing its pure form in true colours after all the shackles has slowly fallen away. We need to purify and to bring into maturity our highest potential being to connect to the Divine. Human being exists for the soul purpose. That is the characteristic property being preserved and attained through human experiences of pure consciousness that are ascribed to the purpose of the yearning for the evolving soul and spirit in reality to my God-given destiny. There must be purity and holiness to worship God, to receive the anointing and abides in my heart with his counsel to walk my journey of eternity.

What do I want in life, and all that I can desire and see with my uplifted vision?

'The eyes of the LORD are upon the righteous and his ears are open to their cry' (Ps. 34: 15).

Feeling down, soaked in my own valley, my heart yearns for the truth and wisdom in the process of my writing; I prayed to God and asked Him, 'God what and who am I? What is my purpose here?' Then he showed me the Bible, I realised that I have not been obedient to Him, so I picked up the Bible, which was neglected and sitting in a corner of a bookshelf, waiting to reveal to me His truth and my truth, to answer my questions.

It came to my conclusion that the only way is being in obedience to Him and I started to read through the Bible to seek Him for an honest answer in detail in my own time with all my mind, all my heart, and all my soul and all my strength. Finally, after reading and understanding the wisdom of God's Word, I discovered that it is only in obedience to God's Word in my heart that I can please Him and receive his life-changing grace. So I decided to live God's word that he promised for my purpose to accomplish the common goal and that is his great plan and my destiny, just by being obedient and humble and repent for my sins to accept Jesus into my heart to have faith and let God lead me in the name of Jesus and Holy Spirit that I am born again to a new level, with new vision, living the Word of God for the divine purpose.

'For this reason we do not lose heart; for though our outward man is perishing, the inward man is renewed day by day' (2 Cor. 4: 16).

Even though I fear Him, I pray every day and talk to him, to create an intimate relationship to know and to hear His word and to do His word wisely. Finally, I feel from my heart and soul that my questions have been answered with conviction. Favour comes from fear of the Lord through obedience knowing and understanding His word and doing it. God's plan is my purpose, by living and doing His word through faith and love and obedience is what and who I become and that is my God-given destiny.

Now having faith in God, I reconciled fully to God; I pray, listen in silence, and humility for his voice, hears his word spoken from in my heart, with obedience, live in His presence of fullness peace and joy.

'To whom God would make known what are the riches of the glory of this mystery in the Gentiles; which is Christ in you, the hope of glory' (Col. 1: 26).

'And God said, "Let us make man in our image, after our likeness, and let them have dominion over the fish of the sea, and over the birds of the air, and over the beasts, and over all the earth, and over every creeping thing that creeps upon the earth." So God created man in his own image, in the image of God he created him; male and female he created them' (Gen.1: 26-27).

'If any man thirsts, let him come to me, and drink. He who believes on me, as the scripture has said, out of his heart will flow rivers of living water' (John 7: 37-38).

Sometimes, we don't even know how significant we are; we pray for something in our lives, but God's answer is simply going to be significant. He has more in mind for us than we have in mind about ourselves. We cannot judge life by things that simply appear to be insignificant. When God has a will and plan for every one of us, that in itself makes your life valuable and significant. 'For in the righteousness of God is revealed from faith to faith; as it is written, the just shall live by faith' (Rom. 1: 17).

A person's value is not determined by their environment. Therefore, we cannot judge or categorise a person by their surroundings and their appearance, what they have, what they do, and what appears insignificant. In the eyes of the beholder, we must understand a person of what he is his value and his purpose in life, the way God loves us unconditionally and sees every person is significant to Him. He often gives His greatest understanding to ordinary people, who are in lower position in life. Sometimes we miss life's greatest opportunity because we don't listen or because we don't expect it. Learn how to listen to God, anticipate what He is showing you, for your success in life because He is significantly walking in your life through the Holy Spirit. What you have asked for you will receive because in the Bible, he said that He will not leave or forsake us.

Let your conduct be without covetousness; be content with those things you have; for he has said, I will never leave you, nor forsake you' (Heb. 13: 5).

The Three Relationships
We Owe To Ourselves

'*If* you send forth your spirit, they are created; and you make the face of the ground new' (Ps. 104: 30).

'Since we keep our eyes, not on the things seen, but on the things unseen; for the thing seen is temporary; but the things unseen are everlasting' (2 Cor. 4: 18).

A human being is related to three things—the body, the outer world, and the invisible world, which is the true-self within, about which we practically are not aware or have no knowledge at all.

Our first definite relationship in our lives is with our own body because the survival instinct drives us to pay more attention to the body welfare in order to survive as a human being.

The second relationship is our lives with the outer world that provides resources to fuel our bodies and purposes.

The third true essential relationship is thy true eternal self (spirit), which dwells in the invisible world, the purpose deep within us that which is the purpose why we exist so that we can create that intimate relationships not only to ourselves and also with God to have faith and walk with Him in obedience, to establish all relationships in the righteousness of God.

'Now we received, not the spirit of the world, but the spirit which is from God, that we might know the things that have been kindly given us by God, except the spirit of God' (1 Cor. 2: 12).

We are not always awake to these three relationships at the same time all the time, but if we focus essentially from within and take control from that well-acquainted higher self (spirit) wisely, it will provide a sound foundation for our body and relationship with anything or anyone in the visible and invisible world.

A strong willed person can also come across being stubborn and controlling and can be hard on oneself and others because he is ruled by the mind and the external influences rather than by the heart and spirit self. To change that, is a challenge but can be done. In reality, the mind is a perfect gift with a free will to connect with an open heart or anything. Through this unity, thoughts are processed from the heart into conscious understanding with purposeful deep feelings, whereby is produced compassionate and considerate actions. This unity also creates peace, joy, clearer thoughts, and developed insight for a balanced well-being and allows the true self to shine with love and light from within.

> *It is the spirit that resides in the heart that rules the inner world and reflects all conscious actions like a rainbow bridge to unite the visible and invisible world of God. (Joo Lian Carter)*

First of all, I have asked myself, and may I ask you the same questions? Are we too busy to spend time for ourselves while catching up with the world we live in, the never-ending progressing technology, all the things we desire, who we want to be, and how to be successful. But are we aware first of all what we are, where we came from, and what is our soul purpose being here and what happen when we leave here and is there life after life?

At some point of our lives, we have to purposely stop to think truly and start to question ourselves in order to realise and seek that transcendent truth first before others and accept personal responsibility, accountability, and conviction. Be kind to our true self and take time to presently love one another. Allow our dreams, hopes, and faith to become our reality and bring forth a new level of angelic living. Through the conscious thought, it rises from an empathetic, pure and aspiring heart which is divine thought so powerful that it can reverse negative to positive, darkness to light to heal miraculously.

'For God so loved the world (every man) that he gave his only begotten Son [to every man, so that whoever believes in [depends on, trusts, obeys him shall not perish, but have eternal life' (John 3: 16).

Therefore, we must seek to understand this eternal truth. It is from our spiritual wakening that we become whole and more conscious in our approach within us to have better knowledge, wisdom and understanding to appreciate the outer things of life. We must realise that we reach God through the heart and not through the mind. Therefore, we open our hearts to love to become more loving, wiser, and purer in our hearts and lives in the power of God in the name of Jesus. It is from within that we connect to our true selves that aspires us to love, appreciate, and enjoy the beauty of Mother Earth, universe, and the creator in a natural way. In this way, we will continuously harvest abundant health and wealth for the body and spirit. Being in harmony within ourselves, with each other, with all living things, and nature, we become attuned to the infinite and more aware of God and see Him in all creation.

> *The capacity for joy and true affinity with the Divine is accentuated in light radiance that creates a personal label and be known by the colour that is able to emit. (Joo Lian Carter)*

My Sanctuary

At sunrise, I ascended with camera in my hand.
Enjoying richer flowers grow here in my land
The light touch my skin with a warm feeling
I walk slowly up the mountain side singing

Such lovely blossoms, pink, golden, and scarlet
met my eyes.
I gazed upon the gardens surrounded by bird of
paradise.
The air is fragrant and my mind is fresh
The grass like velvet to the tread

On a bright lovely morning
The birds everywhere are singing
The sunbeams filtered through the dust
Bringing joy and light as my day starts

Making fire with coconut husk
Smoking cobra from dawn to dusk
Above, the wondrous swifts flying
Looking for food to feed their siblings

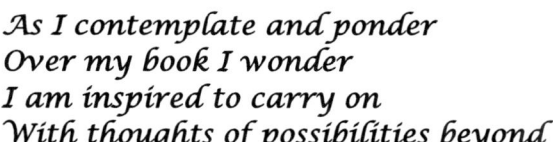

As I contemplate and ponder
Over my book I wonder
I am inspired to carry on
With thoughts of possibilities beyond

Eo, the buffalo whom I am very fond
Wonders into the muddy pond
There he submerge his rocky body
Looking cool rested and muddy

Glittering crystal streams do glide
To comfort pilgrims by the highway side
The meadows green beside their fragrant smell
Yield dainties for them and he that can tell

What pleasant fruit, leaves, and flowers these
trees do yield
Will soon sell all the harvest from this field
Thank you God for thy Divine creation
To sustain me with your blessing of sound foundation

Joo Lian Carter

Introduction and My Life's Mission

*J*oo Lian is my name, and in Chinese, Ziu Lian means 'purification practice'. It encompasses all spiritual, pure energy, and light practices and so it represents the totality of the spiritual journey. I am aware that there is something higher and brighter to live a true and pure or healthy life eternally. I believe that I am individualised spiritual substance from the pure cosmic energy which is the spirit of God in perfection (wholeness). My mission is to attain pureness in the heart and soul over mind, over matter through purification practice.

Purification practice transforms spiritually to attain pureness to evolve my soul, to grow spiritually, mentally, and physically by allowing love and light into me and live my life in reality not to be controlled by the mechanical world of darkness, fear, and negativity.

Do we know who we are and who God is? God is the soul of my soul, and he gives me unconditional love, light, and free will and the strength to find God and return to Him with my soul the same condition to His as One (the pure light). This is my aim in life, to attain that final beatitude which can be attained by faith, constant meditation, and prayer with a heart that is rendered pure and steady through love, light, forgiveness, and selfless service. To attune with the higher level in comparison to what is above me I have to consciously feel I am nothing and be pure in my emotional life in proportion as I feel my own nothingness, humility, and helplessness. Only through real emotions can we transmit higher energy because real emotion requires an absolutely pure and true emotional feeling, otherwise, it cannot reach its goal. So I have to purify myself from the self in my emotional life, which means that I must develop emotionally and eliminate the false emotions based on vanity and pride. Developing from a lower level to a higher level is similar to a vast difference as between a seed and the purity of a white flower. It is not that easy because I know I will have to give up the material or world of vanity, working from my inner world to attain my highest potential and become the flower that bear fruit and always be true to its seed.

I am here for my soul purpose and am one with all things with a principle of living. It is to live by the heavenly eye and the heavenly ear and the discernment of the pattern of things, seeing rather than calculating, allowing myself to be led by trusting, love, and compassion. There is no calculation in the pattern of spirit realm, but this world is running on calculation dominated by machines, which is the law of the earth and are being controlled by our false personality and not realising our true higher selves. My aim is to become conscious to purify or to work to change my life by filling my mind and say yes to the invisible higher influences.

I was born in Taiping, a little town in Malaysia, in 1951. I was brought up as a Buddhist in a large Chinese family and was educated in English Catholic convent school, so my belief is very much influenced by the truth of Christianity because the truth sets me free.

I love my culture in the sense of sharing and caring for one another living in a community fashion, which I hope the new world to be. I was raised and very much influenced in my younger years by my Ah Ma (Granny) who was an osteopath and a homeopathic healer. My sisters and I used to have fun exploring the forest full of plants and home-grown food that nature provides from the divine Creator. When we work in harmony with nature, we reap the results. Nature can be profligate in the abundance it has to offer to those who will work in harmony with it. Whenever we try to exploit nature for the wrong purposes for our own will, we are attempting to interfere with the infinite processes of creation. The result must be disastrous for us. Nature will always continue to fulfill its ordained purpose.

Part of this work is through my granny's inspiration and guidance in the past and present. My grandmother is a much-evolved soul and was a very wise and inspiring lady. In the past, I was sent out to hunt and to collect roots and plants for Granny to knock up her concoction of herbal ointment for massage as well as for healing wounds that showed effective results on my own wounds. I also discovered that the hidden gifts of nature which is a revolution in healing with energy, plants, and flowers or nature as a whole. The profound results inspired me to be a naturalist as well as to write this book.

There was a time when I was a very narrow provincial, but happily the circumstances of my life made it necessary that I should go to a very distant part of the country, and I early found out what a very limited acquaintance I had with the health service.

I worked in a general practitioner's surgery as a drug dispenser for two years prior to coming to UK.

I immigrated to UK at the age of nineteen years. I pursued my career in UK as a nurse in general medicine, surgery, psychiatry, midwifery, woman's health, and conventional medicine promotion for a total of forty years in the health care environment. I was married for thirty-three years and have two beautiful loving sons and a daughter in-law.

Following my service to others in the physical, mental, and spiritual realm, I maintain my well-being and healing in a holistic, preventative, and holy approach.

In my forty years of working as a health professional, I have experienced various forms of services to humanity from delivering babies into this world, nursing patients, laying deceased body ready for the next world as part of my service. My forty years career in the health service has inspired me and taught me a lot in life. I had a life filled with adventure and heartaches, but never with regrets or resentments in my learning and growing experiences physically, mentally, emotionally, and spiritually.

Having survived my confrontation with my illness, I transcended that darkness and decided to spend the rest of my life continuing to care, heal, and inspire people to regain back their power from challenging experiences that drain the life force from their body.

This is one of the reasons for writing this book to honour one another with inspiration from the divine will and the desire to be of service to others. In meditated silence, in solitude, in harmony, and in love, my soul unfolds all the time as I write. Though it may be slow, it is sure and certain.

The divine blessing that is within me, I unfold and evolve, and I am able to express more and more of its divinity. Truths do not change, but our minds change, but truth is constant because it is based upon knowledge and wisdom that comes from the divine and His word. He is the centre and the source of all inspiration so that with His blessings, we can move forward with new strength, with new hope, with new vision, and with new purpose in this new age to purify and raise our souls.

In 2008, when I dwelt in solitude oppressed with sorrow, in stillness I searched my heart and pondered in my thoughts. I prayed for strength and guidance to show me a shorter road by which I may reach my goal more quickly for a purer and brighter future.

Next, I realised that I have to go through a period of deep spiritual reflection, and when the time is right, I will act on my intuitive guidance, experience, knowledge, and wisdom to reach my highest and purest potential. My spiritual journey had gained me independence from my past and from my fears of the future, and a deep faith in myself and God. We are all born into this world on a pilgrimage to learn and care from each other and for the Mother Earth we live in. It is necessary to shed the fears that block us from appreciating the beauty and quality in our lives, and to be in a place of healing, self-acceptance, and realisation. This inspired me to discipline myself to visit my own sanctuary that is my second home. Daily, I am blessed by nature and peace in the privacy of my own prayers and meditation.

I am also a naturist, living life, appreciating the nature and our being that divine has given us unconditionally. Taking pleasure in my physical life is as much as my spiritual goal as achieving a healthy physical body. Most of the time intuitively making choices of how to live and of acting out of faith, trust, love, and follow the will of the divine.

As I am pursuing my spiritual path of true self-awareness during which my inner self-transformation takes place, I have set for myself an arduous journey, and there is no turning back like scaling the mountain towards the divine light to attain mountaintop consciousness. It is seen as the powerful diversity that stimulates my thought and from the non-physical perspective. I enjoy that diversity because everything appears clearer with a bigger picture when I view from the summit of my mountain.

As I progress in my spiritual journey, my purpose is being concerned with the new world and upward journey. With the end of the time, our purification or corrections that need to be met within our polarity consciousness in order to move to a higher level of awareness is achieved. To go on, this simply had to be accomplished and completed. For whenever we act from the cause and effect, we create more karma, but it would last long enough for us to complete our work from polarity into oneness. Therefore, one has to become nothingness to unite into oneness, which is the balancing of nature between the inner and outer worlds in harmony and mark the end of a long cycle and the beginning of a new world of reality. This united consciousness to move and to open up the channel towards the light consciousness is to bring heaven to earth.

Some years ago, I thought to myself that life is too short to wait and never too late to learn and search for the truth, so I became more open to receiving guidance and insight through my dreams and my spiritual reality.

As I become more conscious, letting go of how I thought my life should be and embrace the life that is trying to work its way into my inner awareness of my spiritual journey a process of self-discovery started happening. My spirit showed me not only the outer world, but it also showed me the mysterious inner world of purpose and reality. Living by my passion, my struggle, and my beliefs, this journey brings me face-to-face to my true self in faith and my relationship with God.

The importance and purpose of my true expression in my writing is to demonstrate my physical, mental, and spiritual development and my self-healing journey and discovery that I encountered be shared with others so that they too could benefit and be inspired to become more conscious of the energy within us and begin to care for ourselves physically, mentally, emotionally, and spiritually step by step in a holy approach.

My spiritual attainment is essential to enhance my physical, psychological, and emotional well-being because it is only through this reality I open myself to that higher energy to sustain my personal empowerment, my spiritual strength, and power through the Word of God.

If individuals were responsible for our own well-being, they would not become dependent and, therefore, be a burden upon society. Society would also not become a draining force upon the environment. Through conscious knowledge of our needs and our requirements, we could balance ourselves—organizing the body system to return to its natural equilibrium. By knowing the forces and the conditions within and the environment we live in, we could achieve the ways to restoring the balance. Also by accepting some of the holistic approach techniques, we will have made a beginning in the journey of self-development and healing. Holistic medicine and energy healing might be the gradual shift from reductionism to holism for the new age.

Subtle energy healing methods represent new ways of dealing with illnesses. As individuals, we are all healers within our own rights. Practitioners of subtle energy medicine attempt to correct dysfunction in the human organism by manipulating invisible yet integral levels of human structure and function.

One day, as I was standing on top of the mountain of the land where I live, which is also my spiritual retreat, I was inspired by the natural beauty and the fine vibration of this magical place. As I was enjoying a well-earned rest and peace, a long flock of swift birds fluttered over the lush fields, enchanted with hibiscus flowers, bird of paradise plants, pure white gardenias with a scent from heaven, and everywhere I looked up and beside me was the tree of life (the coconut trees). The sky hung low full of sunshine—an atmosphere of conscious reality, solitude, timelessness, and peace, which connect the earth with a three-hundred-and-sixty-degrees view of mountains, sea, nature, and to top it all, stands the lively beautiful majestic Mount Myon oozing and providing the entire mineral in the ground for healthy growth. The sight and smell of the mountains and sea affected me like nothing else on earth. In some of us, they aroused excessive spiritual energy. I remember one exquisite sunset, one of those superlative sunsets that burn themselves into the consciousness with a joy akin to pain and of which only a few are allotted to each human life. I stood watching the sinking sun over the mountains as the shadow of night crept slowly up the hillside. The sky took on an opal light in which were merged and transcended all the colours of the day. Every pinnacle and rock was lit up against the sky, guardians of that merciful green life from which we spring and to which we return. My friend, the buffalo, my daily messenger from the highest pastures, stood beside me as I pondered. 'Beautiful Hacienda,' I said, 'and in this, I have wished all my life.'

There as I gazed, pondered, contemplated, and meditated everything I knew in the past and present, every bit of experience and observation that has contributed to my levels of what I am, my purpose and my vision has confirmed me in the conviction that the real wisdom of human life is compounded out of the experiences of ordinary individuals and the law of nature. By embracing solitude, I gain serenity and balance in wholeness, which enables me to have greater control over my life, withdrawing the outer desires of life and focusing on the inner life and while pursuing the inner life, I question myself, 'Is desire the source of suffering?'

My answer is if one desires to serve the flesh for the wrong reason and the material world without a true purpose one becomes a victim in bondage to slavery, suffering, ignorance, and sin that will hurt like hell.

The one word that best describes desire is to desire with obedience. For it is only in obedience to the voice of the Word of God in our hearts that we can please God and receive his life-changing grace.

Desire depends on what drives me to make a true purposeful choice to develop my passion to serve my true higher potential and the truth. Usually, the truth comes from the invisible finer vibration from the higher dimensions, and if I progress spiritually with enthusiasm, imagine the impossible as possible, believing and trusting the Creator in faith; to reveal to me the truth and His will to accomplish my God-given destiny. No one is more passionate than God who created us out of His unconditional love for us. His Almighty plan for us is so unique that he created the end before the beginning. The end is heaven on earth if we inherit His eternal life. So I started thinking from the end, my destiny, and then planned forward to act with purpose, living my life that can lead me to the eternal truth by being obedient and what the truth reveals to me with conviction. As I put my trust and my faith accepting Jesus Christ and the Father in revelation, I am a born-again Christian saved by Grace that Jesus paid for us and lived the word of God in faith and in truth, filled with the Holy Spirit. We know that all things work together for good to those who love God and to those who are the called according to His purpose. His omnipotent power overcome us that we have to depend on Him to live our lives in obedience, and I am sure that His hope is that we choose Him through Jesus, who can control everything and anything, who can heal, rid a man of sin, who can change a selfish, profane, evil man to become holy and pure.

What Caused Me to Embark on My Mission?

1. My spiritual needs to accomplish my spiritual purpose, spiritual evolution, and destiny.
2. To attain wholeness, physically, mentally, emotionally, and most important spiritually.
3. Communion with God and to serve Him is to serve humanity. By expressing that beauty of His love and spreading spiritual light into the world as an act of grace all in itself.
4. Wake up call to express my feelings and seek knowledge, wisdom, and truth in order to sustain myself from challenging life situations.
5. To attain self-perfection and maintaining my true nature through purification practice.
6. To seek the truth within me not that which I have been conditioned by others to perceive.
7. To be saved and sanctified for eternal life.

The goal of my individual healing journey is to allow my intuition (third eye), spiritual connection with God, Christ, and faith in the divine will to become my dominant sources of power. I believe that my highest intuition provides the answer. As I become more intuitive and more sensitive to my own best path of accomplishment, my progress will speed up in relative terms, and I will move more quickly towards the spiritual ideal at every level. I wanted to feel, know, and be the truth, and always believe that if I recognise my true self and my true soul, my eternal spirit, which is the direct expression of God as me, will allow my consciousness to attribute my will to determine my demonstrations. As soon as I become aware and enter my inner world, from a sense of my spiritual identity, my whole world begins to change. I discovered and understood that the secret formula for health, wealth, and happiness is to love the true spiritual nature of my being connected to God Christ energy. This inspired me to write a book about purification practice which is my best domain of inspired writing and creativity towards the area of my evolving soul or spirit within to be the life and health of my body. If we are to live the vision that we share and care in society, all of us must be willing to look into our hearts and rid our minds of the fear that keeps us separated. We must re-educate ourselves to the urgency of what we must do to save our souls.

Many times, I talked from another place inside that I know is my higher self which is the identity of oneness, the super consciousness of my individualised being and begin to live. Practicing meditation as my key for opening the doors of mysteries to my mind, connecting to my heart, and in that state, I abstract myself and withdraw myself from all outside objects; in that subjective mood, I am immersed in the ocean of spiritual life and can unfold the secrets of things in themselves.

In reality, life is full of mysteries and invisible possibilities. I never know what to expect, but I belief if only we are aware of that cosmic consciousness and faith every difficult situation can change connecting to the supreme power of divine grace of love and light that can dissolve darkness.

All other pleasures are not worth the pain through pure love that can heal. (Joo Lian Carter)

I know that the spread of knowledge, the awakening of the soul, and the appreciation of spiritual realities, all these I must accomplish for myself, before I can achieve my mount of transformation. Self-realisation must be earned through struggle and toil for only by these means does my soul come into its own.

The future and the future of my descendants are affected by what I do now. Service is my life mission. I have committed my life to serve humanity. For this purpose, I transform my consciousness and build myself step by step in a vertical spiral manner to reach the divine light and develop higher insight (inner evolution) and transform my spiritual journey. Be in harmony with higher wisdom and in touch with my heart and soul through soul communication. By practicing soul communication, I gain virtues, increase my soul's standing and bringing unconditional love and light to my soul's journey and to humanity. By understanding my soul's desires and purpose, my life's journey is to offer good service, including unconditional love, compassion, kindness, forgiveness, integrity, generosity, care, and more with an open mind, heart, and soul.

Soul communication is vital for my spiritual wisdom and for understanding my spiritual journey. My short physical life has the desire to learn and to serve my eternal spiritual journey, progressing to uplift my soul's spiritual standing. Staying in command with my spirit, feeling as I have been conditioned to feel and to shrug off disappointments or misfortunes or even pain because I feel the sense of proportion and never get bogged down to achieve purely personal considerations is inconceivable. I try to see well beyond myself; hence, I am free from fear and well adjusted to be on good terms with time. I try not to allow myself to be ruled and torn, looking for happiness outside rather than within which is peace of mind, a sense of balance, a sense of belonging, and the ability to live with myself and with others.

Through self-knowledge and being analytical, I try to free myself from anxiety by practicing concentration, relaxation exercises, and deep meditation as my thoughts learn to flow where I direct them; I gained a deep awareness of who I am. Without becoming detached, I will, nevertheless, learn to detach myself from my surroundings enough to no longer feel constantly and closely identified with everything that happens around me. I did this for the simple reason that I will no longer have the same need to lean and to meet the world on my own terms but on a basis of spiritual maturity and independence.

Above all is getting the very best out of myself so that my mind becomes my willing servant. Becoming adept at the internal process of self-inquiry and symbolic insight is a vital spiritual task that leads to the growth of faith in me. My intuitive ability helps me to understand the emotional, the psychological, and the spiritual energy that lay the roots of my illnesses.

My Medical Case Study I

'It is spirit that is life-giving.' (John 6: 63)

In 2005, I discovered a palpable lump in my right breast, about 1 centimetres in size. I was very concerned and worried that it could be malignant. I arranged an appointment to see my doctor. She examined and referred me to a specialist consultant for a conclusive diagnosis, whereby I was sent for an ultrasound scan and a biopsy. Following the biopsy result, I went back to see my specialist consultant, and he said that the biopsy result was not fully conclusive and the lump was still present. A decision was made for me to be admitted to hospital for a right lumpectomy possibly mastectomy in case of malignancy.

A few weeks later, I was admitted to a female surgical ward for surgical operation. While being prepared for the operating theatre, I prayed, and deep thoughts went through my mind and heart and felt emotions that made me think and act spontaneously not to go through the operation and prayed to God that the lump will disappear. Then I decided not to sign the consent form and told the doctor and the nurse that I was ready to go home, refusing the operation. I continued to pray and have faith within myself that the lump will disappear, and I will be healed. After a month, thank God, the lump has disappeared, and I felt blessed. 'But he was wounded for our transgressions, he was bruised for our iniquities; the chastisement [needed] for our peace was upon him; and with his stripes we are healed.'(Isa. 53: 5).

My Medical Case Study 2

*O*n 20 April 2009, I was on duty as a medical representative, communicating to a general practitioner who also noticed the lump in my neck while talking to her. The doctor felt the lump and said that it is possibly a thyroid problem and advised me to see my own doctor who sent me for an ultrasound scan and thyroid function test. My thyroxin level was very low 8.7 p mol/l and the thyroxin-stimulating hormone was 1.33 mu/l in June 2009. The result of the ultrasound scan confirmed colloid goitre, a palpable lump in my neck about 3.8 cm. I was referred to a surgeon, and he said to me that the goitre will get bigger, and I have to be treated with thyroxin for life and arranged for me to have my right thyroid removed (thyroidectomy). I turned down two surgical appointments and was adamant that the lump will disappear through my spiritual faith in God that He will continue to bless me.

As soon as I realised that the thyroid gland is associated with the throat chakra, I focused my energy on the essence of the throat chakra (fifth chakra) in faith. Discovering a lump in my dysfunction thyroid in my neck lead me to the faith healing that I will not have conventional healing by surgical removal of my thyroid; instead, I had a faithful contract with the divine will to heal me. My faith is the assurance of things I hoped for, the conviction of things which do not appear or be seen, and God's grace is the possibility or miracle. In faith, I prayed, meditated every day, and aligned my energy flow connecting to the seven chakras, focusing more on my throat chakra, intuitive chakra (third eye), and crown chakra I received power from the light divine to heal my dysfunction thyroid. Time went on following my two surgical appointments, and I was commenced on thyroxin medication to take for life which I only took for two months. By February 2010, the cyst was no longer palpable and decreased in size and the size of my right thyroid also reduced significantly. On 10 October 2011, I had another ultrasound and biopsy taken for a final check up. Evidently, my consultant said that the biopsy result was normal and showed a significant reduction in size to 2.5 cm, which is a normal size of a thyroid gland. Those final results were concluded by my consultant, and he said to me during my last consultation, 'You have healed yourself.' I agreed and thanked God that it is by faith in God that I am healed. Jesus said to the woman, who touched his clothes, 'Daughter, your faith has made you whole; go in peace and be well of your affliction.' (Mark 5: 34).

'It is by faith I understand that the universe was formed at God's command, so that what is seen was not made out of what was visible' (Heb. 11: 3).

Connecting to the seven chakras (and the crown chakra), which represent my connection to the transcendent dimension of life, intuitive consciousness, I evaluate my energy and my connection with God's will and my faith and through will power being healed spiritually brought me back to balance. While my energy system is animated by my spirit, my seventh chakra is directly aligned to seek an intimate relationship with the divine which is the chakra of prayer. The energy I amass through kind thoughts and actions and through acts of faith, prayer, and meditation enable me to gain an intensity of my inner awareness and faith healing process. I realised that the less I hold on to the physical world, the more I position myself to access consciously the energy of my crown chakra that motivates me to seek an intimate connection to the divine in everything I do.

On 23 June 2010, I climbed up a bench to remove a light bulb which was far beyond my reach. I stumbled and fell off the bench landed on my right foot with a jerk and accompanied with a hard blow from the wall and sustained a right side back injury. I felt tremendous pain sitting or standing, following the incident and continued experiencing acute back pain radiating down to my buttocks when I move, causing me a lot of distress and immobility. I decided to focus on the energy flow and position myself in the meditative yoga state to be healed from the power of faith and will. For a week, I continued this form of energy healing process to ease the pain and the stiffness. That which caused me a lot of distress gradually disappeared totally within a week. This made me more convinced that when the energy power flows, it performs certain remarkable phenomena and when conditions are harmonious it allows the spiritual, psychic, etheric, and astral laws to be brought into operation to perform miracles or faith healing. Because of what I experienced, I became aware of my responsibility to be available to serve those who come to me for advice, healing, and light in their darkness. Also through my spiritual experience, I would like to share some of the truth, wisdom, and knowledge that I have gained.

We have to make our spiritual selves prominent in our lives in order to stay balanced. I may say I was afraid of loneliness, but now I have found my true self and with all nature in solitude to attain inner peace and connected to the light and finer vibration. I realised that I was never separated from the divine source, God, and never has been. In reality, I am one with the infinite and can never be separated from my spirit, for I am integral part of one complete whole. The separation which I feel and experience is psychological and is due to my blindness and disbelief. The majority of people are unaware of this intimate relationship with the divine because they are unaware or because they refuse to believe in it, they are, in one sense, separated from the inner life of God. As soon as I realised the truth of my relationship to the infinite, I am able to transcend my weaknesses to strength to gain empowerment within for a harmonious life.

One moment, I am in the desert, far off, weak, separate, and alone, and in the next moment, I realise that I am nothing less than a child of God with all the privileges and powers of His Holy Spirit. I realised in a flash that I am one with my divine source and that I can never be separated. I awaken also to the fact that all the power of the infinite is mine to draw upon that I can never really fail that I am marching on to victory. It is amazing how great the power of your thought is. While thought is not the power of the spirit, it is the power by which you either connect yourself with the infinite power, opening to the divine inflow or separate yourself from your spiritual source. Thus, in a sense, you are what you think you are. If you think you are separate from God and cut off from His power, then it is as though this were really the case, and you are just as impotent and miserable as though you actually existed apart from God. On the other hand, if you think and believe that you are one with the infinite, you find that it is gloriously true, and that you are really the son of God. If you believe and think that you are a mere material being, then you are the limited life of a material being, and is never able to rise above it. But if, on the contrary, you think and believe that you are spiritual being, then you find that you possess all the powers of a spiritual being connecting with God in the name of Jesus Christ.

You must learn to think after the Spirit, as a spiritual being, instead of after the flesh, as a material creature and shine with Jesus. He came to my rescue when I am tempted, tested, and trailed and when I need him to heal me the Lord touches my heart, setting it on fire to revive and heal me from inside out.

Faith and Grace

Our Father will to save us all.
It is our free will to follow His call.
God knows what our future lives may be.
With our faith we set ourselves free.
Grace is free because Christ paid for it.
By not acting in faith, God will forbid.

We all have a part in God's saving Grace.
If we act in the name of Jesus's faith,
He offers salvation for us to repent.
While we sustain in His healing hands,
There is nothing faith cannot accomplish.
If we act from our heart and not being foolish.

Show that you are obedient to our Father.
Like our Lord Jesus who is our brother
God forgive us through his son He sent.
There are things that we need to do to repent.
Show Him that you are obedient to His grace.
Demonstrate deeds of repentance and with praise.

Earning our salvation in good deeds
With courage and endurance till it bleeds
Faith can be contaminated by fear
Act faithful whether we are far or near
By faith, we respond to grace
If we want to be saved.

Until we are born again
Life can be a pain.
Hang on to our faith even in times of darkness.
God's saving grace will get us out of the wilderness.
Those who go on have faith in His compassion.
Then he is able to bring us to perfection.

Great is our faithfulness
Accompanied with righteousness.
We earn in our faith God's saving grace.
Then we will see God face-to-face.
Those who are not saved must not blame God
Because it is His saving grace that you have forgot.

Joo Lian Carter

What Is Grace?

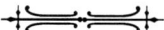

'Faith comes by hearing, and hearing by the word of God. Consequently faith comes from hearing the message and the message is heard through the word of Christ' (Rom. 10: 17).

'For by Grace are you saved through faith; and that not by yourselves; it [faith] is the gift of God, not by works, lest any man should boast' (Eph. 2: 8-9). 'And the Word was made flesh, and dwelt in us; and we beheld his glory, the glory as of the only One to come from the Father, full of grace and truth. 'He who comes after me is preferred before me; for he was before me. And from his fullness we have all received grace after grace and gift after gift. For the law was given by Moses, but grace and truth came by Jesus Christ' (John 1: 14-17).

Faith and grace are the gifts of God and to hear the Word in your heart is to obey. By grace, we are saved. We obey his commands that we hear, which are works we then do in our love for God. Faith is like the salt of the earth and grace is like the light to the world. Grace, paid for by Jesus, teaches us, and then removes even the desire for that sin from us. Our faith and hope increase following each revelation in our heart that motivate us to appropriate a closer relationship with God and spend more time waiting on God's commands and teachings. Gradually we become attuned to the supernatural release from sin and miraculous healing, endorsing our efforts and motivation to endure to the end.

Truth always comes after grace, and they are bonded. Every challenge that you face is an opportunity from God and every trial is an opportunity for you to see Jesus in a fresh and new way. We are justified by faith, just like our hearts are purified by faith, like our souls are purified by obedience to the truth. Faith is the process through which the spirit leads us and is heard from the spirit of God. Faith is in our hearts and mouth to obey by hearing the Word. Jesus says, 'Blessed are those who hear the word of God and keep or practice it repeatedly.'

We are saved by grace through faith. By faith, we communicate with God through our spiritual self. Faith is our response to God's grace. Faith is not something you do to get God to respond to you, but faith is your positive response to what Jesus already did by grace. 'Faith does not move God or make Him do anything; He has already provided everything you will ever need. 'Jesus bore our sins in his body on the cross so that we, being dead to sins, should live to righteousness, by his stripes you were healed' (1 Pet. 2: 24).

When we are ill, God does not need to heal you because Jesus took all the sickness and diseases before we got sick and anticipated every problem you will ever have. He has already paid for your complete healing and your deliverance, and he has paid for the forgiveness of our sins on the cross and all these are grace which is already complete. This is why God does not have to do anything because it is done through Jesus. So we are all equally saved by grace released to every individual. But every individual is experiencing God's grace to a different degree. Faith is how we receive what God has already done for us, 'For the grace of God that brings salvation has appeared to all men' (Titus 2: 11).

Grace is God's part and faith is our part. Got has already provided everything for us but not everybody believes and receives that. This is why we have to be saved by grace through faith, but if you do not respond positively to what God did, then we will not be saved. Grace is very powerful, without grace or faith, you will not survive. This is what the body of Christ does in grace. Faith is our own response, so faith and grace goes hand in hand for it to work. If we just believe that it is totally up to God's grace, we will never see the power of God manifest in our lives.

Definition of faith is not something you do to make God move; faith is how we appropriate what God has already provided by grace. Faith is just our positive response to God's grace. 'Therefore I say to you, "When you pray, whatever you desire, believing that you will receive it, you will have it"' (Mark 11: 24).

If you ignore this principle, you cannot make somebody receive the blessing from God through another person's faith. You cannot make someone believe or receive if he does not want to believe or to receive, unless that person is trying to believe and then you can help him. So by grace through faith whatever you want, believe that you will receive it, and you will have it.

'Death and life are in the power of the tongue, and those who love it shall eat its fruit' (Prov. 18: 21).

We have to believe that through Jesus we are saved by grace; otherwise, it will not come to pass. It is not my faith that made it happened; it's God's grace that made it happen this is why through misunderstanding a lot of people get into trouble. A deeper understanding of the Word will show you how to renew your mind to understand what God has already provided. We built our faith through the understanding of the Word of God. The church can help you with the truth to set you free.

Having faith in God to be healed is receiving the divine healing in His time and according to His purpose, not according to our wishes and demands. We can still be treated by conventional medicines, but it will relieve symptoms and sometimes not completely heal. Faith is the product of clarity, and it is unlimited with no boundaries. Only you can set your own boundaries. 'Let us then approach the throne of grace with confidence, so that we may receive mercy and find grace to help us in our time of need' (Heb. 4: 16).

Sometimes, you have to be courageous to step forward in faith to take risk. Because you have what it takes to endure what you have to do, and there is no such thing as failure as long as you don't give up. It is through the results of your effort and righteous works that you have experienced and learnt to gain knowledge, but it is through faith that you receive result from His grace. Nobody can limit your ability except you. Bible is the factory for building your faith. Trust the Word of God and have faith from your heart, not your mind. When you ask for miracle out of crises, God will give you a divine position to obey. He will ask you a step of faith from your options. With your chosen option, you act to obey instruction to plant the seed. The obedience will be the instruction you follow and that determines the season you create. Obedience is the only proof of faith. Faith will give courage and hope for personal work with a strong, unadulterated confidence which takes God at his word. Faith is nourished by the Word if we feed our faith upon the Word, and exercise prayer with faith, then we shall have the faith and we shall prove the promise of the Saviour. 'And thou shalt write upon them all the words of this law, when thou art passed over, that thou mayest go unto the land which the Lord thy God giveth thee, a land that Floweth with milk and honey; as the Lord God of thy Father hath promised thee' (Deut. 27: 3).

What is Faith?

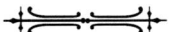

' _Faith_ is the substance of things hoped for, the evidence of things not seen' (Heb. 11: 1).

'Faith comes by hearing, and hearing by the word of God. Consequently faith comes from hearing the message and the message is heard through the word of Christ' (Rom. 10: 17).

Faith is when you bring all your emptiness to divine fullness. Some people may imagine that they know what faith means, but faith is not easy to understand, but if we get to know God's heart is to get closer to Him and have an intimacy with Him through prayer and also to receive His love from Him. Spiritual maturity is based on faith and doing things in God's way.

Faith is a seed in the heart, not in the mind. It is not what you suppose you belief. Faith controls all your worldly beliefs and leads you in a direction that is not confirmed by the ordinary natural beliefs, but faith is connecting within the idea of higher consciousness to transform. Faith is about walking in truth and asking for wisdom. Faith is putting our trust in God to see Him deliver us out of our circumstances.

The quality of faith depends on the level of the conscious transformation of the being with a possibility and attuning into entirely new concept with regard to life in this earth plane. The outcome of possessing faith is that nothing is impossible to us, and it renders what was impossible possible. It is not you yourself, but the faith in you that render things possible. To have enough faith, you have to put your integrity with the divine. Faith power is different to ordinary power, which is more or less connected to violence. When you truly possess faith, all things no longer have its own power and so become possible to you. In this respect, faith is like truth so you can rest in the will of God. 'Now the God of hope fill you with all joy and peace in believing, that you may abound in hope, through the power of the Holy Spirit' (Rom. 15: 13).

Faith comes from believing, and it can be very effective by praying or meditating on the word, saying, and doing. I believe that I have received the answer, and I will see it. Faith is a gift from God. It is a force in your spirit, but I think that when you believe, it's a choice you make and that releases your faith. Place with belief and with confidence and be firm to agree with. If two people live in harmony and agree about anything, whatever you ask, the Lord shall do it. No earthly agreement is as powerful and effective than being in agreement with God because he has great plan for us. The words belief and believe have been mentioned many times in 'John the Disciples', whom Jesus loves because of his belief in his closest relationship with God. The closer you get to God, the easier it is for you to believe what He says in His word.

Jesus said, 'If I have told you about earthly things, and you do not believe; how then will you believe if I tell you of heavenly things?' (John 3: 12).

You must have a revelation on how much God loves you and receive that love. It is not religion it is relationship that counts. You receive God's love and do everything to please Him because He loves you. When I start loving Jesus, I start doing radical things or strange things. Because I love God, I do things what he wants me to do, and not what I want to do. The love of God constrains me in doing what I wouldn't dream of doing, and yet I did it, even though it was difficult, and I did it out of His love.

The Bible says the love of God controls us. It is because I love God and for the love of Him, I am able to shut my mouth and not to have the last word in the conversation. When I love God with all my heart and soul, to serve him with all my might, it means to give Him in every area of my life, give him in my word, thoughts, feelings, and my possession. I receive from God because I believe all things are possible with Him. 'Trust in the LORD with all your heart; and do not depend on your own understanding' (Prov. 3: 5).

Faith is the product of clarity, and it is unlimited with no boundaries. Only you can set your own boundaries. Nobody can limit your ability except you. Bible is the factory for building your faith. Trust the Word of God and have Faith from your heart, and not your mind. When you ask for miracle out of crises, God will give you a Divine position to obey. He will ask you a step of faith from your options. With your chosen option, you act to obey instructions to plant the seed. The obedience will be the instruction you follow and that determines the season you create. Obedience is the only proof of faith. I believe in the saving grace of the

Bible that is all given to us out of the generous heart of our Father's grace. With faith, hope, holiness, and goodwill through prayer, meditation, and contemplation life reaches the level of loving intimacy with God whose healing grace will flow through us to heal. It is through the integration and healing from within of the physical, psychological, and spiritual dimension of life that gives us peace, glory, honour, and wholeness. If life on earth is a dream that we imagine ourselves in and that dream is reality, how could there be death? But a transition of life to the invisible reality that is much greater is possibly more important and eternal.

The most important part of a Christian is the experience of the spirit as an assurance as a true Christian. It is the witness of the spirit that reveals to you that is in you makes you a genuine Christian having faith in God. You will know the presence of His peace and love in your heart.

The issue is your awareness of the spirit in your life, and if you are not, you have no biblical assurance as a Christian. The experience of spirit is your foundation of faith.

In the first baptism, you receive the Holy Spirit and experience the Holy Spirit. The second is the baptism of water. The third baptism is the filling of the Holy Spirit on you to bring you power, to bring the good use, and the power of the kingdom of healing, dominance of light over darkness, deliverance, and authority is for the others.

It is an advantage to be able to pray in tongue and speak in tongue. When I am soaked in the Holy Spirit my body aches because of so much love from God, I was weeping because of the overwhelming love of God flowing through my body. We can grieve the Holy Spirit by our moral actions and we can quench or resist the Holy Spirit or you can have a wonderful blessing experience of this outpour of the Holy Spirit in your life, which is a gift from God. 'For I long to see you, so that I may impart to you some spiritual gift, so that you may be strengthened; That is, that I may be comforted together with you by the mutual faith of both of you and me' (Rom. 1: 11-12).

'The bricks have fallen down, but we will build better with hewn stones; the sycamores have been cut down, but we will plant better cedars in their place' (Isa. 9: 10).

'Whoever comes to me, and listens to my words and does [practices, obeys] them, I will show you what he is like' (Luke 6: 47). Worship opens your heart, brings you back to the presence of God, and wait on him soaking personal time alone or in a corporate meeting sit there and you wait and ask the Lord what He wants you to do and the thought come into your mind, someone needs to be healed. Hear what the father has in mind for you. You might have a prophetic word for someone. You get an impression and then speak it out and follow through and get the flow going connecting with the Holy Spirit. The righteousness of God is revealed from faith to faith; The righteous shall live by faith' (Rom. 1: 17).

Through God's love and grace, we are all unique because God's gift of faith to every human being is unique for a purpose. Laying on hands is to stir up the faith that God has put in you. Be in tune with people's feelings and able to communicate effectively and influence others in a unique way. The anointing comes when you worship God. Worship is the one commitment that opens your heart. You draw God near to you when you choose to communicate and worship God. Soak in your spiritual self and receive the Holy Spirit from Him to empower your life in wholeness. He intercedes our thinking when we have quiet time to soak in our consciousness to have that quality time in his presence is to receive his love and spirit in order we can serve him and others.

I have learnt that I will be nothing without any power as a human being because if God takes His hands off me, the spirit that I depend on will devastate me. I am what God makes me to be a significant human being living and doing His word as my compass to conquer my mountain leading me to the summit of my destiny. It's all about God in his anointing and favour. He so loves us and wants to take us by the hands to guide us back to Him. When we marinate in the presence of God, we become saturated to transform us to become more like Him. Tune in to the same frequency of God, positioning yourself in his presence, and love God with all your heart as we love ourselves and others. God wants to be with us in visions and in dreams. By seeing, hearing, and flowing in the spirit is the key to the anointing. One way to do that is to spend time praying or communicating to ask Lord to teach and show you the things that pleases Him. Through the screen of my mind, and God show us pictures, lights, and images, messages in our dreams. Jesus said I only do what I see the father doing, and I only say what I hear the father saying. First of all, get rid of all the negative things in your life; prune away the useless branches that cling on to you that do not bear fruit. 'I am the true vine, and my Father is the vine dresser. Every branch in me that does not produce fruit he takes away, and every branch that produces fruit, he purges it, so that it may bring forth more fruit. Now you are clean through the word that I have spoken to you and as the Life of God is imparted to you by you are also cleansed. From the Voice of the Lord: 'Like the Apostles, you too must be cleansed.' 'Abide in me, and I in you. As the branch cannot bear fruit by it, unless it abides in the vine; neither can you, unless you abide in me. I am the vine, you are the branches. If a man abides in me, and I in him, he produces much fruit; for without me you can do nothing. If a man does not abide in me, he is thrown out like a branch, which withers; these branches are gathered up, cast into the fire, and are burned. If you abide in me, and my words abide in you, you shall ask whatever you will, and it shall be done for you.' (John 15: 1-7). Faith is a series of revelations as we see Jesus in the word. Faith does not come by hearing from the world but comes as we hear the voice of God speak through the scripture, the knowledge of Christ that renews the spirit of your mind. When you get to know Jesus in his word, faith reveals within you, which is life giving or born again. The Holy Spirit speaks through the Bible to build your faith. As you progress and walk in your faith, then you start to bear fruit in your life. Jesus said, 'Have faith in God, when you pray, whatever you desire, believing that you will receive it, you will have it' (Mark 11: 24).

Faith Healing

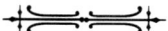

' *H*ave faith in God' (Mark 11: 22). 'For we walk by faith not by sight' (2 Cor. 5: 7). Maintaining the higher principle of God and your faith in Him can release miracles that will turn around the most hopeless situation.

Faith healing is a concept that you belief or your faith can bring about either through prayers that, according to adherents, evoke a divine presence and power towards correcting physical, mental, and emotional illness or disease and disability. Your faith is in His grace. It is the grace of God and His unconditional love that you are healed. You receive His grace with your love and faith to have effect in your life. Receiving his grace through faith is to receive the power of His Holy Spirit. God has no problem; it is you that have problems, and this is why you ask God for His Grace and believe that you are healed. 'For we through the Spirit, wait for the hope of righteousness by faith' (Gal. 5: 5).

A healing journey is a walk of faith you must take in order to manifest the healing, God has provided in Jesus Christ. It is your faith based on knowledge and the ability to receive His Grace to be healed by the Holy Spirit through Jesus. It is the spirit that has the mind with the Christ in it. When you approach a problem and recognize that God wants you to be well, you trust Him to guide you by the Holy Spirit and claim that you are healed miraculously. You need to have direction from God on how to deal with this situation. Through praying in quantity, your spirit that has the mind of Christ in it deals with things that you could not deal with in your natural mind, which is vitally important for healing. This can affect and change your live forever. Once you have experienced the result, and it is no longer theory you have seen it work in your life, and it just gives you a bonus and authority you know that it works and makes the difference.

We tend to suffer a lot of things that is unnecessary that God does not want to see us suffer. It is through our thinking that we expose ourselves to certain illnesses and one of the main contributions to that is stress from unhealthy environment and life style. The mind controls the effectiveness of them all engaging with the heart that approves it for righteousness. Meditation nourishes and strengthens the mind and keeps that controlled mind constantly attuned to God which keeps you happy and successful in existence. In this way, you should gain complete power over the mind before you try to deny matter and material remedies. Until then it is best to take commonsense steps to help the body. The easiest way to overcome diseases, disappointments, and disasters is to be in constant attunement with your own mind and soul and with God.

Self-realization and healing through prayer is already before us and waiting to open the world, only just look more closely, we will find the eyes to see from the first insight. We need to wake up and connect with God and the energy he gives us through nature. We are blinded by the constant demand of the material world and money that takes over our lives. Putting faith before money reduces our status as leader to that of servant, which is a more appropriate position to be in. Faith that transcends money frees us to follow our intuitive guidance without giving over unnecessary authority to financial concerns. When doctors, despite their skills, learning and experience, no longer can do no more for their patients, the power of faith and spirit can often produce results which bring health where it was absent. Thought and energy are two fundamental aspects of prayer. Thoughts of perfection and attunement with the divine's help are needed, and then through performance of the techniques, healing energy is sent forth to those in need of healing and help. Through self-realization meditation, attune your thoughts to the healing presence of the Divine, and then mentally pray deeply for all those who have requested. 'See how faith energized and motivated works, and by works his faith was made perfect' (James 2: 22).

The growth of faith in us is a vital spiritual task because it captures the spiritual essence of honouring our true selves. The thought of releasing our power of choice to a divine force remains the greatest struggle for the individual seeking to become conscious and be transformed. From our spiritual perspective, our highest goal is the full release of our personal will into the hands of the divine to be in complete union with the divine will. This is how I seek my healing miracle for myself and hope with faith for others too. The fear factor becomes the healing factor from divine will. However, we are all evolving in the same path through the medium of consciousness and spiritual awareness, so we must weaken our fear.

If we put right what is wrong with the physical body, and we do not touch the spirit, then the healing has failed. But if you touch the spirit, then the healing has succeeded, for we have helped to fan the divine spark that can now grow in illumination and strength. If we succeed in waking one soul, then our life on earth is enough to justify our existence and strengthen our spirits so that we can transcend every dilemma through the united power of our mature spirits. If only we realised what we are made of and the energy we are connected with, we have no choice, but to live a spiritual life which is ultimately our truth. There are more and more people turning to the power of spirit for healing when convention treatment fails. Health is wholeness of body, mind, and spirit. There are many forms of spiritual healing. Self healing, spiritual awareness, and personal evolution healing, vibrational healing, healing through chakras' power system, meditative and yoga healing, spiritual healing from healers imbued with healing energy, from the Holy Spirit power through faith, a Divine promise. God restores our faith and heal everyone who seeks to be healed and have faith in Him. A person who has strong faith is obedient and believes in his promise to God's commands that he heard spoken to Him and walks in faith, obedience, and seek the righteousness of God as the highest priority in his life. 'He did not waver at the promise of God through unbelief; but he was strong in faith, giving glory to God' (Rom. 4: 20).'Therefore, we conclude that a man is justified by faith, without the deeds of the law' (Rom. 3: 28).

How to Release Faith and Receive Grace

For you are all the children of God by faith in Christ Jesus.
(Gal. 3: 26)

But first seek the kingdom of God, and His righteousness
(Mark 6: 33).

Receiving the end of your faith—the salvation of your souls (1 Pet. 1: 9)
Releasing faith is being moved by what you believe. Faith is released in your action, with words, and deeds of obedience. Destitute of power means you are not producing the works and the deeds. Now your faith is

released, and it can manifest something. Faith is the substance of what things you hope for and the evidence of things that is not seen. Faith gives things substance. When you pray, the prayer is being released or declared, and then you celebrate. Now you have done the celebration, it has no choice, but to manifest. The same with conquering the enemy if you stand steadfast and resist the enemy has no choice but to flee.

'Even so faith, if it is not accompanied with works, is dead, by itself, but if a man says, "You have faith, and I have works"; then show me your faith without your works, and I will prove to you my faith by my works. You say you believe that God is one; you do well. Even the demons believe that and tremble. Are you willing to be shown, O vain man, that faith without works is dead' (James 2: 17-19).

We have to be thankful that God has given us everything including our mind to will freely. So it is up to us to will with faith in Him because it is our choice to receive God's grace and blessing to be healed in the name of Jesus Christ. We want to see miracles happen and be healed. So believe and have faith with confidence in the Lord you will experience miracles happening. What is the point that God has given us his love, his compassion, and his blessing to heal if we do not use it? Be humble, obedient, and faithful to receive God's grace. 'For everyone who exalts himself will be humbled, but he who humbles himself will be exalted' (Luke 18: 14).

How many miracles you see or experience is down to each individual. He said if you are willing through His will, then just bring the motive for it to happen. Jesus's motive of healing the sick was because he wanted people to be whole to glorify the Father so they are drawn to have a relationship with Him. Jesus's motive was not just to prove to us the power of God proving mighty things, it was just he wants us to be made whole or oneness. God's compassion is His love in action. Natural compassion can be very much based on emotion, but God's compassion is not based on emotion, it comes from His Holy Spirit, and God's compassion is love in action and when Jesus healed people, he was moved with compassion and through love being released into somebody's life. It was faith releasing the power but working through love to make somebody whole. 'For the Son of man has come to seek and to save that which was lost' (Luke 19: 10).

So releasing into the supernatural power is not just to see one thing happen in a moment, but it is to see the fullness in God releasing His power into somebody's life to make them whole. We live in a very competitive society, and there can be a lot of insecurity, and sometimes we want things to happen to give us a strong sense of identity in ourselves. If our identity is in Christ, then there is no competition amongst us or between us, and it is that we have seen the greater or the lesser in our natural understanding. In Christ, it is an identity that is not based on performance and result, but it is based on the position that we have in Christ, a place we have him seated in and from that seated place, a position in him with that identity, we are in him or him in us. Then we know that we can step out in faith to activate his love, to bring wholeness to people's lives. That is not just because of the result or to have a great testimony, but his motive is that he wants to see that a person is healed and restored to wholeness or to be in relationship with Him and the Father. Then we live a fulfilling and abundant life which should be our underlying motives as Christians.

Draw a line and refuse to be your old self and change to transform your life into wholeness or Oneness.

If you are living a faithless life, if you are living a self-reliant life, if you are living a life using your human wisdom, a self-sufficient life, you are denying by your very life the very thing that you claim with your mouth. Whether it's a business decision, a family decision, or relationship decision, whatever you do, you do it in your own strength, sooner or later it is going to blow up in your face. But if you do it in the power of Jesus Christ, he will sustain you and he will strengthen you even when you face difficulties. We pray when we are in trouble and even then you are not asking in a faithful way. Not asking God the power and might to demonstrate Him in you. To live and walk in His might and word makes the difference. Why not pick up the cross and stop denying, and honour your own individual true self from your inner being living in God's word and will, to walk boldly with confidence and with certainty.

To operate the will of God is by having confidence. The righteous are bold because they walk in faith. Boldness is not based on your own self-effort. You are bold because of the faith you have in the one who paid the price for you to walk in it. Christ is the object of your faith because he is the expression of the Father who loves you so much that He gave you His son Jesus.

Bold use of the word of faith can raise questions for you. 'Thy kingdom come thy will be done.' In order to operate confidently like a lion, you have to be certain even in your prayer, 'Father, I thank you that you have heard me. I knew you will always hear me.' 'Because He created our bodies, he has the Divine power to heal them, beyond what mankind can do. Now when he had called his twelve disciples to him, he gave them power over unclean spirits, to cast them out, and to heal all manner of sickness and disease.' (Matt. 10: 1).

Prayer

Dear Jesus, I know that you love me and you died upon the cross for me. I confess my sins, and I ask you to forgive me. Please come into my heart today, I receive you now as my Lord and saviour. Amen.

Spiritual Disciplines

'And do not get drunk with wine, in which is excess; but be filled with the Spirit; Jesus told us: you will know them by their fruits do not be misled' (Eph. 5: 18).

'Let every man be swift to hear, slow to speak, slow to anger, for the anger of man does not lead to the righteousness of God' (James 1: 19-20).

*E*very day, I try to practise the spirit discipline, with self-control, peace, and gentleness, which are fruits of the Holy Spirit.

Thinking on purpose and making purposeful decision every morning before I starting the day and dedicating myself to God and putting on my spiritual cloth, I put on righteousness. To receive is as important as to give. 'Every good and perfect gift is from above, and comes down from the Father of lights' (James 1: 17).

Be thankful and say so because I am grateful that through God my faith in him has been accepted, therefore, I am healed by God and the Lord Jesus Christ. I talk to God and seek his advice and walk his way and linger in the house of God. Receive the light of God to protect me from darkness to shine around me. Jesus came to bridge the gap to show me the way back to our Father's kingdom. No matter what condition I am in, seek the Lord for that guidance and protection because He facilitates and realigns my life to God. If I give my life to Christ, He heals, saves, and redeems me. In whatever you do, never give up.

Giving selflessly to others to serve humanity is one example of God's love, when you do something for another person, you say I have done what I am supposed to do with love. There is now a great opportunity for us to sacrifice, in personal freedom, in popularity, in social standing, and personal comfort. No one is too poor and too old, to do something to win souls and to serve God's will.

Personal Spiritual Awareness and Spiritual Journey

$\mathcal{M}$y first essential is an awakening, a sense of the absence of spirituality, the realised need of giving to my life a new and higher quality; first, there must be the realised desire before there can be the satisfaction.

My disharmony was my illness and absence of meaning and purpose in life that impelled me to recognise the crises. Fear and loneliness sets in making me feel as if I am losing touch with a sense of self and hope. When I realised my spiritual needs, I started by give myself the quality time and attention to find that peace within to explore my inner being.

I then become more aware and inquisitive about myself, readjusting my life in ways that removed mental and emotional blockages. Together with my illness, I was going through my spiritual unfoldment to discover the invisible world to seek the truth and the source of healing. It was a life-changing experience, but I very quickly divorced myself from that crisis to the spiritual awakening and embraced that period as a sacred time of forgiveness, renewal, and reassessment and a chance to meet myself anew. I considered personal life crisis as an invitation for change and transformation, to launch my unfulfilled dreams, a time to reflect, learn, and change the direction of my life. It also gave me a chance to transform sadness to joy, anger into compassion, to forgive and turn pain into joy, together it sanctify me.

Faith, hope, love, forgiveness, and spiritual awareness have brought me emotional healing and spiritual transformation. It also allowed me to make peace with my past and to reconnect with my divine nature.

To practice life purification, I started questioning myself—How will my world change as I unfold?

Who is responsible for my own spiritual journey?

Why am 'I' scaling the mountain?

Scaling the mountain is like consciously climbing very steep steps and in every step I take, count the blessings towards the light of God and stay attuned with my higher self until I am luminous by the light of God. If I love God with all my heart, with all my soul, with all my mind, with all my strength, and love the presence of my true entire being, with everything I have got, then I am in oneness with the universe and with God. To love God is to love my god self, which is the true impression of God.

The most effective way to reach mountaintop consciousness is through the process of purification practice. When I realised my love towards that something that is totally pure that my entire consciousness is taken over by it, I know that I have reached the mountaintop consciousness. When I contemplate that presence within my very spirit with great love, this one-pointed love and focus will literally draw the incredible power of the universe right into my thinking mind and feeling nature. I take on the power, and I become the power and speak as the power. All things are made new and I start loving the true nature of my being, my spiritual reality, including my thoughts, feelings, and visions which is the secret key for health, wealth, peace, and happiness.

Regaining my empowerment and development of my inner self, I feel a connection that is more real to me each day that is making me stronger physically, mentally, emotionally, and spiritually. Through the suffering, I went through my spirit being to come into its own. As a result, I am able to unfold my healing gift and know what others feel when they need to be healed. It is this awareness and the realisation that touched my soul. Touching of my soul helps my body and mind to achieve wholeness that brings health, certainty, confidence, inner well-being, awareness so that I am at peace with myself and with everybody else I encounter. Being aware of my own spirituality and still walking my spiritual journey, I feel that each individual must seek a personal and responsible spiritual life. Being responsible for my own, I work on meditation and yoga till I am able to touch my spiritual essence that resides within me. It is a joy to experience this enlightened state and reflect a deep understanding within me. Meditation does not create spiritual essence, but it can lead us to realise that it is already there waiting to be recognised. Becoming more aware of yourself and realising your spiritual nature is something that transcends life.

Through own experiences, the power of love and light, meditation, prayer, and the conscious connection with the true self and the divine being within, the healing energy starts flowing through faith and cosmic consciousness.

In reality, we are manifested beings projected from the spirit (true self). The organic matter form of us is the body congregated from innumerable atoms of life (souls). Each organic form expressed in material state evolves under the control of the dominating soul or atom. Universally, we are true spirits in embodiment from the cosmic energy and consciousness to evolve our unity of spiritual life. Then we will become more spiritual and aspiring for advancement and knowledge, thus, setting up vibrations that will create higher and brighter conditions for the physical being to progress our soul and spirit.

Realization and Awareness

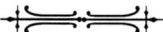

*T*he manifestation of the spirit is given to every man to benefit all' (1 Cor. 12: 7). Everyone must improve their God-given talent; otherwise, in the next life it is taken away. Life is like the contents of a book, it is lived in chapters during the process of the life journey and the lifetime is the book ends. The need for spiritual attainment is to consistently open to spiritual force before engaging into any act. It enables a new way of living by creating a channel in your being that opens you to the source and the multi-dimensional influences with small but significant steps towards a new way of living and a spirit-orientated divine life and existence. The key to the ascension process is through purification practice in various stages of physical, mental, and fundamental spiritual transformation.

Still to advance further is to transform the very cells of the body so that their programming changes from degeneration to sustainability. A truly transformed individual can live as long and fulfilled as desired.

This will require a fundamental change in the nature of human body, transcendence including the shift and expansion of true consciousness into light and harmony within and universally. Many masters have said that the necessities can be done only from the heart, for if from the mental nature, will fail as untruth combative with perceived truth.

There are moments when I catch glimpses of a life, my life infinitely beyond the life I am now living; I realise that I am living below my possibilities. I long for the knowledge, experience, and realisation of that life my soul yearns for. I realised only when I wake up to analyze the extreme, connect, and discover new possibilities and quality in my life as a whole to transform what was old and then I am reborn. From then onwards, I set out on a journey to seek the truth that I know has been hidden within me, and there must be my true self. In order to bring out the divine properties that are within that evolves from the source that connect to my body creating inter-relationship to the capacity for infinite peace, oneness, knowledge, wisdom, power, creativity, beauty, love, and delight. That inner quality reflecting the infinite consciousness is the ultimate source of who and what I am that I was unaware.

From my own awareness, the key to experience any of these spiritual attributes is to realise the divinity that lies within us by bringing it to the surface of life and effecting great progress for ourselves and the universe. To my understanding, this is true for us humans, and our relationship to the divine is one in our being. At that magical fateful point of my spiritual awareness is my own inner relationship with my inner self or higher self. This experience is the glorious moment and the merging becomes one, and my being is filled with the light of truth, accepting Jesus into my life I am born again or re-emerging from the water, reaching a new level, which allows me consciously using my inner power to connect to anything that is alive. Through realisation, I begin to move through consciousness towards the reality within, my higher soul which begins to radiate and moves towards the divine thoughts of Christ consciousness. My life changed the way I think, I feel, and I act and transformed my consciousness, and my world became a reflection of the living truth of fulfilment and harmony. My personal nature which is the essence of my being blossoms with love and light. My feelings and my soul are like a mirror. On the planetary level, there are different octaves and produce astounding and unusual things occur, and I took everything as it comes along then to interweave with the pattern of my life. As I am moving from one vibration to a finer and faster vibration that forms beautiful strands of light, allowing this weaving or work to grow to make my mark with style, I change from within and the light will flow out with the mind totally feeling that unity with all things. My life has been transformed as if my inner self is being rejuvenated.

Within my true self of consciousness, sometime I went through the link between the third and fourth dimensions, and at this bridge, I have to shed my negative karma and separate my ego through purification practice just before uniting my total self in consciousness. This was the most mystical challenge process of my enhancing life that I have ever encountered just like looking at the world upside down from the bottom of my heart. This process of transformation involved having to let go the material world and do without on certain comforts but to focus on natural law. To this, it is as if my old self have gone and became closer to God. One of my greatest trials of life while pursuing my spiritual journey on earth is the increasing feeling of loneliness and separation from people around me which I felt was a necessity at that time for my transformation. It is important for me to pray or meditate at the same time everyday so that my spiritual aspect of life will grow and expand in order to develop the ability to grow and show others as I express the energy of truth. This gives me the possibility of solitude, peace, and upliftment in order to gain enlightenment to understand spiritual laws to progress and to put them into practice with natural laws until I create my own heaven so that I can show the people how rather than telling them that there is no death and the eternal understanding that life must go on. We must understand our soul, who we are, and raise our consciousness as we touch that higher energy of Christ.

Christ paid our debt on the cross, and he has already successfully navigated to the other side. In reality, there is no death if you consider death is another gift from God by which the body returns to matter and the soul returns to God. For those who practice purification and are prepared, the journey need not be feared because death sets us free to reality to go home to God.

During the three years of my spiritual transformation, I have shed more tears than my entire adult life and could not understand why?

This experience and understanding of shedding tears have made me realise that it could be part of my purifying and transformation life process emotionally, physically, mentally, and spiritually to progress my soul. After all, about 65 per cent of the human body and 75 per cent of the earth consist of water. Water symbolizes the soul which is strong and capable of carrying the load. Water literally lifts me up from the unconscious. To stay connected to my soul, my flow of energy in the water must continue to flow preventing the soul from shutting itself off feeling inadequate and turning to ice or a long lost love from a distance star. Only through the conscious attention that flows effortlessly throughout my whole being, I allow my frozen feeling to melt and flow out into tears to keep my soul spirit flowing to purify and to work with my dreams and visions. Dreams have always been an important part of my expanded awareness of the spiritual realm of reality. In reality, I started to observe and pay more attention to my inner self, dreams, and intuition and being able to identify my weaknesses and strengths, creative or spiritual dreams which needed to be realised and frightful dreams that need to be dealt with. In order for me to remember most of my dreams, I decided to keep a diary each time I woke up with a dream still fresh in my mind that I would write down what I remembered. Up to a point, I started to realise the differences of my dreams that can connect me with my higher self and God giving me an opportunity to receive messages in the conscious mind and also provide a horizon of communication from my loved ones in the spirit world.

The interpretation of my own symbols from dreams depends on each individual some are so uniquely our own that only the dreamer holds the key to them.

Whenever we bring light into darkness, we dissolve darkness and gain reality with true colours. Similarly, we are like the sun that presents the new day as it comes up over the horizon which carries and represents constant and actual birth like a new life. For an adult to be like a child again, we must live from the centre. The term midlife refers to more than a person's energy and depending on the relevant state of consciousness. It is possible to grow again and in fact to grow for the first time. This centre of life is independent of a person's age. However, as soon as we have outgrown childhood and adolescence, it takes a conscious act in order to be a child again which is called the rebirth. It means that as adult we initiate the act of coming into life by ourselves and for ourselves. We replace conventional behavior and thought with a lifestyle we choose deliberately as the correct one for us. We select our relationships independent of our blood connections as well as we choose relatives too. We make decisions about large and small events based on our will and by conscious choices instead of living by the dictates of habit and repetition. Living now and spiralling up is the way forward.

Since I became more spiritual and aware of my higher self, I have also noticed that whatever challenges I have been faced with, whether it's a health imbalance, psychological, or emotional, I have been able to solve them much more quickly and successfully.

Whatever is causing this current shift is a direct result of the tireless inner personal work we've been doing on ourselves for many years because we are all connected in one way or another, and whatever is happening in the world affects every one of us like a domino effect.

It only takes one person to begin exploring a path into the conscious truth, or own truest Divine self, a vibration is set out and a space is created for another person to wake up to their own truest self too. This is like sending out prayers or affirmation to connect and heal via the cosmic consciousness and energy or through the Holy Spirit of Christ consciousness.

In this current world, vibration and the amount of light are pouring into our planet from the solar activity and the universal expanding nature is the direct influence causing our ability to adjust and move through challenges.

The way to perceive and attune to this finer vibration is to connect the mind and the heart and then feel and act from the heart. This way the heart leads for the mind to follow. Strong willed persons might find it difficult to start with because the mind is always doing the thinking and impatiently control situations, feelings, and actions. This can easily be done by calming the mind with no attachment from the external world, but to allow your higher true self that is your heart to shine out that finer vibration into action. Then, we can begin to find peace and bliss in the heart.

When we live consciously attuning to our evolving soul and from an open heart, we are able to perceive our true purpose to serve our inner being with more meaningful and fulfilled life. We will also perceive what aspects of our being needs to be transformed into higher quality and soul growth in consciousness, which will also benefit our spiritual journey of discovery into higher dimensions and the invisible possibilities. To attain the highest consciousness and spiritual values, require discipline and conscious effort the most profound conscious effort through purification process with prayer, meditation, and yoga to evolve ourselves. Ultimately, when we have attained our highest consciousness, then our true self becomes the enlightened pure being living like angels of a new divine life on earth.

In May 2010, while I was meditating in my conscious sleep, I heard clear whispers three time to my right ear 'Angelic Living' follow by a bright golden light face that seemed to me like (god head) appeared near my right side of my face. It was a lovely feeling of love, harmony, and hope for that new world to arrive. To me, all things are possible through faith and believe in our pure living.

Life Compensation

They have and they have not
Glows the feud it brought
Shoots across the neutral dark we fight.
Compensate by the glow of Divine Light.

Man's the elm, the wealth, and the vine,
Stanch and strong the tendrils twine
And power to him who power exerts
What he earns is all he deserves

The darkness of fear we try to flee
And like thy shadow, follow thee
With hope and vision in positive thoughts
The happiness that can be brought

The wings of time are black and white.
Pied with morning and with night
The dust that cloud the earth once bright
Thank goodness darkness cannot penetrate light

Mountain tall and ocean deep
Trembling balance duly keep.
Floating in air or pent in stone
True life is what you make it on your own.

Joo Lian Carter

Questioning Values and Purpose

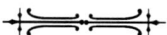

$\mathcal{W}$e all bring something unique into this world, something that did not exist before and never existed without the person. There is a destiny that shapes our ends. We each have a purpose to serve because every individual has a gift within him or her to fulfill our destiny. But every one of us also brings characteristics and qualities that do not necessarily fit into the framework of established norms. These are gifts that remain in the dark where they are ignored considered as taboo. Therefore, we must learn how to take advantage of all the qualities that lies within us when we realise our true nature. It is part of our evolution that we share knowledge and wisdom among our individual qualities to learn from each other, to ease away ignorance and misconception until the process of spiritual awakening takes place to discover reality instead of in the darkness of subjection.

The goal of dealing with the polarities of life is to discover our personal values and to determine what is truly essential for us. That is life compensation. It is through polarity that we can make choices and learn to evolve.

We cannot always get away from the contradictions of life, and we cannot always solve them. Do not be threatened by the challenge of the circumstances or crises that stress us, instead create new determination and enthusiasm by focusing our undivided attention and all of our energies, we will find better solutions. Consciously engage in our relationship in the task to allow our energy to become involved to overcome contradictions and limitations so that we can discover new creative possibilities in them or even a new dimension of life.

The light energy encourages us to deal with the contradictions that surround us which means that to solve problems with conscious thoughts, skills, and effectiveness as well as to complete the task regardless of what the task is.

When we deal with our inner impulses and our external goals and stop projecting, our energy power reaches new levels. When we are in doubt, we make compulsive unfair assumptions and judgements which can be misleading and cause indifference, pride, and prejudice.

The more the spiritual life progress, the more loving and wiser our judgements will be and also learn to forgive without resentment, be more appreciative, and be contented accepting the passion and the simplicity of life. One also becomes more creative and able to express feelings through music and thoughts together through poetry and through inspirational writings. The combination of high thoughts and feelings of high tension leads to a higher form of psychic life.

The element of ideas or knowledge is always linked with the emotional element, therefore, art brings out the true expression of the higher creative being that involve in sensation, perception, and conception.

To create is to express one's potential through actions and aspirations. During creation, we realise possibilities beyond the individual circumstances of our life, this way we live a certain true greatness which transcends what we ourselves may be able to recognize the true nature to make matter what really matters to us. Consequently, this form of valuable time, effort, energy, concentration, and focus create that higher consciousness and noble results.

My purpose of pursuing truth through values is primarily to do what God wants me to do. Through my creative thoughts, feelings, and actions, I focus on my valuable energy of passionate creation to give life and quality that is part of me and separate from me.

For instance, the music that I create is heard in a continually changing reality so that the same recording is not really the same music each time it plays. This also applies to my creative cooking; my successive dishes taste different from the previous for better or for worst. This means that each new moment provides fresh possibilities.

Everything in this world is temporary because it has a beginning and end. In the world of reality, it is infinity, therefore, it is eternity.

We live in a demanding world of complexity, environmentally unfriendly, and social discontentment that affects the daily quality of living. Most disease is due to unhealthy and imbalanced alignment of the body, mind, and spirit that we are aware and yet we are ignorant of how to deal with it wisely.

To attain complete unity, perfect health, stability, poise, and awareness, we have to attune between these three aspects of being. By touching the soul and awakening it so that the individual is conscious of what we have to do, which is freeing the soul, liberating the mind, and then the body will benefit the result which is our divine self. Then we can fulfill the needs of this world with radiance and good vibrations. If we thrive to achieve our higher ordeals, the secret dreams, and prayers which are our great hopes and aspirations, then we have earned our credit. So long as we recognise that we are all instruments of a great purpose, each of us thriving to do our part so as to make it easier, better, and happier to complement each other like our physical body, the temple of the spirit is as pure as you can make it so that we can grow and evolve towards perfection.

Of course, evidently, first, to understand ourselves, we must be conscious and appreciate the power, the divinity, and the truth which is behind all life and to realise the relationship to it. We are not just human beings with passions and weaknesses, but we are spirits and together with the great spirit, the first primal cause, and the supreme arbiter of all destiny. We exercise our spirit within us to fill the world with loveliness, beauty, grace, and splendour and enable all the wealth of the mind and the spirit with knowledge and wisdom to be enjoyed alike by all in the sunlight instead of desire for materialism that cast shadows and imprisonment. We are born to be free with free will to choose to build a new world where there is no hatred, no difference of colour, where the only superiors are those who have earned it by their greater service. Being faithful to our own responsibility, we discharge and spread the light with multi colours with our understanding and knowledge to help ourselves as individual and others where we can.

Solitude

As I evolve towards simplicity
The ordinary life of holiness and sanctity
In the world of external madness and violence
Solitude is the key to explore within in deep silence

You may say I am a hermit
It is true even my star Virgo admits
Do I feel lonely and abundant?
No the company of nature in abundance

In solitude I feel the finer vibration
It gives me peace and rejuvenation
It is through solitude of silence
That I connect with my essence

I went into hiding
In order to come out of finding
I become exposed and vulnerable revealed and nothing
To face temptation in fighting

Now I am ready to face reality
My journey of love, abundance, and prosperity
To share and enjoy the wisdom and my presence
And the love that I have from my essence

The need to know that I am saved
Through my confession to Christ I gave
Reveals the true value and truth within
Now I know I am saved from sin.

Joo Lian Carter

How to Attain the Divinity within Us through Consciousness

Life journey is like playing hide and seek. The invisible world within is hidden, dormant, and waiting to be discovered and connected so that we can explore the divinity within us. Unless we are aware to a certain degree that we are spirit beings, it is not easy to attune to the concept. So it is important to become aware of all the vital supreme power which is responsible for every phase of life. Once the knowledge of spiritual truth has been discovered or consciousness has dawned within our being or to know who we are, we become transformed and view life differently and confidently through new eyes, with new understanding, for its purpose begins to fall into place to realise the divine plan to equip ourselves by service for the fulfilment of our inevitable destiny.

Within us is a spirit being, and when we tune into the spiritual power that higher source can access the divine part of us when we realise and become aware. As spiritual children of God, we are part of him, He is love and love is in us. We must learn to still our physical senses and must learn to be detached from the material world. We must learn how to attain that inner peace and to harness our soul through consciousness, prayer, meditation, contemplation, and pondering.

All these will require patience, time, and knowledge and understanding, which will lead us to wisdom and truth that set us free. But as we become more aware of our subtle vibrations and our higher potentialities of our spiritual life, we will become aware of the spirit within us. Then we have opened our hearts, minds, and souls, and we are ready to attain the divinity within us to our highest potentials. Then you will be ready to receive and be blessed and anointed by God through Jesus for a spiritual revival to be healed.

How often do we listen to that still inner voice?

He, who has ears to hear, let him hear (Mark 4: 9).

Faith comes by hearing and hearing by the word of God (Rom. 10: 17).

Unless we are attuned to that consciousness, how else do we expect to hear that still faint voice of the higher self through that entire outer racket and material distraction that we call the social life of comfort that relax us in a sleeping state? Instead, we find the sacred space and time for communion within to fill our lives with humility to receive the council of God and Jesus. It is through that higher consciousness connection within that enables us to find that peace and hearing of God and that gives us the centeredness and harmony with the rest of our being and the universe. God speaks to us in our dreams, through people, through circumstances, through visions, through thoughts, through natural and supernatural manifestations, through whisper, through peace, and through the Word of God from the Bible. Unless we are attuned sensitively in peace and in faith to any of these ways, we miss out on receiving God's grace and council.

'And the peace of God, which passes all understanding, will keep your hearts and minds through Christ Jesus' (Phil. 4: 7).

'And let the peace of Christ rule in your hearts, to which you are called in one body and be thankful' (Col. 3: 15).

Cosmic consciousness bestows a bliss that is beyond all words to describe. It also quickens the sympathies and attunes the soul to the vibrations of the heart that cries of the struggling and evolving ones who are still travailing in the pains of the rebirth. We must be willing to endure the suffering in order that we may realise the joy and not because joy is the reward for suffering, but it is through suffering that we learn and become stronger to evolve the soul and to develop the spirit, which is immortal and blissful that we are united with all and must feel with all to shine our own star.

> *If I can help only one soul to find itself, to become aware of its latent divinity and begin to express it, then the whole of my earth life is well worth while. But I will be able to help more than one and so can you. (Joo Lian Carter)*

Eternal happiness is when you have purified to please your soul to progress the spirit. (Joo Lian Carter)

Temporary happiness is when you stop wanting from the material world as long as you are contented and grateful. (Joo Lian Carter)

Empowerment

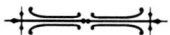

Jesus said, 'Man does not live by bread alone, but by every word of God.' (Luke 4: 4)

*M*y key to empowerment is through purification practice that leads me to consciously see clearly from within with my true self and nature (soul and spirit) in order to bring wholeness to my well-being to attain the peace and freedom to make my own choices relying on my own resources, strength, and wisdom. For me, my soul power in the hands of God is the most important empowerment which is the key to transform my physical and spiritual life mission. Unfortunately, in the days to come, human wisdom will not be enough. It is possible to walk with God filled with and led by His Holy Spirit at a level that I can experience God's supernatural protection and supply by obeying His word from within my heart prompting me with thoughts, words, and deeds to fulfill the destiny that the Father has for me.

'For as many as are led by the Spirit of God, they are the sons of God' (Rom. 8: 14).

'To receive the Holy Spirit, is by partaking of God's nature, expressed in the spiritual principles contained in His Law; the Holy Spirit, whom God has given to those who obey him' (Act 5: 32; 1 John 5: 3).

To be supernaturally equipped and strengthened by the power of the Holy Spirit is to be empowered for protection and the maturity of spiritual life, therefore, also enhance the natural life walking and living in the light, peace, and love.

Before it was mind over matter now it is the truth, the Word of God, the soul and spirit over mind over matter that transforms my life. I follow the revelation of Jesus within my heart, with the energy of love which is an active force through my soul that is what heals me in a light energy or Holy Spirit flows beyond physical reality. Being truly empowered by the revelation of Jesus and my own soul power, this allows me to love with personal conscious attention that is deeply healing and protecting and makes all things bright and harmonious. There is a power lying hidden in us, the true self or spirit self that transcends the finite self of the sense-being, by the use of which we can rise to higher and better things.

It is important that we bring our inward powers of our mind, heart, and spirit into expression wisely and in harmony with the law of nature, to build up character, and to find within ourselves that potential self, which is our true self, and which, when found, reveals to us that we are one with God. Everything happens for a reason regardless of our past and present circumstances. In reality, there are no victims; it is that we simply lose our power by giving it away or have been taken away from us. Our aims of empowering is to find ways of recovering that powerful being that resides within ourselves to bring back balance, harmony, and health into our lives.

To start with, awaken the empowered self that already exists within us to provide the inspiration for us to gain back that lost power of wisdom and confidence. There is no way whereby the discipline of life can be avoided. Every time I rely on the external world or someone, to provide me with love, success, or happiness, I hand over my power that I depend on. As soon as they stop providing me, I am disempowered. Possessing self-reliance, awareness, responsibility, knowledge, and wisdom provide me the inner strength to attain and sustain empowerment. Ending my relationship with the material power necessarily, allows me to walk a new path. Although at first, I struggle this new direction when I finally surrender to it, I was able to see my new circumstance as a blessing. It allows me to choose to view crises as interventions that are part of my greater plan directing me to my next lesson about my own personal power, sacred contract, and ultimately, my soul journey to accomplish its mission. Whenever I feel that I am alone, I engage myself with invisible world; I talk to God and pay attention to his message, meditating and contemplating or releasing a prayer as a personal act of power, then I no longer feel lonely or underestimate how important I am to someone else. I set myself to counteract it by a widespread combination of unceasing work and intercessory prayer. It was an aspiration, but there can be no doubt about the sincerity, the single mindedness and the strength of my urge to serve the will of the Divine.

In my forty hard-working years spent in this world serving, I worked my best to preserve the purity, the unity, and the strength of the sanctity of mind, the tact, the tenacity of will, the patience, the business talent, the endurance, the perseverance, and the sleepless watchfulness that I brought to bear for serving humanity. Whatever the work that my soul has agreed to, whatever its contract with the universe, all the experiences of my life serves to awaken within me the memory of that contract and to prepare me to fulfill it. I will require my true empowerment and will to accomplish fully the mission of my soul. As I move towards that fulfilment of my soul's agreement, I move consciously towards the energy of my soul power that empowers me to expand all aspects of my life now and eternity.

Wholeness

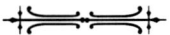

My principle of well-being is to prevent our thoughts from thinking that we are ill, instead, focus on our inner-self and allow our live force to flow freely within us so we can move in faith the direction of greater consciousness. (Joo Lian Carter)

With the power of love, hope, faith, and the power of prayer when used in unity with others is the most powerful force one has to unite for wholeness, peace, and harmony. (Joo Lian Carter)

Preventive action is always better than crisis management. Therefore, prevention is better than cure. (Joo Lian Carter)

Every being has the potential to be a healer and be healed within his or her consciousness. Self—healing is by dealing with your own problems through prayer, relaxation, meditation, faith, and giving yourself spiritual healing and transcendent healing. There are healing with faith attributed to interventions of God, angels, Christ, saints, and other luminary humans or spirits. Healing starts with self-healing and can be enhanced by a healer. Many complementary/alternative therapists, physicians, and nurses are also healers. We can learn to improve our natural healing gifts if we have faith in ourselves and in God's grace, which could directly help us, bless us, and heal us of every disease and illnesses, and then we might actually begin to turn to Him, to ask for blessings, live and walk in spirit. Our physical and emotional stress may affect the psychological states and alter the balance of wholeness and lower the body immunity to protect us from life contradictions.

Spiritual upliftment and faith may make difficult emotional and physical problems more tolerable when natural healing fails. 'She girds herself with strength (spiritual, mental, and physical fitness for her God-given task), she makes her arms strong and firm. She tastes and sees that her gain from work (with and for God) is good; her lamp goes not out, but it burns on continually through the night of trouble, privation, or sorrow. She lays her hands to the spindle, and her hands hold the distaff. She opens her hand to the poor, yes, she reaches out her filled hands to the needy (whether in body, mind, or spirit)' (Prov. 31: 17-20).

How We Live Our Lives Determine
Our Wholeness

Healing includes physical and mental change, spiritual shift, and change of life sources around you that were polluted in the last season coming alive and being healed in this season and nations' change according to individual faith.

It is not what you do in your life, and it is what you are that determine your wholeness.

We are entering into a different season that we have to shift with the source that is inevitably happening. Therefore, we have to shift in a different way. This season of angelic healing is present in our atmosphere as long as you have faith in God. God is opening our eyes to the shifting of heaven, the Lord's will for us to be whole, but we don't experience that often because we live in the world of outer distraction pulling us apart. The world is filled with peace grabbers and faith robbers of everything that tries to create the atmosphere of wholeness. We are instructed to be united in mind, to realign our mind in our heart that sees God. The mind, the heart, and the spirit are interwoven into each other in the work of God.

When we are wounded, we fragment ourselves; let us pray and resource the power held up in that fragmentation of yours. When you lay hands on others, a new flow happens within you from your heart, mind, and spirit because your body is recognizing that new flow, and all of a sudden you are just going to touch somebody and that person will be healed. It's the impurity keeping us from seeing God and new vision. It is vital we ask the Holy Spirit to fill and flow like pure water to purify our heart, mind, and spirit. Pray to God and ask Him with faith to be healed and saved in the name of Jesus to make your heart pure to reunite with your mind and spirit to be renewed for a new life, new hope, new joy, and new peace.

Prayer

Lord, let us hear what is necessary to cause my heart to be pure. We pray that our spirit be renewed. Therefore, Father, we ask you for our united mind, we ask you for a pure heart, and we ask you for a renewed spirit while we are here. Decree that all fragmentation that's dwelling in us begin to let go. Deliverance occurs; the enemy is not just after your soul to fragment. What the enemy is after is your spirit to exit from you so that it can occupy you to cloud your mind. This season, we have entered in the most supernatural season and we must protect our spirit man from vexation because the enemy will start to rearrange the atmosphere around you, getting you all tied up in things that God never intend you to be tied up in and all of a sudden your spirit man is vexed and the spirit become annoyed and agitated, and it cannot allow Holy Spirit to penetrate through your body.

So we have entered in just not to a season of healing the soul, but we enter into the season of liberating the spirit. There is a whole new harvest coming and when you come across who are lost and need to be saved, you are going to say I know how to get you free. You are going to say, let's disconnect the spirit that is in you and send that spirit out of your body and for new spirit revival. Deliverance is now beginning to stir and be released.

'That is, that God was in Christ, reconciling the world to himself, not counting their trespasses against them; and has committed to us the word of reconciliation' (2 Cor. 5: 19).

The key to well-being is to live a well-balanced life to attain wholeness. We can be enlightened only when we have the Holy Spirit light within us. In order for personal light to shine, we must let go of reservations and false inhibitions and open ourselves to our own truth and reconcile with God. We receive from God in faith. Healing to be whole and facing reality depends on our unity with our personal truth with God through

Jesus Christ. The principle of expansion and abundance depends on our values and aims in life. It is a spiritual or material growth, it requires some elements of humility to be able to engage with the Holy Spirit that can help and support you as well as your own strength and great effort to make it effective to achieve the final goal.

We all live in two worlds, the inner or invisible world of the mind and spirit and the outer world that of the body and the physical universe about us. In the invisible world, lies the silent, subtle force that drives and continually determines the conditions of the outer world. As responsible human beings, we should be able to understand and to determine what is right or wrong and whatever action we choose to act, we must accept personal accountability and responsibility for the outcome. At some point in our relationship, we will face problems and our strengths, emotions, and character may be challenged. Personal responsibility and conviction are an obligation to oneself. It is our individual duty to ensure our good character and behavior responsibility also includes being accountable for our health, wealth, success, and happiness.

I pray all the time, asking for inspiration and wisdom to be influenced from the higher level of consciousness because it can perceive what the conscious personality cannot. Our higher self contains all the knowledge and memories of the soul through its journey in many past life incarnation. This returns us to the concept of self-responsibilities in accepting the consequences of our actions whether they originate from this life or past life and our personality remains bonded to the spiritual energy of its higher self through the connection of its higher vibrational bodies. From the higher level of causes, we know how emotion can create normal or abnormal energy physiology in our physical body. Through that it alarms the personality and ego from the higher level before manifestation of illness and knowing how our distress and suffering could be brought back into homeostasis or transformed into positive energy.

The Price of Purification

You can only reap what you have sown
That requires inner awakening and nurturing of your own
The flower will always be true to its seed.
Like how you inherit your breed.
However low you have descended,
So equally high can you ascent.
Without the shadow and the darkness,
There will be no sunshine and brightness.

If only you understand the function and necessity
for pain and suffering,
The greatest crises lead you to learn with greater
understanding,
If there were no rough stones in your way,
There will be nothing to conquer every day.
When blinded by the tears of grief and joy encountered,
Automatically, it touches the soul and be rewarded
In this world, there is no justification
Unless you go through the wisdom of purification

The more you have experienced and tested,
The more you will appreciate the perfected.
Once the cup of sorrow has been void,
The joy and the laughter can be enjoyed.
When from within that you can be trusted,
With the secrets of your inner mysteries seated,
You have wisely purified to attain your divinity,
Evolved and attain heaven now and eternity.

Joo Lian Carter

Purification Practice

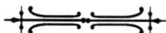

*B*ut as he who has called you is holy, so you be holy in all manner of conduct (so you must be holy, perfect, pure, and righteous. You must be perfect holiness). Because it is written, 'Be holy; for I am holy' (1 Pet. 1: 15-16).

> *Purification practice involves everything to do with life physically, mentally, emotionally, and ultimately the spiritual attainment, which is reflected in light and purification in obeying the truth by faith, so you may best purify to perfect your spiritual purpose. (Joo Lian Carter)*

'Your souls are purified in obeying the truth, through the spirit' (1 Pet. 1: 22). To have a perfect heart, to grow spiritually, you need to be loved and edified. Be in the right environment and be with someone where you are being inspired to grow. Trust the Lord who is full of grace and truth, to work through you because anything He wants you to do, you will be given the strength and blessing to towards the mark of perfection. 'God make you perfect in every good work to do his will, working in you what is well pleasing in his sight, through Jesus Christ; to whom be glory forever and ever. Amen' (Heb. 13: 21).

Strip yourselves of your former self that controlled your conduct, which corrupts itself through lusts and desires that spring from delusion, and be renewed in the spirit of your mind, and put on the newly created nature of Christ, which is created in God's image of the righteousness and holiness (Eph. 4: 22-24).

'For God, who commanded the light to shine out of darkness, has shined in our hearts to give the light of the knowledge of the glory of God in the face of Jesus Christ' (2 Cor. 4).

The main purpose of purification practice is to purify or to heal obscurations and to set the mind free of delusions and focus on reality and knowledge of truth through the spirit. I would like you to understand that within us there are realms of consciousness and truth untapped by us before, and now through our spiritual journey of awareness within, in search for the truth our perceiving realities become possible in the light. Everything we paid for the result of our efforts become worthwhile and real. Through realisation and accept eternal progress which is open to every human soul, and each individual will aim to progress at his own individual pace. There are many levels of progression to be encountered and conquered. Naturally, the more evolved the soul, the spiritual release and fulfilment is higher at the divine ladder of sanctifications. All souls come here with a choice to purify and to develop a certain quality, which is to weave into the higher self to attain that divinity (God-conscious being). From this, divinity, there will be no more necessity of reincarnation for the soul, but only through choice that it comes back to assist human kind.

'We must be perfect as our heavenly Father is perfect' (Matt. 5: 48). We must be merciful as He is merciful (Luke 6: 36). We must become pure as He is pure (1 John 3: 2-3).

How to attune towards this inner light and be sure that the truth has been discovered. One main essential is the purity of life by living the Word of God to transform the mind. Fear and struggle is through our own self-imposed judgment and punishment because we choose from our own free will and nobody can live your life and tell you what to do. However, we can serve and give our best to each other to progress life physically, mentally, and spiritually.

'If we confess our sins, he is faithful and just, and will forgive us our sin and purify us from all unrighteousness' (1 John 1: 9).

The process of purification practice is not only to set ourselves free from fear and faults, but it is also the healing of the senses, and a formation of the body and spirit. It is a transfiguration of the consciousness or to be born again.

As valuable as the knowledge and understanding is, they are not enough to purify without love, compassion, and forgiveness. We develop harmony out of love for one another, and through that love, we are guided towards an activity that is relative to spiritual experience because we share that common experience in everything we do.

The only way that we are kept pure is by keeping the energy channels open, so that nobody may deem himself so humble as not to constitute a part of the life force system so that there will constantly becoming a new flow of the Holy Spirit, love, and energy to become righteous to have peace and joy.

Let us cleanse ourselves from all filthiness of the flesh and spirit, perfecting holiness in the fear of God. (2 Cor. 7: 1)

Nothing can prevent a man's hope to progress forward if he but attends to the purification of his vehicles. That requires work and effort.

The light within will shine forth with ever greater clarity as the refining process continues until when atomic matter predominates great will be the glory of that inner person. We are all graded, therefore, if it may be so expressed, according to the magnitude of the light, the rate of vibration, according to the purity of the tone, and the clarity of the colour. This light puts out the lesser lights through the pure radiance of its power. Then you are luminous and empowered with light of knowledge, the light of wisdom, and the light of intuition, and these are the three definite stages of the divine light or one light.

The day of purification depends on the equilibrium, that is, the balance of the nature and the degree of violence will be determined by the degree of inequity caused among the people of the world by war and natural catastrophe. At this point of crises, everyone will be forced to struggle as equal to survive. It is vital that we live in harmony and appreciate the nature that requires preservation and the natural resources protected with responsibility and respect.

We conquered many battles in life, and now begin to take victory for granted; we just presume that God is going to keep on blessing. We've been mighty warriors for the Lord, but now we're getting careless, and we never dreamed that we would have done such a thing. God will rebuke us when we sin. We will put his finger on the sore sport and say that was wrong. If we are living in sin, high, wide, and low, God does not rebuke us, there is no conviction, and I wouldn't give half for your hope of heaven. If we are children of God, He will rebuke us and then there were arrows of conviction. God will squeeze, and put pressure on us, if we are living in sin and know that kind of pressure, we better thank God for it. If he has word of rebuke, if God has arrows of conviction, if he has a hand of pressure on us, thank Him because he loves us too much to let us go in this way.

Now this is a mark that a person is saved.

The Bible says, 'If we be without chastisement, then we're illegitimate, we've never been saved' (Heb. 12: 8).

For truly for a short time, they chastened us according to their best judgment, but God chastens [rebukes and disciplines us] for our benefit, to enjoy a share in his holiness' (Heb. 12: 10).

Day in and day out the thing you have done or said is in your tongue, in your heart, and in your mind. It affects you so much that you have problem sleeping; a clear conscience is better than any sleeping pill. Seek righteousness and justice, then peace will bless you.

Unresolved guilt will sap the strength out of your life. The burden becomes too heavy for you. In general, sin constantly weighs you down and weakens you. Save yourself from sin and focus on giving your strength to productive purposes. Sin blinds your spiritual eye, deafens your spiritual ears, you become spiritually dumb that leads you to danger, and you do not know how to glorify God.

Sin wearied David. He said, 'There's no soundness in my flesh because of your anger, neither is there any rest in my bones' (Ps. 38: 3).

What would you do if there's sin in your life?

The Bible says in 'If we would judge ourselves, we'd not be judged,' (1 Cor. 11: 31).

'Therefore since we are surrounded with so great a cloud of witnesses, let us lay aside every weight, and the sin that does so easily entangle us, and let us run with patience the race that is set before us' (Heb. 12: 1).

It may be just the sin of coldness, but you deal with it immediately and ask for forgiveness.

God is not trying to get even with you; he just wants to correct you, to give you second chance. God is more concerned about your holiness than he is your health. He is more concerned about your righteousness, than your worldly possession or living in a big house having business success. God is more concerned in your eternal life than your reputation, and he will appropriately chastise you, not because He doesn't love you, but because he does love you. There is no perfection in this world, but if you are willing to shift and adapt to change and transform within your own drive and let go the unpleasantness in you to pursue righteousness with the help of God, then perfection becomes a reality.

'As he who has called you is holy, so you be holy in all manner of conduct because it is written, 'be holy for I am holy' (1 Pet. 1: 15-16); so that we walk as he walked (1 John 2: 6), and as he is, so are we in this present world' (1 John 4: 17).

Purification of Thoughts

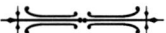

Nothing is at last sacred but the integrity of your own mind, heart, and spirit. (Joo Lian Carter)

*B*ut Jesus knowing their thoughts said, 'Why do you have evil thoughts in your hearts? (Matt. 9: 4).

'For as he thinks in his heart, so he is. "Eat and drink," he said to you, but his heart is not with you' (Prov. 23: 7).

The mind is the doorway of the soul, the heart is the mirror of the soul, and the eye is the window of the soul. What we think is so important, and, therefore, we need to choose our thoughts and discipline our minds, reflecting in our hearts to select and meditate on, and the Word of God is the key to live a righteous and fulfilled life. It is our thinking that creates the conditions of our lives, therefore, it is essential to understand and self-observe our own mind. We are light beings, and we change the way that we shape the light, which is the energy flowing through us by changing our consciousness that shapes our thoughts and crowns our minds or oneness of consciousness. This increased awareness will help us to understand contradictions so that we may find new solutions and make clear decisions for a more worthwhile and peaceful life. Sometimes we misuse the power of our own thoughts. The mind will only attain full power when we free it from all limitations of thoughts and venture forward into the unconditional and absolute which connect us to the necessity of our personal existence to gain fruitful mental abilities.

'And do not be conformed to this world; but be transformed by the renewing of your mind, that you may prove what is the good, acceptable, and perfect will of God'(Rom. 12: 2).

One of the unhealthiest prospects of man is his negative thoughts, emotions, and actions. Not only these emotions in action affect him in a bad way, but also affect everyone around him.

You are what you eat, think, feel, and act that define your values and integrity. Everyone has a right to choose to be a positive or a negative person. If you are being constantly negative and mould your life in a negative fashion, you become an unpleasant habitual negative person to serve your life purpose. If you choose to stay positive, it becomes your focus in a purposeful life with more and real possibilities. 'Casting down all our own decisions, and every barrier that is raised up against the wisdom from God, and bringing into captivity every thought to the obedience of Christ' (2 Cor. 10: 5).

We are rational human beings when our cognitive function is performing correctly. The mind and mental process starts with the study and understanding of mind, both in its normal and abnormal state, along with the interaction between objective and subjective and between thought and reality. But most of the time, we are more optimistic than realistic as suggested by both neuroscience and social science. There are also some who are more pessimistic than optimistic with no conception of reality.

Optimism induces positive attitude and enhanced thinking with clear benefits in the present and a better future, which is an illusion or a hope, but can be a process for manifestation. Hope maintains a peaceful mind or lower stress and improves well-being. Optimism and hope leads to faith that dwell in the process of now, progressing to imagine alternative realities and possibilities with believe and clear vision that we can achieve them. It is so important that such faith helps motivate us to pursue our goals.

'Strip yourselves of your former nature that controlled your conduct, which corrupts itself through lusts and desires that spring from delusion' (Eph. 4: 22).

Instead of living and enjoying the present moment, most people are constantly being clouded by the past and shaped by the future. There is no past or future without the present. The past experience can be valuable if applied appropriately that can help to progress further the present to a more promising future and reality. This is where the purification of thoughts applies. It is the thoughts that project from the mind that shapes the condition of our life. Therefore, to attain a clear mind for pure thoughts, one requires to go through purification process in our thinking. It is the free will, the ying and yang of life from the cause and effect of the natural law that we are able to evolve through our personal choice. It is so important to make rational or righteous choice to create a sound foundation in whatever you endeavour because the result of any choice manifested is the consequences that one has to take responsibility and accountability with conviction.

In real positive thinking now about our prospect, we must be able to imagine ourselves in the invisible future and reality, and then with a creative higher mind the true self is the reality. This allows us to project into our mind in time travel, which is the ability to travel back and forth through time and space which is essential for our survival in evolution.

Our expectations can change the future, but the intuitive sense activated by the pineal gland can see the future.

In order to attain these qualities of well-being, we have to look at the basic reasons that cause the suffering. This solution was helpful, and it worked. It still works. Responding like this, the mind feels free from agitation. However, at the conscious level, the mind can be free from agitation and negative influences by facing the problem and then observing and exploring the inner truth and experiencing the reality of mind and matter within.

Habitual negative emotion is usually embedded in the unconscious mind, and by the time, it reaches the conscious level. it has gained so much power that it overwhelms us, and we cannot observe or control it, but we can consciously pay attention with close self-observation in reality by focusing the inner truth. We must learn to transcend all aspects of the negative ego thought system, not just have one profound Revelation.

It is through self-observation and realisation that we become aware within and we recognise our mental impurities or negative emotions and be willing to change our way of thinking and start paying attention to our own emotions regardless of how the exterior affects us. Whenever negative thoughts fill your mind, do not become the victim, become a master to control that thought process and in your heart, see things differently through your spiritual eye. The negative thoughts will disappear and then positive feelings and emotions will appear to change your attitude into action of compassion or love.

Like before, we sow the seed for it to grow successfully and fruitful, and we first have to get rid of the weeds and cultivate the land on good soil. 'To the pure all things are pure, but to those who are corrupted and do not believe, nothing is pure. In fact, both their minds and consciences are corrupted' (Titus 2: 15). Another way of purifying the impurities of negative emotion is to live on a higher level of ourselves where we are in the position of making realistic inner decision and inner choice and be able to protect ourselves from external negative influences without being affected and not worrying what others think of us. This way, it allows us to maintain a better state of mind belonging to the higher level of ourselves. We have to learn where to live in oneself and then whom to live within oneself.

Through observing the reality within, it enables us to act and to react wisely without hurting ourselves and others unnecessarily. When we stop reacting blindly to stop creating negativities, then our minds become balanced, understanding the truth, seeing situations more clearly, therefore, we are capable of real action and also to react wisely from within and from others.

This observation of truth from within reveals the reality and knowing of oneself for the higher level of control over mind and over matter. As we practice this process, we continually free ourselves from the misery of mental impurities. Then one transcends this and experiences a truth beyond time and space, beyond the conditioned zone of relativity, freedom from defilements, and all sufferings and all impurities which is the final achievement for everyone. We have to experience and attain the correct cognition of this mental-physical phenomenon in order to free ourselves from diseases, suffering, and heal our body. It is necessary to have the ability to control our thoughts to free the soul from bondage and attain control on the spiritual life.

When the ultimate truth of the psycho-physical system have been purified and we start experiencing this truth, we are free from misery and experience a mind free of defilement and live a pure spiritual life and can become more sensitive to the sufferings of others and do our best to relieve suffering with a mind full of love and compassion ready to serve humanity. Be steadfast, don't worship your feelings, and focus on maturing your spirit and your higher potential self, and when you are spiritually matured, you do not allow your feelings to rule you instead you will think, feel, and act wisely, godly, and victoriously in the mind's battlefield.

If there were no higher levels, there could be no purification of the emotions beyond the self-emotions. For instance, when you challenge a negative pattern, such as anger and impatience and consciously choose from your higher self to understand and consider the needs of others. This you create and purify your negative thought or energy to positive forms of thought, feeling, and action by stilling the mind and focusing on here and now, pay attention on what is happening to your mind and the result is stability. When you are paying total attention, there is no thought and, therefore, there is no greed in the mind, so you cannot be greedy.

Freedom is when there is full attention to the mind with no thoughts and free from delusion. Peace requires stability and freedom of the mind. A pure and peaceful mind can create clear positive thoughts and good intention, therefore, progress to positive action purity of thought, truth in motive, and unselfish benevolence. Spiritual leaders and healers from around the world use the powerful technique called Energy Redirection Technique to break out of bad situations. By thinking creatively about a solution to the problem, and taking action to turn a negative into a positive. This requires taking focus from the negative and working a positive solution instead, and by law of attraction, the positive will come to you.

The mind is the best transmitter of thoughts and faith which ensures success. When you purify your thoughts, then your mind transmits these into your body to make all activities successful for you. It encourages your body to move in positive direction. By giving training to the mind, it can be vastly developed. Your immense powers can be awakened and can be made active in this way. When faced with a bad situation, turn it into a challenge, think creatively to make it an exciting challenge something that can motivate and inspire you. This redirects your thoughts from negative to positive.

During the first ten minutes, with positive thoughts, meditate on the soul over the mind and over the matter, and in the state of relaxation, feel the soul power and concentrate your mind on the immense power and confidence within.

During the next ten minutes, feel that your powers have arisen and have become active.

During the third ten minutes, make this promise with concentration 'I am powerful, and I can use my powers. I can solve my problems.' With this, your resolving power would increase. New faith would be build up. View the world of thoughts and separate the false out of the truth. Concentrate on the thinking principle and be the master of your mental world so that your physical self is the servant of your mind. Always observe closely the gates of thought and cast out all fear, all hate, and all greed. Pay close attention to your words and speech that will indicate your thoughts. Think pure and positive thoughts, then it will lead to good positive effective actions. See to your motives and seek to use those words which blend your lives with the large purpose of the will of God.

Prayers and meditation are ways of guiding our thoughts and energy in a certain direction to help us transform our mind. Thus for a person dedicated to developing his or her highest potential, prayers, meditation, and the activities of daily life complement each other.

Heart of Gold

When first my heart learns to beat
It seems strange, yet sweet,
Listening to my heart beating
How it quickened, loud repeating
What I have seen and felt,
With confidence, I tell.
From a pure open heart I fight
Winning will become a real love and delight.
The witness of the Holy Spirit in non-sinners
Will give a holy confidence to the soul-winners
Often do I hear it throbbing?
As I've heard it, after sobbing.
Why so wild, so swift, and so heated,
Is there something in me seated?
Pain with all my throbs is blended
Often life seems suspended
Then I grow so still like ocean
Till I scarcely can feel a motion
When my own good time arrives
From the load with which I thrive
That light feeling when I first begin
That there are hidden depths within
To know what love alone can teach,
Which friendship never yet could reach?
In every contraction my heartbeat
For the pure love that we all seek

Joo Lian Carter

Love must have that seed that germinate within you and the flower blossom and spread fragrance and delight in solitude. (Joo Lian Carter)

The light is brighter when I look with my inner eye which is heightened and enlightened and that which is also the eye of my heart that make me see the true meaning of love. (Joo Lian Carter)

Our most divine gift from God is that spark of light and unconditional love with the mind to will freely so all we have to do is love with an open heart and live in the light of God's will. (Joo Lian Carter)

Purification of the Heart and Soul and the Power of Love

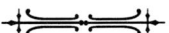

The heart will take you some place where your head cannot take you. If you follow your heart, you will find a sacred place of love peace and hope. (Joo Lian Carter)

'Your heart is purified by faith' (Acts 15: 9). And above all these things put on love, which is the bond of perfection, and let the peace of Christ rule in your hearts, to which you are called in one body and be thankful (Col. 3: 14-15).

'Beloved, let us love one another, for love is from God; and everyone who loves is born of God and knows God. He who does not love does not know God, for God is love. This is how the love of God was shown to us: by God sending his only begotten Son into the world so that we might live through him.

In this is love, not that we loved God, but that he loved us and sent his Son to be the propitiation for our sins.

Beloved, if God so loved us, we ought also to love one another.

'We ourselves have come to know and have believed the love that God has in our case. God is love and he that remains in love, remains in union with Him' (John 4: 16).

'God does not see the same way people see. People look at the outside of a person, but the Lord looks at the heart' (1 Sam. 16: 7).

Learning how to communicate with your heart and not with your mind opens the doors to God because He speaks from His heart, He listens to your heart not your head. So if you want to find God, look for him in your heart and when you have found him, receive him into your heart. If you want to grow your relationship with Him, listen to him, love him and feel him with all your heart and soul. Ask him to purify, to cleanse and to open the eye of your heart so that you can see him within you. There is a place where God wants you to take a journey to, your sacred heart, where you will see his place in you. When you give up with a broken heart, he will fill your heart with love and truth, showing you how to live with a broken heart. Let the Word of God speak to your heart when you call on him. Sometimes when you feel God so deeply, tears flows out for no reason because God is digging into your heart, where in return, you desire to love and please Him to repent and be healed.

Jesus have saved us from sins, but it doesn't mean that we don't have temptations, trials, tests, and afflictions, but we don't have to go through suffering and agonizing over failures and unforgiving sins and trying to live a life in our own will power because Christ have already done it for us.

'He has made everything beautiful in his time; he has also set the world in their hearts, except no man can find out the work that God makes from the beginning to the end' (Eccles. 3: 11).

We need to pay more attention to love than anything else. Love towards God, love towards people, and also the love for you in a right and a proper way not to be in love with yourself, but to love yourself. 'No man has seen God at any time. If we love one another, God dwells in us, and his love is perfected in us' (1 John 4: 12). An open heart allows us to love unconditionally, deeply, feel compassion, and have a deep sense of peace and centeredness. Allow that vital life force energy and light to flow freely to attain a pure heart. After all, the heart chakra is the centre of all the other six chakras which is the centre of the human energy system. Perhaps the most critical chakra imbalance is of that which affects the heart chakra as this is the centre associated with the issues of self-love and love towards others and God. It is essential to have the capacity to give and to receive unconditional love. The most gracious characteristic of God is that it offers us an experience of unconditional love that is a feeling of once being so fulfilling that emanate so vibrantly that touches the heart and soul. This is a kind of love that exceeds other romantic love at an ordinary level. While it is true that love can be twisted because of its human characteristic, it is also true that love is the very godly nature implanted into the human race. Love is devotion, loyalty, tenderness, and attachment of the inner heart, mind, and soul of one person for another. It is a feeling of oneness being with the vibrations of the Holy Trinity, for it comes from the Holy Trinity. Is love the God-nature implanted into the human race? Is biblical love a feeling? How does God define love? 'This is the love for God: to obey his commands and his commands are not burdensome' (1 John 5: 3).

Love is feeling of the vibrations of the Holy Trinity within. When thought and emotion mingle, the thought is conceived and will come forth. When they connect with the feelings or emotions, they become living vibrations, generated unto growth and power, expanding into life and will surely grow into their full stature of fulfilment. A thought must be harboured as an emotion, such as a fear or a deep desire that resides in the vibrating essence of life and then only is it liberated into the forces of creation. At this point, where thought and emotion meet is also the place where vibration is released and vibration is life. 'But those who wait upon the LORD shall renew their strength; they shall mount up with wings like eagles, they shall run and not be weary, and they shall walk and not faint' (Isa. 40: 31). When we are being discouraged in flesh with frustration, fatigue, and feeling demoralised, we submit to failures like a coward. But the spiritual wealth increases day by day and become your strength and moral support. 'But you, brothers, do not be weary in well doing' (2 Thess. 3: 13).

How to Deal with Discouragement and Weaknesses

'*Apply* your heart to instruction, and your ears to the words of knowledge' (Prov. 23: 12). First cry out to God; continue the work He has given you to do. Do not get demoralized, do not lose sight of His purpose and go by your pure conviction of the Holy Bile, endure to the end, you will succeed and be saved. Learn how to receive the supernatural love from Him, and He will give you the deposit within you that divine emotions, to apply to your life from the instructions of your heart. When you wake up in the morning, you will start to feel things in your soul, and a renewed mind that you did not have before. 'For this reason we do not lose heart; for though our outward man is perishing, the inward man is renewed day by day' (2 Cor. 4: 16).

Learn to receive and be touched by the Holy Spirit and this will equip you with the supernatural love in your heart and the knowledge and the wisdom in your mind to increase your experience. Your replenished and renewed self is your privilege in your new experience as your reward and glory from God in the name of Jesus. Lose yourself to find eternal reality and freedom and be born again in the glory of Jesus Christ to walk the Father's will and shaping history through prayer and fasting in holiness, in the spirit of revelation and concentrate on the big picture which is the key to accomplish your true purpose. 'Nevertheless we made our prayer to our God; and because of them, we set a watch against them day and night' (Neh. 4: 9). 'And I have declared to them your name, and will declare it, so that the love with which you have loved me may be in them, and I in them' (John 17: 26).

As we reach out to each other with love, hope, and faith, we can help each other's burden and suffering. Recently, in October 2010, thirty-seven men (miners) in Chile were entombed in a coal mine, and great crowds gathered to help clear away the earth and rescue the miners with unity, hope, light, and love. The love that gave them the strength of many men began working aiming for one common goal that is to rescue the thirty-seven miners from the dark pit, and yet the love and light from within themselves gave them hope. The unity of the people's hope and love brought the thirty-seven miners and their families back to light.

> *With deep conscious thoughts and deep emotions, I learn to find God in the sacred space of my heart. Every moment that I enjoy, the smell of the flowers and the beauty of nature, I see God in it. (Joo Lian Carter)*

> *To feel the beauty of love up to the spirit level is to open our heart to God's pure love and share that love in our actions. (Joo Lian Carter)*

Divine healing is repairing the body with the Holy Spirit. God heals in His time and according to His purpose, not according to our demands and wishes. Faith comes from faithfulness; just believe and you receive the gift of the spirit to heal you. Be strong and courageous and meditate on your word. Do not harbour fears; instead, receive the light from the spirit realm. The spiritual field is made up of four or more layers, which help us to relate to our higher self and spiritual realm. It is activated when we meditate, pray, or channel. To evoke the best from the Holy Spirit, you must find a vibration that is a match to you. The feeling of peace with God and receive His grace to be healed.

Peace and Love

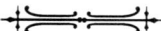

' *L*ove is patience, love is kind. It does not envy; it does not boast; it is not proud. It is not rude, it is not self-seeking, it is not easily angered, and it keeps no record of wrongs. Love does not delight in the evil but rejoices in the truth' (1 Cor. 13: 4-6).

There are two kinds of love.

Need love is an experience like we need food. Love of friendship, erotic love or sex love is release of energy and substitution, which is transferable and it is not true love.

Gift love just gives. It is a sacrificial love. When you truly love a person, you give unconditional love.

Sometimes, when I feel insecure with frustration, not feeling being loved and has no confidence of proceeding forward, I would reach out for attention. Unfortunately, one cannot ask for unconditional love and peace here. Then, I would turn to the heavenly Father, who loves me with grace without conditions; I would soak in His presence of peace and love with good response. The presence of His peace and love has made a difference in my life, providing me with strength and feeling a deep sense of security and safety. He gives me renewed hope, thoughts, encouragement to have that determination and righteous character to complete His great plan which is eternal love because; 'love will never come to an end' (1 Cor. 13: 8). Faith, hope, and love last forever but the greatest of them all is love. Put love first above all things because love is the arbiter of life, this connects life and conquers death to eternal life.

'Pursue peace and love with all people, and holiness, without which no one will see the Lord' (Heb. 12: 14). The more trust and reliance you develop in God, the easier it becomes to deal without worry or fear with the struggle and the inevitable challenges life brings. 'Do not be anxious about anything, but in everything by prayer and petition, with thanks giving, present your requests to God. The peace of God, which

transcends all understanding, will guard your hearts and your minds in
Christ Jesus' (Phil. 4: 6-70).

World peace depends on every individual to create his or her own
true natural peace from within and then be capable to influence the
peace vibration around us, the world, and with God. As well as praying
for peace, become that natural peace that resides deep within and can be
found when you allow your true self to emerge into the surface of your
life to the real feeling of peace to everyone and everything around you.
Let go of your fears and your doubts and that of others. Be extreme in
what you focus your attention upon right now and question the messages
and reflections. If it is loving, critical, or in any way invokes hatred,
fear, or anger release it and return to the fruit of righteousness, which is
peace. 'And let the peace of Christ rule in your hearts, to which you are
called in one body; and be thankful' (Col. 13: 15).

Create your own pictures of reality with commitment and fill them
with peace and love. Love is how you express your emotions through
your actions and treatment towards yourself and others. Love is not a
feeling, it is an action of treatment that express love, regardless whether
you like people or not, you love everyone all the same by your action and
how much you love them like how our Father loves us unconditionally
with grace and mercy. To love requires personal responsibility and
personal action to treat and express the love you receive from yourself
to love God and others with all your heart and strength, feeding on the
Word of God. Love is the most important thing for us and God. Love
with all your heart, and He will give you what you need, not what you
want for no purpose. Through love, we receive the peace of God to live
in wholeness.

If you cannot take responsibility and afford to buy what you want,
it is wise to do without, instead of depending on others and credit card
everywhere you go. Keep away from debts which rule your life and rob
you from your peace. Walk in joy and harmony and know that all is well
and be contented to experience the peace and love. You can put your
energy to this by contemplating peace and tapping into higher desire
for peace and at any moment focus on here and now. 'He who does not
love does not know God, for God is love' (1 John 4: 8). The natural part
of your existence is a loving life which you have inherited from God,
so beautiful that you have to accept to love yourself for what you have
within is what you can then give out. 'We have known and believed the

love that God has for us. God is love, and he who dwells in love dwells in God and God in him' (1 John 4: 16). 'Blessed are the peacemakers, for they shall be called the children of God' (Matt. 5: 9). When you have built an innate love, wisdom, and sound foundation, you become the privileged and conscious being of your wondrous world of peace and love. Jesus said, 'Peace I leave with you, my peace I give to you; not as the world gives, do I give to you. Let not your heart be troubled, neither let it be afraid' (John 14: 27).

Jehovah Shalom means Lord who is our peace.

Divine Heart

In a being, the heart is the centre of attraction,
The heart directs the light and fluid of life compassion.
Call it the pump or the compassionate mind.
For certain, the heart rules mankind.

It converts thoughts into feelings
With emotions into actions with meanings,
It stirs up emotions and love,
With burning desire or flutters like a dove.

It murmurs in silence deep within,
It connect us to all things,
It pounds with fear and palpitation,
Causing arousals and jubilation

It connects all energies into light glow.
From its chambers, the energy flow.
When it is blocked and stopped,
It responds magically to electrical shock.

It hides your feelings and yearns for truth,
From feeling to action it reveals with proof,
It is a sacred place for all.
It aches for the love that toll

When I see, hear, or feel nothing
My heart tells me something.
When I am alone and out of reach,
My heart acts like a rainbow bridge.

Do not forsake the tender heart.
It can be broken and stay apart.
Fill it with love and compassion,
Till the day of resurrection.

God gave me a mind and free will
And a heart to live His Will
If I think and feel from my heart into one,
From the bottom of my heart, I have won.

Joo Lian Carter

Purification of Emotions and Actions

The truth is how one act now, determines one's
life, and karma that affect one's eternal reality.

(Joo Lian Carter)

'And he said, "Whatever comes out of the man is what defiles the man. For from within, out of the hearts of men, proceed evil thoughts, adulteries, fornications, murders, thefts, covetousness, wickedness, and deceit, lack of restraint, an evil eye (envy), blasphemy, pride, and foolishness. All these evil things come from within a man and defile him' (Mark 7: 20-23).

Purification of emotions involves the awakening of the psychic centres or intuition and an open compassionate heart so that we can look forward to that lovely colourful feeling with joy and anticipation. We must also allow our essence to be alive to trust and feel deeply without inhibition.

Unless we are intimate with our emotions, we cannot perceive the concept that lies behind emotions, and how it serves us. In real emotions, only when we allow our feelings to flow freely can we clearly define the natural boundaries of our intuitive abilities.

Like the mind, there are also methods of engaging and disciplining the intuition, which is at all times to honour emotional purification. Very often when we are emotionally blocked, we do not know what we are feeling and become a negative person that we manifest a physically diseased body. By purifying your emotional flow of energy, we open our intuitive system to enable us a clear sense of loving and brings us closer to unconditional love as well as harmony within ourselves. This requires time to get rid of the emotional impact that resides within us just as we require purifying our body from toxin and waste which also interferes with intuition. One of the effective examples that I have experienced which might be helpful is being able to forgive and to let go of resentful emotional baggage. As soon as I forgive the person who have been affecting my emotion that imprison me, I become free, lighter, clear of negativity, and resentment, and the result is peace.

Trust our essence and allow our authentic self to be alive because that is pure with no pride, instead of inhibiting and minimising our true emotions. If we want to experience happiness, we must acknowledge the shadowy side of each person and accept even if we cannot identify with those feelings as long as we understand our own and others needs. Sometimes, we have mixed feelings and become confused; in this case, it is good to follow your own heart instead of depending on someone else's approval to validate our own feelings.

Emotions are waves of energy that flow through us. Being aware of this energy is the initial learning of how our experiences manifest into being and why. Awareness of intentions is reflected from the awareness from emotions. Feeling with reverence is a perception of the soul with an attitude of honouring life. Therefore, we have to be conscious of our emotions to be able to experience reverence. The need for spiritual wholeness and openness, and at the same time, allowing privacy to protecting our soul is essential for a sound spiritual life that will allow us to consciously use our inner power and connect us to everything that is alive with passion. Our passions shape our feelings and project into actions which determine our moral attitude. From our creative passion no matter what the changes, we keep things moving, creating lasting moments and treasures. As long as we do not turn our crystallised feelings into fixation, realise our weaknesses and turn them into strength, we are able to control our emotions to satisfy our feelings and attitude.

Our emotions and feelings are also constantly affected by the cause and effect like the moon which brings hidden, primeval feelings and darkness to light the journey of life, providence, and many layers of energy just as on a night of full moon, our emotions are easily stirred. Sometimes we need to confront our overwhelming feelings because the danger lies in allowing ourselves to be absorbed by the emotional roller-coaster. The ability to put ourselves in the shoes of every living being can help us to see more clearly about others from their point of views. Nothing that is human is foreign to us, and we will be equally at home in the past, present, and future. We will learn to move and stand securely on a firmer footing. You will acquire an expanded ability to recognise what is godly and what is private in each human being and in every event. Open our hearts and let go of apprehension and let the Word of God lead you, the key to a successful and prosperous and godly life.

'To the righteous, light arise in the darkness of his heart; he is gracious, and full of compassion, and righteous. A good man shows favour, and lends; he will guide his affairs with discretion. Surely, he shall not be moved forever; the righteous shall be in everlasting remembrance. He shall not be afraid of evil tidings; his heart is fixed, trusting in the LORD. His heart is established, he shall not be afraid, until he sees his desire upon his enemies' (Ps. 112: 2-8).

The problem is that we do not know what to do with our desires and feelings. We are more likely to judge others for their sinful actions, but unaware of our own. Jesus says, anyone who sins is a slave to sin. 'Do not judge, and you will not be judged; do not condemn, and you will not be condemned; forgive, and you will be forgiven' (Luke 6: 37).

'For the wages of sin are death; but the gift of God is eternal life through Jesus Christ our Lord' (Rom. 6: 23).

'All of us like sheep have gone astray; we have turned everyone to his own way; and the LORD has laid on him the iniquity of us all' (Isa. 53: 6).

How can we accomplish our aims?

'Whoever looks into the perfect law of liberty, and continues looking into it, if he does not forget what he heard, but he does the work, this man will be blessed in his deed' (James 1: 25).

When a person is blessed, when he seeks, he will find and when he asks he will be given.

What does not fit any more and which fruits are ripe now?

Be wise and courageous to let go what does not fit that was in the past, anything false, nonessential, negative, and fruitless. By eliminating these impurities that cling on to our emotions, then by replacing what is ripe to bring new light to our feelings. Let go completely so that you may harvest that which is ripe and worthwhile. If life is to be fruitful, we must do what is necessary to harvest what we want, including the big tasks that are results of a lifetime of efforts which leads to productive future accomplishment.

'Blessed is the man who endures temptation because when he is tried [and has stood the test], he will receive the crown of life, which the Lord has promised to those who love him' (James 1: 12).

Which result are you yet to achieve?

'His delight is in the law of the LORD, and on his law he meditates day and night' (Ps. 1: 2).

It is essential that we mature our spiritual life. Meditation or prayer is the key and technique of seeing oneself to attain spiritual awareness to ask questions, to think, and to observe and hear what God says and apply it to our lives. It sharpens our perceptions and clarifies our directions and increases our faith. Through meditation, prayer, and contemplation, we quieten our spirits and stabilise our thoughts and free our mind to feel peaceful to purify our hearts. The purer the heart, the clearer we understand the Word of God. Feelings can be purified in many ways. It is a system to be free from misery and sorrows which enables the individuals to achieve complete harmonious evolution of the body, soul, and spirit.

'If anyone is only a hearer of the word, and not a doer, he is like a man looking at his natural face in a mirror' (James 1: 23).

What we wished for to succeed?

'For this very reason, make every effort to add to your faith, virtue, or excellence; to virtue knowledge; to knowledge, self-control; to self-control, perseverance; to perseverance, godliness; to godliness, brotherly kindness; and to brotherly kindness, love' (2 Pet. 1: 5-7).

Through prayer and meditation, a person increases physical energy, releases tension, improves health and self-defence, and achieves the ability to heal the physical, mental, and emotional level. Fear begins to dissolve, confidence and wisdom emerge and then the spirit, mind, and emotions and heart are purified living a godly life after life lead by the Holy Spirit to prosper in the peace and love of God.

Prayer is another form of purifying your emotions, memories, and thoughts. Traditionally, I have always encouraged myself to be in holy familiarity with God or intimacy with God with satisfactory results because He listens, sympathises, understands, and gives with unconditional love, compassion, inspiration, wisdom, knowledge, and truth through prayer and in any state of mind. Very often spontaneously at any time and place, I communicate about my desolation, success and failure, anxiety and fear, praise or thanksgiving, adoration, questioning, requesting for help for myself and others, and reflection of my life and the world. God is one controlling power of human life and emotions, and I sense things clearer and more peaceful in His presence. If emotions get purified, our thoughts become clearer, confident, and positive. The results of purification of emotions are right attitude, success, and simple contentment, peace, and wholeness.

'And do not be conformed to this world; but be transformed by the renewing of your mind, that you may prove what is the good, acceptable, and perfect will of God' (Rom. 2: 2).

While going through my spiritual journey, I was experiencing a progressive transformation of my external whole being and insight involving my six senses, thoughts, attitude, and habits. It was necessary during the transition to the new level of mystical or interior feeling to face the psychological and spiritual challenges. During this transition period, I went through a period of solitude to allow me for consistence deep meditation, where days and months pass, time and space, external and material perception become less significant to me. The senses from my heart and my insight accompanying with spiritual sense of Christ consciousness become more apparent. I sense deep feelings and emotions to the core of my being more than before to a point I can feel the Holy Spirit, overwhelm me with the electric shivering sensation in my head and down my spinal cord, and I was unable to control those overwhelming emotions of love following torrents of tears of joy that just roll out of my eyes and sometimes from only my right eye when I sense Christ consciousness and peace.

What Happens When Wound Does Not Heal?

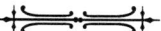

'For a just man falls seven times, and rises up again; but the wicked shall fall into injury' (Prov. 24: 16).

'Come now, and let us reason together,' says the Lord, 'though your sins are like scarlet, they shall be as white as snow; though they are red like crimson, and they shall be as white wool,' 'If you are willing and obedient, you shall eat the good of the land; but if you refuse and rebel, you shall be devoured by the sword' (Isa. 1: 18-20).

There must be something and someone responsible for healing your wound that is your own self. No one can heal you unless you want to be healed, even God cannot help you if you are not open to Him. Wound has to heal from its core, by encapsulating out the part that is hurting you or a broken heart. All these are psychological, emotional, and spiritual wounds, and it all come down to insecurity and not being able to forgive and let go. Sometimes it is self-inflicted and sometimes inflicted by others through their selfish attitude or action. When somebody hurts you, response in touching people's life is more important than revenge because forgiveness with love heals wounds of both parties involved. Being resentful does not heal wound, instead, it makes you cold and calculating, which can be soul destroying.

'And above all these things put on love, which is the bond of perfection; and let the peace of Christ rule in your hearts, to which you are called in one body; and be thankful' (Col. 3: 14-15).

Trust, Betrayal, and Forgiveness

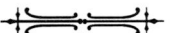

𝒯rust always contains the seeds of its own betrayal; the taboo implies and requires its own transgression. Betrayal allows for the coming of reflection and therefore of consciousness. And with consciousness you can transgress, transcend, deceive, evoke, evade, create, enter, and exit. The loss of the primary attachment allows the entry of the gods and more of insights and knowing that you could not assimilate before. In this type of betrayal, one is forced to the terrible awareness of disappointment or feeling being let down, deceived, and being used. The love or trust has been refused, the message mistaken, unattended and fate announced. Most betrayals break the tender heart until forgiveness sets in to free you from the heartache. 'Bear with one another, and forgive one another. If any man has a complaint against another; forgive him, even as Christ forgave you' (Col. 3: 139).

There are different types of betrayal. Betrayal from parents who do not keep their promises, by lover who finds another, by the child, who never calls home, by the close professional associates who abandons the dreams or project you had together. You really begin to grow through the betrayals, and you lose your sense of intimate linkage with the other who betrayed you and are thrust out into an unprotected existence. Yet this lead into the greater reality is not always made. Sadly, at the point of betrayal, you can instead become calcified in the hard shell of alienation and unable to forgive, unable to love, and unable to grow. If you fall into this, you will not grow in the state of revenge, and it can only have an insidious effect. Another self-defeating choice is denial. The supreme and most dangerous disease of betrayal is paranoia which leads to revenge. Jesus said, 'Be on your guard. If your brother sins against you, rebuke him, and if he repents, forgive him' (Luke 17: 3).

How to Change the Pattern and Transform the Suffering?

*J*esus said; 'Everyone who exalts himself will be humbled, but he who humbles himself will be exalted' (Luke 18: 14). Allow your love and humility to forgive and to heal your wound, and then you will be healed and exalted to find your peace and wholeness. Consequently, the person who intentionally goes round hurting others and not feeling any regrets or remorse due to their action and pride will be made humble by God. But it does not stop you to let go and forgive without him being involved and then your forgiveness is a gift to the person who hurt you.

However, you will grow and expand your consciousness until the wound is healed and reach a deep and conscious trust may be born. 'Have not I commanded you? Be strong and of a good courage; be not afraid, neither be dismayed for the LORD your God is with you wherever you go' (Josh. 1: 9). But the key to redeeming betrayal is forgiveness. The only way to be ennobled and to forgive truly is through love. Then love is restored, revealing the larger consequences and the deeper unfolding by giving yourself beyond your protective shell and see the others in wonder and astonishment. These bring love into darkness and grow the world and yourself in and of itself, leads to the development of compassion both for yourself and others, releasing the capacity to love. Following, you will find that the healing process of the wound to forgive takes a while so that the resulting changes can become integrated into your daily life. However painful, are profoundly healing. Instead of only focusing on the pain and problems that can imprison you release the energy stored in you for development and transformation.

The process of betrayal always has consequences not just of pain and suffering, but also of widening the contexts of opportunities in your life. You then focus on remembering your betrayals and discovering your capacity for forgiveness. As soon as you forgive the person who have been affecting your emotion that imprisons you, you become free, lighter, clear of negativities and resentment and find peace again.

Betrayal can be a sacred wound that may be suffered by the soul. No matter how painful and awful, it has a luminous quality surrounding it. It represents the end of primal unconscious trust and forces upon you, those terrible conditions that enable you to take the next step to respond consciously to new situation that has been blocked within the old conditions to a deeper level of relationship. Wounding involves penetrating into the soul or human flesh by a force coming from beyond our ordinary recognized boundaries.

Forgiveness

Forgiveness with love and compassion brings freedom, peace, kindness, light, and wholeness.

(Joo Lian Carter)

'Be kind to one another, tender hearted, forgiving one another, as God in Christ forgave you' ((Eph. 4: 32).

'If we confess our sins, he is faithful and just to forgive us our sins, and purify us from all unrighteousness' (1 John 1: 9).

Forgiveness between two parties is more than saying I am sorry; you need to ask one for forgiveness with remorse. Don't say you're sorry; it needs to be a two party transaction; you ask, the other forgives. When a sinner feels remorse, he is in a state of overwhelming regrets that can turn him away from all hopes, until he repents and ask for forgiveness and knows that he is forgiven. When you repent, you let the regret turn you back to God. If you can see the difference, you can understand what it means to us today it really change everything in your life. 'Godly sorrow produces repentance leading to salvation, not to be regretted; but the sorrow of the world produces death' (2 Cor. 7: 10).

What does one do when you find yourself in a relationship where there is no forgiveness?

'For if you forgive men their trespasses, your heavenly Father will also forgive you; But if you do not forgive men their trespasses, neither will your Father forgive your trespasses' (Matt. 6: 14-15). Unable to forgive and bitterness can corrupt one's life. If there is a person in your life who has betrayed you, instead of feeling angry and resentful towards the person who hurt you, it is best to pray to let go that negative feeling with forgiveness so that you can move on in a positive way. You have

129

to consider the situation and make a decision based on love because love releases your negative feelings to set you free from the person that hurt you. You cannot go back to change what happened in the past, but you can change how you look at it and change the present situation and feelings, and where there is forgiveness you set your mind free to focus on progressing in the future. Then you can be more in control of your thoughts and feelings to live a life of freedom, peace, hope, and love.

'When they came to the place, which is called Calvary, there they crucified Jesus, and the criminals, one on the right and the other on the left. Then Jesus said, 'Father forgive them for they do not know what they do' And they divided his garments by casting lots' (Luke 23: 33-34).

'Then Peter came to him and said, "Lord, how often shall my brother sin against me, and I forgive him; Up to seven times?" And Jesus said to him, 'I do not say to you, up to seven times, but up to seventy times seven' (Matt. 18: 21-22). Very often, we forget how easy it is to hurt others by thoughtless words and actions. Learn how to forgive instead of getting angry and resentful because the person, who hurt you, may not even be aware of it, instead you will only hurt yourself more. No one can heal your wound unless you willingly set yourself free from all the negative emotions inflicted on you, which can affect your wholeness.

'As Jesus told Paul; I am sending you to open their eyes and to turn them from darkness to light and from the power of Satan to God so that they may receive forgiveness of sin, release from sin's slavery, and an inheritance among those who are sanctified and purified by faith in me' (Act 26: 17-18).

Forgiveness

It is time to forgive one another,
Like we are forgiven by our heavenly Father,
Seek not to hurt but to heal,
Because we know how the pain of deep wound feels

Seek for pure love and the divine spark
From the sacred space of our hearts,
Seek to love and not to hate
Forgive with love that it takes.

Tears

'Those sowing seed with tears will reap even with a joyful cry' (Ps. 126: 5).

It is time to weep a river of tears. If we don't, if we stay as 'dry-eyed' as we are today, it will be like the drying up of the River Euphrates and 'the kings of the East' will come marching across to our destruction (Rev. 16: 12).

I was moved by my experience of overwhelming tears of love from God and Jesus Christ, I began to research into tears, interestingly enough; there are three kinds of tears

1. The exterior tears that we all shed when we are experiencing grief or frustration. Tears of pain, fear, broken heartedness, and anger.
2. There are those overwhelming torrents of tears that stream down the face when the mind and heart are filled with peace and joy and heartfelt unconditional love of God.
3. There are those other tears that pour forth abundantly and powerfully from the inner eyes even when the outer eyes are dry.

As I have shed so much tears while going through change and my spiritual journey of transformation I felt that it is also a process of purification. Experiencing the love of our Father and Jesus is like awakening within oneself the realisation to transform, connecting the body and mind to the spirit within to attain consciousness and wholeness. From the time, I was a child till now, I am very naturally sensitive along empathic level, and I would get upset or cry when things and influences are not balanced especially those with whom I am closest are the one I will feel the most empathy for and with. At this stage, my five senses deeply crave for peace and harmony within to unite and progress to the sixth sense or intuitive sense to satisfy my soul.

Empathy is the key to kindness and compassion. Empathy is an infinitely intensive response that affect me more intimately and its effects enables me to experience others as they are beyond their outer faces and see myself through the eyes of others. Empathy is often considered the most ancient of the healing art for psychic healers. Empathic people have a strong dynamic electromagnetic quality to their energy and constantly absorbing and giving off energy.

God bathes our lives in tears to make us more Christ-like so He can use us for His will. Perhaps those who shed tears from only the right eye and sense Christ consciousness in the right hemisphere of your brain will understand me. To me, these are subliminal feelings that we are ordinarily aware of or ignore. Allowing these holy feelings to flow freely leads me to self-realisation and inspires me to connect to a higher level. To me, this is a very precious and delicate feeling towards peace and pureness that we must relish and cultivate. Be aware of that gentle warm and light feeling that enter your heart and ready to absorb like a sponge and flow. The level of the being is characterised by the impure state of the emotional life. Purification of emotion means converting impure emotions into pure emotions. Emotion is a powerful motive force which can lead to negative or positive feelings. Pure emotion is like a well-polished glass which can give you clear pure image for your knowledge of which it is intended and process it into light experience. Impure emotions put you in bondage to the dark, causing you fear and lack of self-empowerment and misunderstanding. Envision yourself as being a luminous mind and entertain luminous thoughts which lead to pure emotions leading to conscious moral action. This requires one to purify emotions of resentment, vanity, and self-conceit or negative attitudes.

To be purified, it is not good enough to envision light, one also needs to cleanse one's psycho-physical from its defilements. First, it is important to know and love yourself as well as others, also to clear the mirror of the soul by cleansing the mind with the light from the higher self or spirit self. That is to work on the emotional centre, which requires efforts to observe and realise the existence of these emotions in you and being aware of their origin, the course they take, and the effect they give rise to. When you possessed some real knowledge of your own being and have consciously worked on it, and then you will understand the position yourself, of another person and so help yourself and him as much as you know. Amongst other things, you will be able to know when you are speaking from negative feelings and be able to distinguish between the pure and impure in yourself better and be able to speak more purely to one another as well as seeing in yourself what you are seeing in the others.

Very often, we become victims of our own actions especially the ones that make us feel uncomfortable and we have aspects of ourselves that we do not like and wish to change.

Purification practices are excellent ways to remove negative emotions such as guilt or resentment, as well as to clear the path for our happiness and self-improvement created by the imprints of our destructive actions. It does not improve anything by continuing to feel guilty, feeling helpless, and hopeless over past actions and old wounds. However, willing to be healed and be detached from past actions is to purify negative imprints and afflictions, and this is very productive and rewarding with a sense of empowerment. It helps us to change our bad habits and subdues barriers to long life and progress in our spiritual development.

'You number my wanderings; put my tears into your bottle; are they not in your book?' (Ps. 56: 8). How comforting it is to know that God records all our tears as we struggle in our lives.

Purification practice consists of four opposing powers

1. The power to change is the realisation of the consequences and feeling remorse for having done the negative action and willing to change life style for good, seeking help from counsellors, spiritual teachers, healers, specialist family and friends who have been in that same situation that can give empowerment.

2. The power of reliance with altruistic intention by being in the right place, with the right people, to restore and generate our conscious relationship with our own true self, with God, and other sentient beings.

3. The power of meditation and prayer that can guide and connect us within to attain our inner awareness and inner peace. Reading

or contemplating the Holy Bible helps to develop faith and hope to gain back our empowerment.

4. The power of the promise with remorse not to repeat the negative actions.

In order to purify negative actions completely, one need four powers or strengths: the power of support, the power of regret, the power of the antidote, and the power of resolution. When all these have been achieved, it may not have been easy, but rewarding when we experience the new change of a higher level of life. We will begin to perceive most things with an understanding and compassion in a bigger picture with no limitation but more possibilities.

To get people to wake up is to get rid of all their embedded negativities because they are filled with association and self-love and wakeup to attune to the light of consciousness by keeping the internal account active.

Going through purification process will need strong support from within to express our remorse, make our confession, or ask for forgiveness and repair the effects of our past negative actions. Being spiritual and apart from life, think of God and fear Him so that we are strong to attain pureness, peace and love with God. 'Flee the evil desire of youth; pursue righteousness, faith, love and peace, along with those who call on the Lord out of a pure heart' (2 Tim. 4: 22).

Some of you may want to try the emotional freedom technique (EFT), which is an alternative healing technique that offers great healing benefits and often works where nothing else will. It applies to just about every psycho-physical issue, including emotional freedom, health, and disease, and to enhance performance.

This technique may help you to achieve your own reality to manifest things into your life, provided you can overcome your weakness like emotional doubt which obstruct your affirmation, believe, and faith.

Therefore, it is important that you fully believe your affirmations with all the emotional content, and without any doubt, you need to ensure you have full congruence in your thoughts and actions and make sure that doubt is eliminated from your mind and body.

Emotional freedom technique may also help to set your manifestations in motion for a happy, healthy, stress-free life. EFT reduces stress, accelerates healing process, frees you from fear, and passes negative emotional baggage, managing anger to increasing emotional intelligence and motivation and finally clearing all your past negative karma.

Intuition

*I*ntuition is developed through strict rationalism, and it is an important perception and it is meant to assist us to perceive beyond the physical senses. Intuition does not depend on the five senses. In fact, everyone has this sixth sense, but it needs to be developed through superconscious awareness, meditation, and prayer. Intuition is an inner response which serves many purposes to understand people or situations and when rightly used, it enables human beings to grasp clear reality free from glamour and illusions.

It is possession of a clear analytical mind with recognition of similarities. During intuitive function, in any human being, he is enabled to take direct and correct action for he is connected with his true-self pure and unadulterated fact and untwisted ideas free from illusion and coming direct from divine or universal mind. To attain a conscious mind, it is necessary to focalise on the psychic intuition which is the most powerful way to separate the conscious mind from the collective mind of humans. Quite often, we are guided by our own intuition and seek within our own mind for the knowledge. An intuitive human can learn more rapidly and the personality can understand more quickly the meaning of its experience, how he comes into being, what he represents, and his role in creating them. He can also make wiser choices and with more compassion. Intuitive insights are registrations within its consciousness of a loving guidance that is continually helping and supporting its development.

Through our emotions, we connect to the force field of our own soul. In my experience from my true nature, during the state of awareness, my natural knowing can sometimes be obstructed by my emotion. When I let go my emotions, with some attentions, I realised that I was uncovering my intuition which at the same time becomes clearer, the more I release my emotions. This also allows me to clear my negative energy and unblock my chakras thus allowing the free flow of my vital energy for my well-being, spiritually, mentally, emotionally, and physically. Meditation and prayer are the keys to activate and to develop our intuition, and at the same time, promotes psychic and phenomena awareness.

Progressive unfolding of this faculty will manifest the world and the recognition of the plan, which can be the great achievement of the intuition in this current world cycle. People who have much experience living in this world and intellectually engaged or interested with a lot of people can usually gather problems and disposition of others. An interested intuitive person can usually help others for their best interests at heart. Being a psychologist, a medium, a psyche, and the capacity to attune at either higher or lower level has nothing to do with intuition. Intuition is the perception of artificial understanding and only become possible when the soul is reaching towards the Monad and the integrated, which indicate a deep subjective combination resulting in consummation at the third initiation. Naturally an identification with all beings at their highest points is universal love which is true compassion. Light itself is intuition, and when it is functioning, the world is seen as light bodies with the ability to contact the light centre in all forms with a sense of superiority and separateness.

Understanding, illumination, and love are the three qualities of intuition, which is an inner wisdom and reality. Opposed to intuition is illusion, which can imprison a person's mind that prevents him from discovering his inner and higher realms of awareness or consciousness. The progressive understanding on behalf of humanity, the law of the spiritual life, and of the ways of God in the world is through intuition. An intuitive reaction to truth will take place when we move along a particular line of approach to truth and has succeeded in quieting the thought forms making propensities of the for the mind so that light can flow directly and without any deviation from the spiritual world. When a human being's consciousness is illumed by the clear light of intuition, his window of vision becomes clarified and his sight into reality is unimpeded, sees all life and form in their true relation and can even comprehend and see the passage of energy.

Intuitive people whose minds are so subordinated to the group good and so free from all sense of separateness that their minds present no impediment to the contact with the world of reality and of inner truth. They will not necessarily be religious people, but spiritual men of good will with high mental well-stocked and equipped mind, and they will be free from personal ambition and selfishness, animated by love of humanity and by a desire to help them.

> *An intuitive person attunes to the bigger picture and is spiritually wise with love and perceives supernatural possibilities from higher dimensions.*
>
> *(Joo Lian Carter)*

Third Eye

The third eye is a very important tool for sensing or perceiving finer energy and higher knowledge of truth. Higher energy and higher knowledge expands consciousness which is the very purpose of the true self-enhancing and the spiritual life.

By practicing progressive meditation, the energy flow activates the function of the third eye. When the third eye is being activated, I can feel tingling sensation around the forehead and starts to see glimpses of various colours moving like clouds around you. Unlike the normal eyes, when the etheric body gets sufficient cosmic energy, the third eye becomes perfected and, therefore, sees many things clearly that cannot be expressed with words.

My hearing become more sensitive and hearing noises which I wouldn't normally be conscious about. As the meditation progress, I feel like travelling in a tunnel finally merging with the light.

During this transcendent stage, the third eye can visualise the masters like bright lights who are not there as physical forms as I know them. I can also hear messages from the masters.

Through third eye experiences, I am able to perceive things clearer in a bigger picture and realistically get answers for most of my problems by seeing other frequency of reality as a feeling. Through all these experiences, my perceptions, actions, beliefs, and understandings will change and be able to conceive reality with more understanding and knowledge for my well-being mentally, physically, and spiritually.

Purification of Spirit

Everything good and well balanced in the light is healthy. Over indulgence is unhealthy, to resist temptation is holy fasting.

(Joo Lian Carter)

*B*ut Peter said to him, 'You shall never wash my feet!' Jesus answered him, 'If I don't wash you, you can have no part with me' (John 13: 8).

When you boast of the love of God, know that He loves you and feed on His love, then your heart is open for Him to purify you in wholeness.

Progressive healing of the spirit in growth, grace, and prayer is founded in the divine Holy Trinity that dwells in your heart. When you seriously convert into gospel living, and in doing this and the ordinary duties of the state, embrace this by first of all addressing those areas of your life, where you have weakness and then, secondly, perhaps the most powerful of doing this is to remedy your weakness, by emphasising your strengths or practice the contrary virtues to whatever the sins that you may have. Then repent with humility and ask God for forgiveness. This helps you to resolve those spiritual weaknesses within. When you begin to get used to this, you open yourself more to your part, to prepare you in your will to receive God's grace. He, who has given you the grace, takes you at your word and He begins to give you an influx of His light and His love, which is infinite. What God is trying to do is to raise you from the human way of looking at things to a divine way of looking at things, which is the perspective of faith.

Grace and divine dwelling of the Trinity is given to you, to change your way of looking at yourself in the world, put yourself for heaven so that you on earth can adopt God's perspectives to know as God's way. When God finds your soul prepares to receive Him, He takes your soul towards Him, to develop until you are no longer looking up at the cross, but you begin to adopt Christ attitude from the cross, looking down. This involves you a in a further growth in life spiritually in comparison to the physical being. As the body develops further, the emotion begins to fully realize and blossom into fullness.

Living this godly life towards self and others can and will bring you inner peace and holiness guided by Christ consciousness, the Holy Spirit, and your own awareness in the mighty presence of God. This thought system will build your light body and activate your higher chakras to become spiritually mature. The Bible is the mind of God in print. The more we study the Bible, the more we give God the opportunity to renew our minds, to wash our thoughts in His truth and His deep thinking. Contemplating or meditating on God's Word, requires interior solitude to enable us to think and to reflect deeply to understand the wisdom of God. God's Word is food for feeding our spiritual mind a healthy diet of information and knowledge that is true, pure, just, and honest. 'And do not be conformed to this world; but be transformed by the renewing of your mind, that you may prove what is the good, acceptable, and perfect will of God' (Rom. 12: 2).

Things happen in the spiritual life when God begins to give you a great influx of the divine knowledge which is faith and divine love which is charity and hope, and we begin to be lifted in our perspective towards the world. The important spiritual truth is that you cannot judge your progress in how you feel about it because you are infinite spirit. We communicate with God in spirit and in truth.

Therefore, until you develop a deeper communion and understanding through your mature spiritual being, then God in the spiritual life begins to communicate with you as you and you learn in receptivity to receive Him in His language in your spiritual maturity. As this is happening, the relationship becomes more intimate and deeper, and you learn to understand what he is trying to tell you.

One way to communicate with God is to think of Him through prayer or meditation in a deep interpersonal union of spirits of hearts. Feel the experience of the presence of God coming on you in many ways. It is not what you have produced; it is what He has given you to work in you in an illuminative way. All you do is remain open, be obedient, and pay attention to Him and wait till the presence of him using you His way, not the way you would have Him communicate himself in your way. This is a deep surrendering of the ego. To say that you have to be willing to open yourself to allow God to lift you in His way means you must lose yourself, a suffering, but it is joyfully won from love as you slowly being transformed into him, like pulling out the roots of your ego and pride.

Why does God allow that to happen to you? It is to purify you until you are ready to be used at His will to become a channel of abundance in life to serve Him and others in the world. Now the world is thirsty for grace, when you allow Christ to break you down, you allow him to lift you to his perspective and his way of life so that you can truly become a channel by which you participate in the reign of grace of the crucified Lord through his word. The sacred heart of Jesus, overflowing with love for mankind, as he crucified his life to you, makes his heart a channel to make your heart like his. It is your hope that his sacred heart will transform you to be like him.

When you are feeling the spiritual needs and the spiritual desire, it is your soul that yearns to explore a new level, which is an awareness to seek reunion with the inner life and the divine, acknowledging that glorious feeling and act on it with passion, will shape your feelings and consciousness. You become aware of that conscious belief, and in many ways, meditation or prayer can help you to attain your pure sensation and state of mind while transcending the spiritual path. Striking the right balance in life determines your wholeness and offering of righteousness and is worship in spirit and truth.

To reach the higher form of activity and to find God is to truly pray or meditate and concentrate solely on your inner self and being spiritual. Each aspect of your life is connected with other aspects of your life and the truth in you is awakened to life which is the spirit in you. Spiritual activity can contribute to improve mental health and heal mental illness. Sometimes, the lessons and experiences that you have build up in your life somehow lack meaning and fulfilment. Then you become deeply concerned to find something on a far deeper and fulfilling level that your true heart's desire may be found. This journey is not easy but effort is required to clear the false or superficial personality so that lessons may be more effectively or consciously learned to discover and understand deeper meaning that becomes the compelling vision towards an important goal.

Further on the journey, as you become attuned to the actual struggle and pain, perception changes even if the intensity of your feelings has actually intensified. This will enable you to penetrate, to separate, to define, to gain insight, and to form concepts to gain clarity and to make conscious decisions, find new fulfilling solutions, and creativity for a more worthwhile life.

Through faith, our energy level will escalate to a higher level to guide you from your true self or soul to accomplish deeper fulfilling journey. What counts is how you live your daily life constructively with the resources that you have and how loving you treat people around you.

The two keys to successful and deeper fulfilled living is attunement to spirituality and service to humanity and the two go together. One way of protecting, is to keep your surroundings and the state of your body in your higher conscious mind. Another is to follow your heart and allow it to protect you with hope, contentment, love, compassion, and forgiveness purely in the sense that you cannot hurt another, but will help them.

Prayer and Fasting

'Therefore I say to you, whatever things you ask when you pray, believe that you receive them, and you will have them' (Mark 11: 24).

Fasting together with prayer or meditation is one of the ways of purifying your body. You can also say that fasting is praying practice of the presence of God or the divine. It is important for health reasons that you understand the concept of fasting. Fasting does not mean starving to endanger your well-being, instead to purify or detoxify your body with respect and to the divine as one. Fasting is not confined to restricting your intake of food, but at any time, being able to say no to the temptation of naughty, but nice food. It is very important to understand how food and drinks affects your body and mind. Most of the time, I watch what I eat and how much I eat; appropriate food taken in proper quantity the body needs which is light, easily digestible, and plain vegetarian food which does not contain much of tempting spicy materials and drink plenty of water. Sometimes I eat too much because I feel it is wasteful to throw food away and then I suffer the discomfort and sluggishness which does not help in any way.

The fear of starvation also drive people to eat more and inappropriately because of the survival or the collective unconscious of human instinct. During praying or meditating, it is important how food affect your mind and body. When I eat the wrong food or too much, my stomach disagrees, and I feel lack of energy and the mind gets dull with lack of concentration and awareness. If I eat the wrong kind of food or potent alcohol drink, it becomes poison to my body, mind, and spirit. After all, you are what you eat, you act according to your thoughts, your emotions, and your senses, depending on your consciousness.

Periodic fasting and less sleep weaken the body and thereby strengthen the spirit. During my fasting, I drink only water; to go without water for more than three days is extremely difficult and can result in dehydration. When I am asleep, I naturally fast from 8 p.m. until 7 a.m. During the awake state, I pray or meditate to assist me to sustain my period of fasting and totally depend on the Lord. Ask in prayer and you shall be given, prayer with fasting and with giving are dynamic tools. In faith, I pray and fast for three days in holiness and for purification purpose to receive the Holy Spirit because prayer creates channels to invite glory to the house to be renewed and receive the Holy Spirit and anointing. When I pray, it changes my heart to become humble and merciful to have a relationship with God.

Prayer has an effect in the spirit; God has invented prayer for a reason to bring about his purpose on the earth. Prayer is feeling in your heart and in spirit realm. To create the feeling of healing, we must create a feeling without ego but with humility and compassion and feel that your prayer is already been answered. In your desire, when you can marry the thoughts and emotions into one, in your prayer, feeling as if it has already happened and give thanks and gratitude for what has happened.

Prayer in Agreement

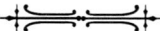

Travailing in prayer brings something to God. Pray earnestly with passion because God loves passionate people. When you pray, you release the seed and wait for the harvest of that prayer.

Prayer has an effect on the spirit, and God has invented prayer for a reason to bring about his purpose on the earth.

'Again, I say to you that if two of you agree on our concerning anything that they ask it will be done for them by my father in heaven' (Matt. 18: 19).

Prayer

Heavenly Father, I ask you to touch everyone and the sound of my voice right now, and I pray for an increase in their prayer life and deepening their relationship with you. Lord, I ask you to touch and to heal, to restore them, and to heal those who need healing. Put your hand on your body now. I rebuke sickness and disease of peoples' life. Lord, I ask you to release your healing power into people's life, right now, and be healed release from any inflammatory in Jesus's name. Amen.

When you pray, you edify yourself to lift your spirit. Pray through and with intimacy with God until you get an answer from God, he is much more to give that we are to receive. It's usually when we are desperate, that we are ready to do whatever we need to do. It doesn't matter what your problem is, you have to reach that stage at rock bottom that you are prepared to cry out for help. The way to live your life at this moment in time you need him you need supernatural power, you need the peace that Jesus can pour into your heart so that you can live one day at a time and stop your mind from raising to solve all your problems because joy has reached a place now you know you can't, but he can, and so Jesus is the answer to your problems, and one day, you might even be glad you had the problems because your life will be so amazing. It will take a wonderful turn around to a new life and joy in your heart will free you and will know the truth and the truth will set you free.

Go to church to preach the Word of God to receive Jesus in your heart and receive the Holy Spirit and start reading Mathew start reading the prodigal son and see what happens to him and forget the problem all out there. You can say Lord will answer your prayer in his own time, and he will give you hope in Jesus's name. Read the scripture and the Word of God and seek yee first the kingdom and all this will be added on to you. So if you seek Jesus, he fixes everything else and he will deal with all your things, I know. I was in a place that I had to do everything. It was only after I surrendered everything to him and got to read Bible—Mathew, Mark, Luke, and John. Read the prodigal son scriptures out loud because it is in your spirit that the power of God will manifest.

Not only food and drink but what we see, poisons our mind as well. We think so much about our body and how we look but not enough about our mind. We are careful not to poison our body with junk or wrong food, similarly, what we must be careful of what we see, hear, and feel. We must also be able to resist seductions that gain power over you to corrupt your mind. For example, addictions is an indulgent habit that you allow yourself to be irresponsible over the impulse that you desire that you cannot resist, that you surrender yourself to the wants of the personality to empower you, which is very strong and resistant to your soul energy. Allow yourself to follow your intuition, which is your soul energy to guide you to make your conscious healthy choice in life. We are constantly influenced by the dark and light force in this universe. So we are experiencing the cause and effect of our own choice. It is necessary to take little exercise, little rest, and meditation, which will regenerate and harmonise the energy within you for well-being. Perception of cleanliness and clarity is one of the basic necessities for purification practice.

Physical life is very short, and its purpose is to serve the learning and karma of the soul, the eternal spiritual life and in return, it is essential to attune to the spiritual self for support and empowerment for a balanced mental and physical life. Soul growth depends on how the soul learns the lessons that it must learn to balance its energy those characteristics becomes unnecessary, and are replaced by others.

The extent to which your light shines is the width and depth and breadth of your karmic influence. The quality of light depends on the frequency of its consciousness. A great soul shines powerfully and has significant potential to affect the lives of many globally. When a soul chooses responsibly to evolve consciously through a vertical path, it becomes capable of liberating itself from its own negativities. It reaches for the soul energy and takes on its own negativity, and as the personality becomes conscious as it evolves to its higher self and becomes integrated, the frequency of its consciousness increases and becomes whole and able to see itself and those around it with clarity, wisdom, and compassion. 'When you pray, whatever you desire, believing that you will receive it, you will have it' (Mark 11: 24).

Prayer is one of the great works of the kingdom. It involves accomplishing certain things for the kingdom within its content. There is something that can only be filtered into your life in prayer by seeking the Lord. 'The eyes of the LORD are upon the righteous and his ears are open to their cry' (Ps. 34: 15).

When you fast, do not make a sound about it, instead, meditate in silence and in holiness. Fasting builds your faith with God. Because you are composed of the spirit in your true self, the body shrinks down, and your spirit becomes alive with God's Holy Spirit within you, where you seek that dynamic breakthrough. Thirst for God is a new dimension enthusiasm for faith. It is almost like a mystery, and I think it deals with things in us to a brokenness and realisation of ourselves and for God. Really our imperfection before God does not change God, but we change. As we change, our spirits become more alive with God's spirit so that we hear God much more, and we get a feeling of what is in His heart.

Fasting is like purifying and humbles the body, soul, and spirit, preparing your heart for greater intimacy. Fasting and prayer create a fresh, clean joyful lifestyle and relationship with us and with God. When was the last time you took beyond quiet time to seek God? To create the deeper level of prayer, where on a regular basis to be alone to seek God and find Him so that He can filter his goodness, vision the detail of your destiny into your life. Because He has a plan and a destiny for you, so in order to hear God you have to seek Him. 'The young lions lack and suffer hunger, but those who seek the LORD shall not need any good thing' (Ps. 34: 10).

Prayer to Our Lord

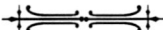

When we pray with intercession, travail, crying out, fasting, and intimacy with our Lord and surrender our life humbly to Him, the Lord listens and have mercy and grace. At the same time, be in silence to hear the Lord's word and feel the holiness and His moving flame from within.

'Have mercy on me, oh God, because of your unfailing love blot out the stain of my sin and wash me clean from my guilt. Purify me from my sin, and wash me so that I will be whiter than snow' (Ps. 51).

Prayer of Repentance

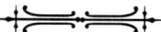

*H*eavenly Father, we come before you today to ask for your forgiveness and to seek your compass and fill us with the Holy Spirit. We know your words, but we disobeyed them, and call evil good but that is exactly what we have done and we have lost our spiritual equilibrium and transgressed our values, we have exploited the poor, and called it the lottery. We have not loved our neighbour's possession and called it ambition, we accept abortions and called it justifiable, we have awarded laziness and called it welfare, we have neglected the discipline in our children and called it self-esteem, we have killed our emblem and called it choice, we devout and abused power and called it politics, we polluted the air with fantasy and pornography and called it freedom of expression, we ridiculed and devoured the values of our forefather and called it enlightenment. Bless us, Father, and know our hearts today, purify us from our sins, and set us free in the name of Jesus. Amen.

'The righteous cry and the LORD hear, and deliver them out of all their troubles' (Ps. 34: 17).

Our personal relationship with God is a very special way and do not be deceived. Evil companions corrupt good manners, morals, and integrity. 'For I know the thoughts that I think towards you,' says the Lord, 'thoughts of peace, and not of evil, to give you a hopeful future. Then shall you call upon me, and you shall go and pray to me, and I will listen to you. And you shall seek me, and find me, when you shall search for me with all your heart. And I will be found by you,' says the Lord, 'and I will turn away your captivity and gather you from all the nations and from all the places where I have driven you,' says the Lord, 'and I will bring you again into the place where I caused you to be carried away captive' (Jer. 29: 11-14).

It's usually when we are desperate that we are ready to do whatever we need to do. It doesn't matter what your problem is you have to reach that stage at rock bottom that you are prepared to cry out for help.

Jesus says, 'Come to me all you who are burden and worry, and I will give you rest take my yoke upon you and learn from me for I am gentle and humble and you will find rest for your souls for my yoke is easy and my burden is light.' (Matt. 11: 28-30).

The way to live your life at this moment in time you need God, you need supernatural power, you need the peace that Jesus can pour into your heart so that you can live one day at a time and stop your mind from raising to solve all your problems because you have to reach a place, and now you know you can't, but he can and so Jesus is the answer to your problems. One day you might even be glad you had the problems because your life will be so amazing, it will be a wonderful turn around, a new life with joy in your heart and will free you and you will know the truth, and the truth will set you free. Go to church to preach the Word of God, to receive Jesus in your heart, and receive the Holy Spirit and start reading Mathew, start reading the prodigal son, and see what happens to him and forget the problem all out there. In the Word of God, seek yee first the kingdom, and all this will be added on to you, so if you seek Jesus, he fixes everything else, and he will deal with all your things. I know, I was in a place that I had to do everything. It was only after I surrendered everything to him, and then I can say Lord, will you do for me what you did for that prodigal son and the answer is yes, he will, he will give me hope in Jesus' name. Read the scriptures out loud because it is in my spirit that the power of God manifest.

'May the God of hope fill you with all joy and peace as you trust in Him, so that you may overflow with hope by the power of the Holy Spirit' (Rom.15: 13).

Prayer is a conscious exercise of will and knowledge. Quite often, when we encounter challenges in life, we try to solve them from within and with the help of others. Some resort to prayer only when in dire trouble and unsuccessful with other options. It is necessary for a harmonious everyday living by attuning in with God's thought patterns of health and then use will power to channel energy to help manifestation of these patterns. Therefore, when we pray, the mind is attuned and will to the consciousness and will of God and thus attuning us to form a loving personal relationship with Him whose blessing response is unfailing.

In the angelic and spiritual realms, Christianity recognizes the existence of the higher classes of intelligence, the nature of their work, and their relationship to human beings. There are many types of intelligences that exist in the invisible world, which come into relationship with human being. Our constant creator of invisible beings, for the vibrations of our thoughts and desires create forms of subtle matter the only life of which is the thought we create and an army of invisible servers, who range through the invisible worlds seeking to do our will. God Himself potent and responsive at every point of His realm welcomes every conscious vibration in the universe, which is oneness, and touches the consciousness of God, and hence, draws responsive action. It is the awareness that Jesus saved us to listen and follow the Word of God all we have to do is with no choice to obey God and open our doors to Him to work on us through Jesus dwelling in us. 'Humble yourselves in the sight of the Lord, and he will lift you up' (James 4: 10).

When you are pursuing this kind of spiritual life, seeking God's power with Jesus dwelling in you, you become conscious in your prayer and will feel the inflow of the power of the Holy Spirit that God has sent down to your heart and know that your prayer has been answered. 'God resists the proud, but gives grace to the humble. Therefore, submit yourself to God. Resist the devil and he will flee from you. Draw near to God and he will draw near to you. Cleanse your hands, you sinners; and purify your hearts, you double minded' (James 4: 6-8).

If you separate from the earthly force and submerge and submit yourself to God, be in your communion with Him, God will listen to you and work on you to lead you to the right path in life and His promises. With His Holy Spirit power within, you become stronger, loved, and love, hope, and peace and wholeness. When your will has been separated from the material external force, you are ready to offer your life to God. We have no power to live eternally by bread alone, but by the Word of God. The Holy Bible is your answer in your prayer to live a righteous and abundant life and attain oneness with God. The Lord helps those who help themselves to serve the divine purpose with faith and then the power of God's grace pours into you. God Himself, potent and responsive at every point of His realm welcomes every conscious vibration in the universe, which is oneness, touches the consciousness of God, and hence draws responsive action. It is in the awareness of feelings and actions that this vibration of intelligences is from God, who knows all the answers to everything. It is in the realisation of this delicate omnipresent consciousness. Nothing is as great as to transcend to it in a remarkable way, the possibility of existence of beings to rise to their highest potential.

We cannot play games or compromise with God. Whatever you compromise to keep, you will eventually loose. We have to change our lifestyle to conform to work in harmony to serve the purpose in God's law and plan. Handle your affairs with good judgment; handle decisions wisely and effectively without drawbacks. Earnestly, pray for God's strong will in the power of His Will. Faith causes this thing to connect to you. With a determination, work in the power of God's blessing, which money cannot buy or earn. Gain new perspective and live the Word of God, instead, of failing your way to success. The only way we can learn is by having it. We seek God for who he is and love him just as much he loves us.

There is no such thing as failure if you are willing to learn from it and make a success out of it. The only time you fail is when you stop trying. Nothing is more frightening than never changing. Believing in God, at least, you are spiritually active before your enemy steals your destiny.

The Word of God is the greatest blessing in our lives that shows me the way and allows me to press forward with confidence and not to draw back in fear. The Word of God has changed me and offered me so much possibility into a whole new dimension. Prayer is a sacred time and a holy communion with God, and it give us confidence that the answer is on the way. The more we prayer the more we experience that prayer has power. That supernatural power, it is the connection that you have with God or your creator and pray all that we believe in so that the prayers we pray are not falling on deaf ears. Depending on when you accept Jesus Christ into your life, you prayer passionately for anything and for anybody, you will reap the result. In the Bible, a mother is a woman who decorates her whole life around her children and is always praying for her children. It was said that the hands that rock the cradles will rule the world. No matter what job or position a mother is in, there is no greater or important than a position of a mother. A mother is happy when her children are happy. God loves all praying mankind. Because through our faith and belief when we pray it can work miracles in our lives. 'Ask, and it shall be given to you; seek, and you shall find; knock, and it shall be opened to you' (Matt. 7: 7). Nothing is impossible when you ask and put God into your passionate prayers. Pray by the will of God and with the power of His name surround by the power of blood of Jesus Christ.

Praise and Thanks Giving To God

'Every good and perfect gift is from above, and comes down from the Father of lights' (James 1: 17). Therefore, we must be grateful to pour out our thanksgiving, praising, and worshiping the God, our creator, who gives us life, breath, and grace. We need to trust, thank, and accept Jesus into our life who is our Saviour and Lord.

Who and What Are We, What Is Our Purpose in Life, and Vibrational Relativity?

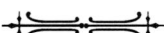

*K*now thyself so that you can consciously love, respect, and serve thyself before others. We may be affected by light energy and the vibration that we inherit in our metaphysical being. We are on a life-long journey in search for what we are, who we are, and why we are here.

It is a journey that expands our consciousness to move forward personally and spiritually to become more whole, to find more meaning, and to realise our true and higher self, and eventually, to help others and evolve our souls to become one with God. The essence of our nature is who we truly are.

The natural man is not saved, perceives by five senses, slave to the law of sin, and doomed to death.

The carnal man is saved, perceives by five senses, is subjected to God's law as a rational being, but still susceptible to transgression and slave to the law of sin and works of the law. You walk not in Christ but still walk after the flesh according to your carnal mind in your lusts, desires, pleasures, pride, affections, anger, vanity, fear, worries, plans, etc.

The lower nature has no claims upon the spiritual man, not subject to the law and is lead by control of God and by the spirit in thoughts, words, and deeds. 'By this we know that we dwell in him and him in us because he has given us his Spirit' (1 John 4: 13). 'There is therefore now no condemnation to those who are in Christ Jesus, who walk not after the flesh, but after the Spirit' (Rom. 8: 1). To those who by perseverance in good works, seek for glory, honor, and immortality, he will give eternal life' (Rom. 2: 7).

When we wake up and see who we really are and why we are here and what we are associated with as the vibrational relativity, then we are truly interested in our beings. When we are ignorant of what we truly are, we are asleep or being hypnotised by the kundalini force. Kundalini force can act in all centres, which takes the place of a real function. Instead of acting, we dream in our present state. We fully realise the difficulty of awakening and understanding the necessity of the long and hard work in order to be awake to connect to our true self to realise our highest potentials.

As my own spirit takes command, I hope others will also yield to its vibration from the source. While experiencing self-consciousness, I realised my very feeling of the path of inner self-development and empowerment needs, and allowed myself to choose the path towards spiritual consciousness and thus rebirth into a new relationship to physical, emotional, and spiritual encounter purpose in relation to the universe.

Primarily, we have to know what we are as individuals to become aware of the fundamental value of life in order to become consciously spiritual, loving, respectful, serving, and living righteously first to yourself and then to others. We may be affected by light energy and the vibration that we inherit in our metaphysical being. When we say we would like to find out who we really are, first, we have to be aware to discover which one is us and which is not us as an individual altogether. We are so much more than what we think we are. Being aware who we are cannot only change our lives, it can save our lives. For instance, we may even see a deeper truth about ourselves and that the important value we were so eager to explore and to discover our true nature. We will also feel that valuable something else arising, something more real, sensitive, capable, compassionate, and strong which is who we actually are in true essence without false personality.

In proper perspective, we must be aware that we are spiritual beings expressing ourselves through physical bodies and that the spirit is the supreme part of us which is divine. We are more than matter, we are mind and spirit, and there are vibrations that belong to the mental and spiritual life. Considering we are spirits in a body which is the infinite omnipotent energy being defined as the vitality of expression which pulsates to the supreme vibration of the mind and emanates from the heart?

The spirit, the soul, and the body are all energy of God in different degree of vibration. God is unconditional love, omnipotence (all powerful), omnipresence (present everywhere simultaneously) and omniscience (all knowing). The soul is the energy of universal love, compassion, and wisdom. With this energy as we grow attuned with our spirit self, we begin to experience energy or light power, through our immortal choice to live according to that before physical which is an illusion life controls by personality. What we are aiming for is to understanding reality and seeking forth the truth and develops our essence to evolve our souls and spirit growth.

Our body is the temple our spirit lives in, so give attention to our bodies keeping it well maintained and in good condition so that our spirit can be well looked after which is the supreme master. If we allow the innate divine strength to rise to the surface, to dominate our lives, we would ease every care, worry, and anxiety because we would know that there is nothing that could happen in our world over which we could not triumph. That is what we have to learn. It is not easy, but with realisation, responsibility, courage, and strength we can accomplish it into a light house that sheds the beams of truth and vitality to sustain to weary souls still in the darkness. When one is spiritually ready without asking, the door will open because of the recognition of our common spiritual nature. Do not be afraid, the journey has just begun, we do not need a map or a compass it may be dark, long and difficult, but our spirit, divine light, and fulfilling our own destiny will take us there. The rewards of the spirit are not easy to be won, otherwise, they would not be worth winning. If we make no effort to win, what is our victory?

Our bodies are fashioned to serve its purpose for our higher nature and our spirit which is the reality and the purpose of our existence.

We are on a life long journey in search for who we are and why we are here. If we can consciously receive this knowledge, then the divine has awakened within us. We must operate beyond the mind to the spiritual higher self instead of allowing the domination of our ordinary, lower and emotional state of being. Then we know beyond all doubt that there is nothing in this world that can take away the real us and the power within us that shaped the whole of life.

Don't be too proud of being a man and don't be unhappy about being a woman. Nobody is better. It is our practice, it is our understanding, and it is our hearts which really counts. We are source energy and collective consciousness. We are spirits with bodies incarnate on earth that the real individual is the deathless spirit to gain the experience to equip ourselves for a larger life in the spirit world. We must understand that we are not created out of dust and matter but are spirit of our spirit and may live and regulate our lives accordingly; this knowledge then the divine has awakened within us. Once the soul become its own, it realises its powers, and we begin to make a channel through which guidance, help, inspiration, wisdom, and sustenance can reach us from the divine spirit. Obtaining this power as we build ourselves, we become solid based on confidence, peace, and resolution.

The whole problem of our own states and levels of consciousness is, therefore, the centre of attention of our understanding and our awareness. To understand consciousness involves the necessity of realisation and purification of conscience which leads to the opening of the subtle faculties of spiritual and psychic perception. When we have no clue about who we are as an individual how are we going to live? We need to prepare ourselves to new meaning. Take the time to understand ourselves and find the new truth within us.

How to Progress Within Our True Self?

$\mathcal{P}$ersonal responsibility first to yourself as a whole and then only you can be responsible to others. One person cannot change the world at once neither can you change people, but the only way to influence them is to change yourself. You know within yourself that you are responsible for what you do, and your own health, wealth, and soul evolution. When you enter consciously into your own evolution, you consciously impose your will into the creative pattern through which your soul evolves and enter with awareness into your own evolution which is the vertical path in your physical and most important your spiritual life. Being aware of your vertical journey, you think, feel, listen, see, and act consciously through the support of your light energy or soul compassion which is your own empowerment the response that will create the karma you desire which requires effort. When you choose the horizontal path confronting with a choice between the needs of your soul and the wants of your personality, you will have to choose through temptation which is a compassionate way of allowing you to see your potential pitfalls to purify yourself. This is an opportunity for your soul to challenge the parts of the soul that resist light or an opportunity for the soul to learn and evolve through conscious choice without creating negative karma.

Do the best you can, help wherever you can and serve wherever you can and offer what you have received. For us and the world to be healed, you must have increased awareness of yourself and what the problem is. You know within yourself what the problem is if you face the truth. Moreover, it is important that you are aware not only of the signs and symptoms, but also of the origin which is the soul energy. Then you will make progress with the help of one or another, health care professional, healers, and teachers.

As children we are in essence. It's a gift of live before we come into this life. The purpose of life is to develop our essence, unfortunately, false personality then surrounds the essence not allowing it to grow. When false personality develops through imaginary 'I', then we are in trouble. We are born to this world to awake, but our false personality put us to sleep. The struggle is our commitment to false personality that controls. Positive ideas make things possible and negative things makes things unbearable. Our minds are so twisted by the imaginary 'I' and false personality that we need the amount of positive power to get us out of this dark pit. Positive ideas set us free from this imprisonment so that we can even begin to see ourselves and stay in the right mind and recognise the real in us to develop and grow stronger physically, mentally, and spiritually. The development of essence depends on the strength and growth of the true personality.

Negative ideas put us to sleep and positive ideas bring light to keep us awake so that we are able to see, acknowledge, and accept to allow the real us to grow. Positive idea is letting ray of lights into our inner darkness. When things go wrong in our invisible world, we have no knowledge what is unless we are fully conscious. We are focalized consciousness, specifically responding to the vibration that we manage in our asking. Learning the human energy system is the key to understand ourselves through our spiritual challenges. By identifying energy patterns of life and the intricate networking connection of our mind, body, and spirit, it can bring us pleasure and peace of mind and guide us to emotional and physical healing. With this knowledge, we can also become more aware of our body as the manifestation of our spirit. At the same time, we will be able to read and understand the energy pattern that enables us to see our own spirit in our personal power in our body. It is also important being able to identify what weakens our spirit and personal power so that we can prevent further loss of energy.

The idea of vibration through energy healing has not been well received a decade ago, yet as a society, we have since become more and more open to the medical treatments that use the ancient knowledge of energy flow in and around the human body. The conventional medical world is gradually recognising the link between energy or spiritual dysfunction and illness.

We are pure positive energy that translates into the human emotion of joy. When we love ourselves first, we are in the same vibration of alignment with appreciating who we are, then we are attracted to all good things in a very powerful way. When we feel a positive or negative energy, there is a surge of personal power within our body that registers a memory in the cell tissue as well as in the energy field. Chemicals triggered by emotions are thoughts converted into matter which is present in the brain and throughout the body. This is why our mind cannot be separated from the body. Each organ and body system is calibrated to absorb and process specific emotional and psychological energies in detailed frequency and when we are healthy, all are in tune.

We suffer in ways that we will not understand. If we choose the thought that makes us feel good and develop that healthy positive pattern as part of our daily routine, then we will understand. When we find vibrational alignment within us, we personally thrive and feel energised, well, and balanced. A loving thought can relax and produce positive power for our entire body which is essential for healing and maintain healthy well-being. When anger and resentment remains obsessive, we are more likely to develop a disease because the energy consequence of a negative obsession drains power from our current body and can lead to illness.

Everything affecting us is a reflection of the vibration that we are emitting. Spend more time focused upon our own well-being and our dreams.

Our emotions are always about our relationship with our own desire. There is nothing more important than that we feel loved, healthy, and happy. We have absolutely the free will to choose the thought that puts us into action to find a way to relax into your natural birthright of well-being. We are responsible in creating our own vibrational relativity.

If we get a diagnosis that is not what we want to hear, how do we feel? We would start to say to ourselves what we did not do to look after our well-being and start to change our vibration of positive thought and action, then we will receive what we want for our well-being by restoring it into balance. The universe is responding to our vibration and the way we feel.

When we feel unwell, the illness affects us physically, mentally, and spiritually.

Physical sickness is due to different forms of toxic conditions, infectious disease, and accidents. Mental illness is caused by worry, anger, and fear and other emotional imbalance. Soul sickness is due to man's ignorance of his true relationship with himself and God.

Ignorance and fear manifest the prime disease, which generally also produces unwanted side effects. The body requires rest and care, but behind every aspect of the health is the energy of the soul.

Why Are There So Many Sick People?

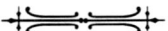

$\mathcal{I}$t is because we have found many excuses to hold ourselves in vibrational disconnect with our well-being, which manifest to sickness. Forgetting who we are creates thoughts and actions that lead to an imbalanced unhealthy lifestyle. The imbalanced living is the precursor of physical, mental, emotional, and spiritual illness. We have the choice to create conditions and experience in our lives, according to the thoughts we think and accept as true. Therefore, we manifest our own illness by objectifying negative thoughts like fear, hate, worries, and so on. But we can also be healed through the right state of mind. Just that people learn through trial and errors and through experiencing from each other, patterns of thought that don't let it in. There are increasing numbers of diseases caused by stresses and strains of the inharmonious conditions in which too many people live. Our civilisation has disconnected us from nature that provides some of the sources of our energy. We manifest disease when the natural unity of our body, mind, and spirit are out of harmony. There are alternative, natural methods by which all disease can be arrested, helped, and cured. We fail to promote health and well-being if we ignore natural methods of healing. We will achieve health when we learn to live in harmony with the natural laws of the universe.

The most important awareness to heal is to turn our attention to needs of the soul. Then we will die physically of old age because our bodies have served, we are extension of this powerful pure energy source, and we are our full creative power within us are thriving, with our clear mind, joyfully filled with love, and we are allowing who we are. If we could just think of pleasant positive thoughts, our body would reclaim its place of well-being.

Act a little less and think a little more with visualisation to allow ourselves to find pleasure from some vision which will cause a focalisation of energy within us. Then we will die physically to serve its true purpose that is evolving the soul, and we are ready spiritually for the next phase of existence. It is the health of the soul that is the true purpose of the human experience in harmony, the correct alignment of mind, body, and spirit. When this harmonious energy balance is right, then our health is balanced. Psychosomatically, the body reflects what happens to the mind and spirit. When we are in good spirit, we are also mentally and physically well. To heal the body, we have to touch the soul which is more important and the key to health and spiritual wealth. If we approach healing based on the perception of external power, this healing may help the body, but it cannot heal at the level of the soul.

Very often physical pain is an extension of emotion. There are two emotions feeling good or bad, we are connected to our energy flow. The only source that flows is the source of well-being. When we reach the thoughts that feel better, everything responds differently to us and because of that effort, we are on an improving platform that feels better. When we realise that by working to achieve our feeling of well-being, it is then impossible for us to ever rendezvous with anything other than well-being that is the only place that freedom will ever be. Wellness that we allow or deny ourselves is all about our mindset, the attitude, the practiced thoughts, and our mood. There is one exception in human because we can patch them up repetitively and will just find another way of reverting back to the natural rhythm of the mind. Treating the body is about treating the mind. It is psychosomatic. If we stay connected to the source of energy, we will remain peaceful, flexible in thoughts, balanced and in the state of grace and well-being. Then we will make wonderful choices. Our lives are all about now so start enjoying ourselves right now. A well being is one who is healthy, happy, and whole and perceives life as one with meaning and true purpose.

We control our own well-being by allowing the wellness into our physical body or allowing the wellness to leave the body. As we focus upon the well-being, we will find that we can grasp that attention and we can convince ourselves that there is no illness.

Spirit is really who we are, death is a withdrawal of consciousness. If we are standing in our physical body and are consciously connected to the eternal spirit, then we are eternal in nature, and we need not ever again fear any tenderness because from that perspective we understand that there is life after life, except the body returns to matter and the spirit move on to further evolve the soul. With the positive attitude, the belief, and the faith that you hold, be familiar with our own positive expectations and be familiar with knowing that all is well, then you will attract more chances to be healed.

Trying to overcome various kinds of suffering by the limited power of material curative methods is often disappointing. While receiving treatment from conventional drugs one has to weigh the balance of benefits and side effects. Only in the unlimited balanced of will power of physical, mental, and spiritual methods may man find a permanent cure for the disease of body, mind, and soul. The boundless power of healing is to be sought in God. All things are possible with His help when a request is made through actual realisation, and at the same time, one should never doubt God, but should constantly affirm our faith in God's omnipresent divine power.

Physicians and surgeons try to learn the prevention and causes of disease and to remove those causes so that the illness does not recur. They are often very skilful in the use of many specific material methods of cure. However, not all diseases respond to medicine and surgery, therefore, these methods are limited.

Medicines and chemicals affect only the outer physical composition of the bodily cells and do not alter the atomic structure. In some cases, the cure of disease is not possible unless the intelligent life energy in the body is brought back to balance. The two causes of disease are over activity and under activity of the life energy that structures and sustains the body which leads to malfunctioning of the body's vital organs. So long as the natural harmonious balance of the subtle energy is restored, the balanced vitality is maintained by right living, proper diet, meditation, and God's divine power, and the body's own life energy prevent manifestation of the disease.

Medicine plays a part in treatment of diseases, but the unwanted side effect accompanies the treatment and the continuous dependency of potent drugs will prove their limitations, and a time will come when they will lose their former efficacy in restoring the body to health. For these reasons, the mind has much greater power with no undesirable effects than medicine.

Each one's mindsets, attitudes, and beliefs affect one's own life journeys. They also affect profoundly one's healing journey. My experience along the pathway, not only is my own journey being affected, but they also affect other people's life journeys. The more beliefs I release, the more wisdom I can access. I can manifest this wisdom to others in many ways.

As I was researching and writing this book from my life experiences, it became very apparent to me that I am blessed by the divine to be in a place of paradise which enables me not only to heal myself, but also to mature my spiritual transformation. My first real clinical experience is the acknowledgment of my physical and emotional weakness that has leads me into manifesting a lump in my thyroid and affecting its function and another at the back of my neck. The realisation of my physical energy's response to the emotional aspects of illness made me aware of my energetic presence that I need to focus on to improve the flow of my blocked energy in my throat chakra to heal myself. My acquisition of this spiritual knowledge is not easy to be obtained. It is accompanied inevitably by physical, mental, and spiritual hardship. The journey to spiritual attainment is not a straightforward road, and there is no short cut either with increasing loneliness, which I chose to tread. There is retribution in the earthly life equally there is compensation for me to attain my spiritual path. My increasing awareness brings with it an inner life, an inner glow, and an inner confidence. It also increasingly brings me an awareness of the eternal foundation on which my life rests and increasing awareness of the divine light and protection. My greatest discovery of my life is awakening to my invisible world of spirit which is the greatest and richest prize that is worthy of possession. This must be earned by every individual for himself. I cannot convince or convert people to spiritual truth; they have to be responsible and accountable for their own spiritual path, and then can only they convince and convert themselves. Spiritual power must work its own will, and not until the soul is receptive can the individual accept the truth. Never be too weary to serve one another in sickness and in health and lead those who are unaware of the healing light to realise their own true power within themselves.

Preventative Medicine
and Complimentary Therapies

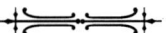

*P*revention is always better than cure. Wellness is the true natural state of our being. It is human nature to strive for a sense of well-being within each of us to move forward to become more whole and balanced. The healing principle within is the cause of the physical, mental, emotional, and spiritual well-being. If we realise the true nature in our feeling and thinking that physical and psychological perfection is the natural state of our being, the body will change accordingly. The negative energy force field within our individual begins to change. Meditation is the key for restoration and preventative medicine regime for health and healing.

The three way of working principles on our spiritual, emotional, mental, and physical bodies are, respect, consciousness, and responsibility.

Respect and value yourself, others and God with love.

Be conscious of what you are and connect with your true self.

Be responsible and be conscious of all your thoughts, emotions, and actions.

To maintain well-being, one has to constantly restore the balance of our psychological, biological, and spiritual self before the damage is too great. To attain self-responsibility for own well-being, you can seek education and knowledge from physicians and practitioners, advisors, and most important from your own intuitive self and the divine who can show you how to prevent disease. If you knew and understood the internal and external forces, and how these could be adjusted for optimal well-being, diseases could be prevented. You require knowledge of your power centres of your body. These centres are crucial regulators of the flow of energy.

Honour and secure your sense of self so that your personal power base is not affected by money, sex, and external authorities instead develop your own intuitive abilities. You can also be inspired spiritually by the essence of alternative medicine with the seven energy centres of the body that will awaken you to the miracles of self-healing.

Intuitively, we can learn how to develop self-diagnosis skill by focusing on the energy of your eight chakras or in each of these aspects of holistic approach, the primary thing is to find the Ying condition or the Yang condition and push the whole organism in the direction of balance.

The whole body is covered in the meridian system and is cyclic. The meridian has no beginning, no end, and represents the pathways in which the chi or life force circulates freely throughout the body.

The chi drives the blood circulation, and when there is a blockage of chi, the balance is lost and result in manifestation of disease. The blockage might have a psychological and biological cause, but the solution begins with the restoration of chi circulation. Whatever we believe about how we exist, mankind has a fixed self-healing system which is the self-organization and spontaneous self-healing behaviour which are used in different ways to control the unbalancing process. Most of the time, we do not realise the slow process of disease manifestation until there is sign and symptom. Personal responsibility and self-consciousness in physical, mental, and spiritual are the keys to excellent health, long life, loving relationships, and successful career endeavours.

Discipline is another key to well-being and success. For the moment, all discipline seems painful rather than pleasant. Later, it yields the peaceful fruit of righteousness to those who have been trained by it and will be healed.

For example, the origins of any herbalist are obviously linked to diet, in the search for nutritional food and water.

As societies are formed, the position of healer became one of importance to provide cures for all levels of disease. Some healers provide herbs and techniques for use in two main ways: internally for purification and the removal of toxins, externally for treatment for wounds, massage, acupuncture, yoga, or any form of exercise, cranial sacral therapy, reflexology, crystals, minerals, feng shui, colours, sound, mud therapy and spiritual environmental effect through vibration energy, soul communication, vibration healing through energy, light (angelic healing), Chi Gung, yoga, and meditation. All these therapies assist you to find out what it is in your future that your present needs to heal. At the same time, you also receive healing blessings and wisdom to make it possible for you to release what needs to be released in the present for preventative measure.

Holistic Medicine

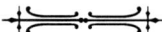

The oldest forms of medicines are enjoying a comeback. Modern holistic medicine is an approach that treats the whole patient, not just the disease. It is a way to maintain good health rather than cure illness. The development of new technologies has allowed traditional medicine in treating serious illness, providing relieve from various types of cancer and heart disease as well as controlling kidney ailment and hypertension. One of the influences on today's holistic medicine is ancient Chinese medicine and Indian Ayurvedic medicine, both of which promoted whole well-being. Holistic medicine usually combines diet, physical exercise, and meditation, together with other alternative techniques such as aromatherapy, reflexology, and acupuncture.

Meditation and contemplation have an important role in holistic therapy. The holistic approach has made conventional doctors look at the whole patient, not just the disease. Lifestyle, emotional issues, and diet are just some of the factors that can affect a person's well-being. Some clinics now offer holistic therapy along with traditional treatments, to allow the patient the choice of combination treatments. There may be issues with seeking holistic therapy due to difficulty for people to be certain that a therapist is qualified and reputable. To overcome this, many countries impose alternative therapists to form professional bodies. These bodies can support and recommend registered qualified professional therapists or healers.

Healthy diet awareness is a major contribution for well-being. Most people know that they should cut down on sugar, salt, unhealthy fat, alcohol, cigarettes, junk food, if they want to reduce the risk of health problems later in life. A well-balanced diet and fresh vegetables and fruits are an important part of a healthy diet. Good diet, exercise, fresh air, water, and meditation contribute to good health.

Dealing with stress is very important because stress can cause many diseases and mental illness that can be avoided.

The Health Care System plays a leading role in the public well-being.

With all these pressure points, the health care system will have to provide more choices, just as in every other marketplace in the world. They will be augmented by people who actually get back to the principles of service because health care is not simply the clinical act of dealing mechanically with people's bodies. It is a broader sociological act of dealing with people's bodies, souls, and minds.

Surviving and thriving to stay healthy in the future drained or squeezed one thing out of health care in the 1990s; it is this broader service-based definition. Responsibility for health is a two-way street if the health authorities want the public to be more responsible, they need to respond to the public concerns, understand their needs, and information for promoting health are easily access. The cornerstones of the society have changed in ways that presage a radical change in values. The new values include an emphasis on self-reliance and personal empowerment, and growing scepticism about government, business, and expert advice. Consumer and patient demand are going to become pivotal factors, marked by a new assertiveness.

Alternative Therapies

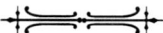

*S*ome people do not depend on modern medicine. They believe that prayer and faith can cure diseases. There are more and more people turning to traditional treatment for spiritual reasons. Some people find that their condition cannot be cured by traditional medicine, so look for an alternative. Also, while many people still respect a doctor's advice so much so that they would never dream of questioning it, others may be sufficiently well informed about their illness to wish to take treatment into their own hands. Since the 1990s, there is an increase in alternative or complementary medicines. There is a difference between alternative therapies in which a person reject conventional medicine and seek some other form of therapy, and complementary medicine in which patient take extra steps in addition to the treatment prescribed by their doctors. The doctors are aware that their patients are seeking alternative therapy and do not mind as long as there is no interference with the conventional treatment. Alternatively, some doctors do refer patients to complementary therapists. The choice is there for patient to seek extra therapies if required. Personal awareness and choice in seeking the appropriate healer is the key for healing and be healed.

Lifestyle Changes

Lifestyles can be changed to include a healthier diet, regular exercise, and spiritual attunement to balance vital energy. Regular exercise, aside from relieving stress and depression has been shown to increase endorphins in the brain that alleviate pain, both physically and mentally. Exercise also strengthens bones, muscles, heart, increase mobility and boost self-esteem.

Hydrotherapy

This form of therapy uses hot and cold compresses, whirlpools, saunas, and alternating cold/warm showers or body wraps to reduce the soreness of aching joints, inflamed muscles, chronic muscle strains, and backache. Some of these treatments can be done at home.

Aromatherapy

Smells have a very powerful effect on the body and on mood. In general, aroma from different essential oils from plants can stimulate and lift your senses to lighten your emotions. Aromatherapy depends on massaging the body with scented oils or on breathing in the fumes of heated oils. This helps the patient to relax and have an effect of some illnesses.

Why not incorporate deep breathing with aromatherapy while we are meditating, performing yoga, deep breathing exercises, and recreation.

The healing art of aromatherapy is the application of essential oils. There are many ways essential oils can help to enhance the body and mind to relax achieving state of balance and perhaps can lift the spirit too. Smells have a very powerful effect on the body and on mood. Aromatherapy depends on massaging the body with scented oils or on breathing in the fumes of heated oils. This helps the patient to relax and have an effect of some illnesses. Massage is the usual method of treatment in aromatherapy which is a subtle form of healing. Perhaps healing comes through the therapist's intuition in pairing the essential oils with the client. Personal preference in selecting combination of oils with confidence and guidance enhance healing.

Deep relaxation is the key to serenity and health. Massaging and inhaling the healing properties of essential oils into the physical and mental self, improves the quality of well-being.

For the mind, certain essential oils containing properties that have a calming effect on the nervous system, acts as a palliative for tension and stress. It brings comfort to the sad, lonely, and depressed to let go of worries, instils confidence and eases exhausted, emotional and psychic states. Bergamot oil has a sedative yet uplifting effect which is brilliant for anxiety, depression, and nervous tension. The combination of the refreshing and cooling quality seems to allay anger and frustration, probably decreases the action of the sympathetic nervous system. The therapeutic effect of hydrotherapy promotes none bearing movements suitable for all ages and disabilities.

Reflexology

Reflexology is based on the idea that different part of the feet represents different part of the body organs. Massage and stimulation of these areas can help treat illness and generally improves health. By massaging and applying pressure point to the various parts of the feet, it stimulates and balances the flow of energy to our vital organs.

Shiatsu

Shiatsu is a technique to relieve pain by applying acupuncture point in your body, using a shiatsu massage technique. This point is a great eliminator. It helps you eliminate the discomfort indicated by your sweaty palms as you anticipate a contentious meeting. For ten seconds, press the point in the middle of the web of flesh between thumb and forefinger of your dominant hand, using the fingers of your non-dominant hand to apply pressure.

Vibration or Energy Healing

*Everybody works on a different energy vibration
to achieve finer, faster colourful strands of light
that weave our eternal life pattern to give us a
perfect finish.*

(Joo Lian Carter)

Traditionally physicians can treat the effects of disease but can they really approach the emotional, mental, bioenergetics, and spiritual precursors of disease? Homeopathic remedies, flower essence, healing power of crystals, and vibrational medicines may be more ancient but possibly a remedy for treating emotional, mental, biogenic, and spiritual precursors of disease.

One can always utilise his organisational self-healing system (holistic approach) by paying out of his pocket to seek products and homeopathic remedies. Generally any subtle energy and natural healing remedies tend to be much less expensive and have very little side effect than conventional treatments. When I was growing up, my granny's homeopathic remedies influenced the treatment that I was treated with and healed my wounds. I can more or less be confident to say that nature heals. Holistic and vibrational medicine is a type of healing system which should apply to everyone and is something that should be available and affordable should they be open and interested enough to try it.

It is necessary to wake up and consciously pay respect to that spark of the divine within by connecting to the individual spiritual energy patterns in their thoughts, emotions, and actions. Negative thoughts create dense and heavy emotions leading to weaknesses and manifestation of diseases. To become whole and well requires total responsibility of self-awareness and the breakthrough incarnation of old habits, fears, and limitations. When the spirit of a being is lifted up, both the mind and body begins to lighten and feels well and balanced both internally and externally. It is important to become conscious of how and why we create imbalance in our life.

The majority pushes away issues like rejection and abandonment that lead to deep-seated hurt and feeling of being unloved. They deny that the problem will resolve itself, but as long as the negative energy patterns persist, issues remains unsolved and unbalanced and become deep-seated wounds. To regain your energy balance, you have to be conscious of the issues through self-questioning, address the disturbances then take responsibility to act on your behaviour, thoughts, and feelings that you have created to affect you. Once you have transmuted the negative dense energy into light and love within every part of yourself, you have identified who you are and can begin the process of healing by becoming conscious of the underlying cause that need to be healed. This requires accepting total responsibility of self-awareness of thoughts, emotions, and actions in order to shine the light of truth from within you and emanate to others to heal.

There are three sources of energy:

1. The highest source is the spiritual energy emanating from God from the archetypal sphere and reaches us from the level of the monadic plane.
2. The sentient energy makes man's soul. This is the faculty of consciousness when brought into relation with spirit. It awakens responsiveness beyond an outer field of contact.
3. Inherent in matter is the vital force which is the pranic energy in which all forms are immersed.

There are three levels of energy, the absolute, the energy of action, and the energy of awareness. The first level is the energy as the absolute, the pure life, pure love, and pure intelligence of your god-self, the reality of you. When you tune into your higher self and take on the Christ vibration, you are literally moving out of the relative energy and into the energy of absolute.

The second is the creative power of the lower plane called the subconscious or the subjective mind. When the subconscious mind receives instruction from the awareness energy, it will begin to form subjective patterns based on relative conditions, qualification, and precedents.

The third level is the energy of awareness referred to as the objective mind.

Celestial space is emptiness for us and is precisely what matter would be without time.

Inside the atom, electrons do not change in the density of matter. This is the transition from the solid state into the liquid or gaseous state and does not reach them and does not affect them in any way. Orbiting in the atom is the electron, just as planets moves in the solar system. We don't realise how much energy is locked in our flesh. Matter is nothing but congealed energy, which is the light that illumined us.

Man's body is made up of sixteen basic material elements supported and activated by nineteen elements of subtle energy which can be condensed into pure consciousness. They are feeling, ego, intelligence, mind, the power behind the five senses and five instruments of action and five life forces. Our physical body is surrounded by an energy field that extends as far out as your outstretched arms and full length of our body. Through this energy field, we are constantly in connection with everything around us. This energy force is a kind of conscious electricity that transmits and receives messages to and from other people's bodies from the vibration. This vibration from and within the energy field are what we perceive intuitively.

There are energies we come into contact with every moment of our lives. Everything we do become mechanical so what do we do? We set ourselves to become aware and set with our command with profound state of quietness and nothingness into meditative state to attain peace and enlightenment.

Chi Gong

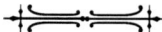

Chi Gong chi adjustment is best illustration in chi gong, which is a blend of meditation and movement exercises to achieve bodily health and harmony. Chi gong practice releasing of chi, which has mass, and thus could accumulate over time in an external object such as the chi gong master's jacket. Chi adjustment is a high-energy stimulation received from auspicious surroundings. Open space with lush green parks and beaches are ideal outdoors to perform chi gong.

Zero Point Energy

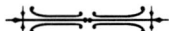

Zero Point Energy or (chi, prana, aura, or chakra) Chi is the source of everything that we see and experience. We are surrounded by much more than air. We are surrounded by a bioelectric energy field which affect our health and wellness, facilitating the body back to a state of balance and harmony. Quantum Medicine is an informational medicine from the science of consciousness, awareness, information, possibilities, and intention in wellness.

Quantum physicists around the world now accept that Zero Point Field Energy exists, and they agree that the field is not a vacuum at all.

Quantum medicine uses the science of energy and mirrors Chinese medicine which uses chi meaning energy. They use energy to remind or facilitate the body back to a state of balance and harmony. Quantum medicine uses the idea of waves of possibilities, Zero Point Field energy, and the principles of transforming with consciousness, intention, and energy.

From the field of nothingness, the void seen as an empty space or vacuum, is the source of Zero Point Energy, the building blocks of everything, from the interplay of negative and positive contrary forces, which interconnect and are interdependent, yet give rise to each other. Zero Point Energy therapy is the most exciting self-care therapy and is an alternative medicine approach to self-care from Quantum medicine, where anyone can use energy to address their health both in prevention and recovery.

Zero Point Energy is a new technology which is now available to you. As an alternative medicine energy healing product, it demonstrates its power as quickly as Zero Point Energy infusion products.

Chi and Zero Point Energy is used to remind or to facilitate the body back to its original state of balance and harmony. Traditional ancient

Chinese medicine has been around for a long time using chi or energy in the healing arts. Zero Point Energy is the source and building blocks of all energy and is reflected in everything we see and experience. Zero Point Energy is sourced from Zero Point Field or simply the field. In Chinese medicine, it is sourced from the Tao.

New discoveries of non-intrusive methods are presented by Quantum medicine in relationship to Quantum physics. A multitude of technologies and products using energy medicine, energy healing, and Zero Point Energy therapy are available.

Zero Point Energy therapy provides a broad spectrum of multi-disciplines and protocols to address the complexities of the human body for prevention, to facilitate energy, to address disharmonies, as well as chronic illness and pain.

Just how can Zero Point Energy help you? Let's start with computers and cell phones. Most of us have heard of the results of research on the use of radioactive devices and most recently the cell phone. We are aware that we are being bombarded with electrical waves from radio waves to microwaves now we have cell phones, but we won't experience the harmful effects for years. Like cancer we don't catch cancer, we grow it.

Our cell phones are radioactive devices and most of us are completely unaware of the impact they have on our health. Our immune system and our first line of defence are under attack by radioactive devices. Do you know anyone that uses a Bluetooth in their ear?

Yes, we have cell phones, so do our parents and now so do our children. Today about 63 per cent of children under ten years old own a cell phone, 77 per cent own a laptop, while 62 per cent have a game console.

We are not going to stop using our computers and cell phones!

Zero Point Energy Therapy can address this issue before it becomes a health problem for someone we love in our family.

I know that the body has the innate ability to repair and regenerate itself and believe anyone can transform their health, using energy and intention. Quantum medicine's energy wellness technologies fit right in with the paradigm of alternative medicine.

Alternative medicines use energy healing technology, techniques, tools, and products that actualised our body's own energy medicine for balancing, cleansing, repair, rejuvenation, regeneration, endurance, vitality, and longevity. Alternative and natural medicines have used energy healing for centuries with the language of vital life force.

Alternative medicines include consciousness and energy healing principles and techniques. Traditional Chinese medicine includes a tool and technique called acupuncture to facilitate and manipulate Chi or energy. The needle is the tool used to direct the energy flow in the body along the meridians. The body's own energy does the work necessary to cleanse, balance, strengthen, rejuvenate, repair, and regenerate itself.

Western medicine, however, has a different perspective on consciousness or belief system, which is based on science that is physical studies, tests, reports, counting, measuring, drugs, and surgery.

Quantum medicine realises that connectedness, information, and intention has everything to do with our experiences, and therefore this new technology has emerged with methods and devices that apply quantum principles.

Zero Point Energy Therapy is a wellness evolutionary new technology and approaches the wellness. Using Zero Point Field Energy Therapy is not only a possibility and affordable, and what is really exciting it that it is available in the USA now. Take a moment and think about what the impact of this technology is going to be on our health care and our planet.

This wand has Zero Point Energy Field Infusion technology embedded it. This technology is one of many products available using Zero Point Energy Therapy. The wand is a tool that looks like a pen, with Light energy infused. There are no batteries or anything to charge or maintain. Zero Point Energy comes out of the tip of the wand and can be used like an acupuncture needle or by simply moving the wand over the body. The Zero Point Energy reminds the body of its original source to accelerate the body's own innate ability to rebalance, repair, rejuvenate, and regenerate itself. There are many wands on the market and Internet today. Make sure the energy source is certified or you may end up with an empty wand.

Feng Shui

Feng Shui means 'wind and water' and is the ancient Chinese attunement of harmonizing your surrounding through the subtle manipulation of chi or universal energy. Attune to feng shui teaches you how to sense and balance chi in your body and your environment creating a calming, free flowing and balancing situation. Certain environments drain you and others lift your spirits cause by earth energy. To overcome the negative energies, the ancient Chinese developed the art of feng shui which creates a surrounding chi energy that will increase and support your sense of well-being and protect your soul from negative influences. It is important to maintain the chi flow in our surrounding and environment that partly affect our physical mental and spiritual health. Our chi should be smooth and balance as long as we maintain optimum health and live in serene surroundings, but the chi can become unbalance from time to time, much to our discomfort. Before you are affected, seek ways to prevent discomfort by eliminating first the unbalanced chi and then some objective confirmation that the chi is back to its normal balance.

All things have chi, which is an unseen energy and like air, it has mass as a quantifiable physical attribute. The chi energy is everywhere and when you feel right, you will sense a positive vibration. Feng shui creates a sense of balance and harmony in an environment and draw upon the subtle energy that will nurture our health, wealth, and happiness.

Chi has no shape, size, sound, colour, or smell. Eight to ten hours of daily sleep are required to boost your chi.

In Chinese, positive energy is called sheng chi and negative form of energy is called shar chi. The Taoist express ying and yang symbols as the duality of the universe which is an important aspect of feng shui. The ying and yang are complimentary forces, moving and altering each other in an eternal process of change which gives rise to all things.

Balancing the ying and yang is the primary objective of feng shui which can improve health and protect us spiritually, mentally, and physically.

The simple tips to improve feng shui are remove clutter, surround yourself with high chi things, living in an auspicious area, surround in setting that have gentle natural curves, visit places high in natural chi, surround by positive people, dress appropriately, decorate your home with positive symbolism, flow of water and moving objects.

Yoga

$\rightleftharpoons$

$\mathcal{Y}$oga is a technique of mental and physical disciplines to obtain control of one's latent powers that may readily be incorporated into everybody's day-to-day existence. It can be practised at any age, and it offers the means to reach complete self-realization which is the key to unlock our hidden vitality within us. A number of research studies have proven the effectiveness of Yoga Therapy as developing exactly that type of awareness.

Yoga is not just an exercise for physical and mental health but also reunites the soul and the spirit and also to regain the lost paradise of soul consciousness by which man knows that he is and ever has been one with spirit. Yoga enables man to perceive the truth in all religions. Yoga teaches the method and shows the way. Man lives in the body as a prisoner; when his term is over, he suffers his indignity of being thrown out. Long accustomed to living in the body, we have forgotten what real freedom means. It is crucial to every man that he discovers his soul and knows his immortal nature. Yoga is withdrawal of attention from external self in order to focus it on the inner source of truth.

Yoga therapy is also a new form of alternative medicine created by the merging of traditional yoga practices, Quantum Medicine and energy healing with intention, combined with modern medicine therapeutic disciplines. Medical assessments are taken into consideration to tailor yoga practices to individual therapeutic needs. Yoga therapy is more effective for specific conditions with the help of a professional. Self-care yoga practices have always been energy healing medicine with intention for balance, concentration, meditation, breathing, or exercise conditioning.

Since yoga is a therapeutic technique within itself using consciousness and intention from ancient traditions, makes it a form of Quantum Medicine and energy healing self-care approach to energy wellness and balance and a medical discipline. It is easy to see how yoga can be integrated with Western medicine therapeutic methods. It is widely known that Yoga can enhance mental, physical, and emotional well-being as a self-care approach to wellness that can help anyone to achieve a balance between mind, body, spirit, emotional, and soul states of being. Yoga has been practiced for more than 5,000 years. It has its earliest roots in the Yoga tradition of Patanjali and the Ayurvedic Alternative Medicine system of health care.

Child yoga is on the rise. It really does help the kids with sleeping, and helps parents with bonding. As a parent, you are constantly in search for the best activities and healthy lifestyle for your children. It really help you just feel better to be able to be present and involve in teaching techniques that calm and comfort your child. This kind of connection is very special for your child to bond with you creating mental and physical health development, and emotional security for both parent and child.

Many new mothers looking for a gentle exercise class that will not only help them ease their post-pregnancy bodies back into shape, but will also improve their confidence, posture, and flexibility are using self-care yoga therapy. In fact, studies have shown that the more babies are touched, the more secure and loved they feel. Needless to say, the faster a new mom gets back to her pre-baby shape after giving birth, the better she feels as well. Therefore, baby yoga is a win-win for both baby and mom. Yoga is also on the rise for seniors and children.

For beginners, meditation and concentration may seem difficult, however, once one has practiced and mastered concentration, posture and the positions of meditation, it is easy to move to the next level. This is to master breathing patterns and once, one has mastered breathing patterns, then mastering the mind is not far out of reach. It takes discipline and many steps to reach each level of meditation with yoga. With practice and concentration, anyone can experience the benefits of self-care energy healing no matter what level one is on. Correct breathing during meditation or yoga can restore the sense of being present, energizing, and balancing, therefore, improves your consciousness or mindfulness to achieve wholeness and a balanced well-being.

Yoga is being practiced by children, teens, adults as well as seniors to maintain balance, strength, and flexibility. Be amazed and experience self-disciple that can be fun. Take time out with this self-care natural approach to energy healing. Be amazed at what you can do and what can be accomplished with continued practice.

Meditation

$\mathcal{M}$editation is the key for opening the doors of mysteries to our inner world of reality. In that state, we abstract and withdraw ourselves from the external world. Only in that subjective environment, that our mood are immersed in the inner world of spiritual realm to unfold the secrets of things in themselves. Meditation can restore that part of us that has been embedded within our true self. Meditation brings back the creative power and peace that is ours so that we can be truly happy and in position to control our own life back into balance.

Part of true spiritual mastery is to learn to quiet one's mind all together so that we can hear the still small voice within of the Holy Spirit and the presence of our true selves. Most people are completely dominated by the mind, driven by the mind, and do not know how to quiet the mind. True meditation is using the mind to get to a state of consciousness of no thinking at all and nothingness. This is a lesson that is moving us towards lessening the influence of the mind over our reality. Meditation enables us to recognize and discipline our various states of mind. The more we meditate, the more we are able to quiet the mind to harmonise all being and be in a state of peace and tranquillity.

The Benefits of Meditation

Meditation is essential to attune us to attain and sustain concentration and energy balance within us for a harmonious and creative well-being. It means thinking about the system trying to connect ideas and reconstruct the system from within.

Meditation is an important method of opening, activating, and cleansing the chakras of the body, especially when practiced in active form of visualisation. Overtime and with repeated meditation, new neural pathways are established which prevents the accumulation of stress effects and actually promotes inner stimulation of pleasure centres within the brain. Thus meditation is a natural stress release mechanism.

When we enjoy meditation and communion more than anything else, then we have found God. Meditation causes many changes to occur at both the physical and the higher vibrational levels of human multi-dimensional anatomy. Meditation promotes subtle energy connection of learning and communication which connect the physical personality to knowledge acquired within our higher vibrational system of consciousness. Consistent meditation accompanied with various sounds and mantras can have powerful effects in lifting consciousness to a higher spiritual level of being. When we are experiencing physical discomfort or emotional stress, our energy is not allowing us to create that resistance in our body. Our solution is to relax and to reach for that feeling of relief by meditation.

During the daily meditation practice, we evaluate our body, mind, and spirit by drawing our attention consciously into each of our chakras starting with the first chakra and working upwards to the seventh chakra. Seclusion is the price of greatness, so be alone within and meditate in an appropriate comfortable place or your own sanctuary that you have created.

The majority manifestation of diseases is due to the imbalance of our energy system within and trying to seek cure or treatment can be disappointing. It is through spiritual influence together with other alternative measures that enable the body to eliminate diseases, through the healing power of faith, self-realization, true self-consciousness, and allowing God's energy to the mind, body, and spirit. Therefore, the practice of meditation and correct breathing is the key.

Meditation has a much more profound effect on the evolution of human consciousness. Through meditation, many secrets withheld from the conscious mind may be discovered.

The two kinds of energy that can overcome various kinds of life energy are cosmic energy, the omnipresent source of all life and vitality permeating and surrounding all living things, and the specific life energy pervading each human body.

Through positive life energy control, we are able to control our life energy in the sensory and motor nerves and thus free the mind from body consciousness during meditation. We are also able to use this life energy to heal or vitalise our bodies at will which is the power of will consciousness.

During meditation, we still our thoughts and sensations consciously, we experience first the state of peace and smile develops that reflects the peace of our hearts. In order to behold, undisturbed by sensory stimuli and motor reflexes from sense-associated thoughts, the purity of our souls, must look beyond peace. Then we will feel bliss. All grief can be elevated when we live with God in our heart and have no fear in the world and free from this cosmic delusion.

Types of Meditation

Transcendental meditation is one of the best known of these techniques. People repeat a mantra chant inside their head to reach a state of deep relaxation and transcendental meditation is a passive form of meditation. Meditative treatment is a form of meditation recommended to realise nature of wholeness. When you are experiencing ill health, there is a false belief in your consciousness. It is not just a question of building greater resistance to emotional storms with a possible aftermath of psychogenic illness.

Yoga Nidra is one of the deepest relaxing forms of meditation, channelling awareness through many levels of mental process to a state of highest stillness and insight and can be used as a purifying process system. During this type of meditation, you are in a waking state of consciousness and drift into a deep sleep yet remain awake.

Nirvana

As we progress with regular and consistence meditation, we receive higher level of cosmic energy, which will heal whatever we are in. By total involvement of the body and the spiritual self, we understand in total about the situations which is knowledge. A person who is not conscious of his true self will get only experience, but fail to perceive the knowledge in that situation because he experiences the situation only in physical understanding.

But a meditator will understand the situation totally because he knows that he is not just the body and knows his true self and stays in the body and understands that his true purpose is to evolve his soul which then opens up to beyond this world of higher dimension of possibilities. This leads to an expansion of our consciousness, which is wisdom. We experience this state of wisdom as a thousand petal golden lotus. Each and every petal is a new dimension of understanding. By perceiving further dimensions, we understand more extensive knowledge and other existence, we come to understand that there is no death. We are eternal beings and understand what birth and death means.

Dynamic tranquillity: the Buddha in contemplation. All Buddhist traditions recognize that the path to enlightenment entails three types of training—virtue (sīla), concentration (dhyāna), and wisdom (paññā). Thus, meditative process alone is but one aspect of the path to enlightenment.

Eternal Pure Light

I was as a spark in essence concealed,
Me my burning ray of light revealed.,
My soul project like a hologram,
Into time and space program

Glowing from the mist of my heart,
Vibrating light to penetrate the dark,
I walk my journey here in the dream,
To grow in reality my soul to pure beam

From essence to personality.
From true personality to divinity.
Thriving to live the divine will.
Through love, compassion, and goodwill.

Matter of time will come to an end.
With amazing grace and united hands.
I will and have fulfilled my own destiny,
Attaining to shine with God eternally.

Joo Lian Carter

Colours and Lights

'*But* he who practices truth comes to the light, through God' (John 3: 21).

White lights of the Holy Spirit or God which is the pure white light cosmic consciousness.
White lights also represent the Christ light of love.
Gold lights of Christ consciousness.
Purple light is the royal colour of spirituality.
Green light is the colour of healing.
Pink is the light for love.
Orange is the light of wisdom.
Indigo light is the colour of the third eye or intuition.

Each of us is a tiny spark of colour of brilliant complexity and God is the pure white light of potential out of which we manifested.

One light is the light of knowledge, the light of wisdom, and the light of intuition, and these are three definite stages of the one light.

Lights

'God is light, and in him is no darkness at all.'(1 John 1: 5)

'While you have light, believe in [depend on, trust and obey] the light, that you may become the children of light.' (John 12: 36)

The light of the body is the eye (spiritual eye, the eye of the heart). Therefore, when your eye is sound (clear without beams or specs), your whole body also is full of light; but when your eye is evil, your body is full of darkness. (Luke 11: 34)

'He drew a circular horizon on the face of the waters, at the boundary of light and darkness.' (Job 26: 10)

'Unto the upright there arises light in the darkness; He is gracious, and full of compassion, and righteous.' (Ps. 112: 4)

Everyman has a small measure of the true light that enlightens and shines within their true self. Jesus is the true light who enlightens every man who believes the light to be the son of the living God.

We are able to assimilate energy and information from the highest levels of being through our interconnection to the chakras and the higher frequency bodies of lights. The higher dimensional energies realm is invisible to most people.

Then Jesus spoke to them again, saying, 'I am the light of the world. He who follows me shall not walk in darkness, but shall have the Light of Life' (John 8: 12).

You must have light within yourselves in order to be enlightened. In order for your light to shine, all you need to do is to bring it out. Open your heart to receive and emanate light to others. This means that you must let go of all false inhibitions and reservations and open yourself to your own truth. When this light shines, at night and brightens up your day, your wisdom will show itself in all its splendour visuals. Some individuals with clairvoyant perception the invisible realm can be perceived.

Some researchers have suggested that resonant stimulation of the limbic brain might be an important phenomenon underlying the effects of kundalini through meditation. Meditators experiencing physio-kundalini syndrome often describe sensation of brilliant light accompanying the so-called state of bliss.

My Perceptions of Light

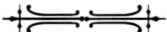

'*G*od is light' (1 John 1: 5).
    'Do not be yoked together with unbelievers. For what do righteousness and wickedness have in common? Or what fellowship can light have with darkness' (2 Cor. 6: 14).

I realise that I am constantly challenged by the viewer's perception just as I am tested by the image in my own inner eye, the eye of my heart. This is why beauty is in the eyes of the beholder but striving to represent reality one must transcend one's own perception. The canvas of the brain is the retina. The phenomenon of 'blind sight' establishes that the cortex is the zone of conscious perception but some kind of sensory function can continue without it. It constructs a description of outside reality, an object in which it has confidence and enough faith to accept. The image of truth is when I believe everything possible through my transcended perception which I trust as a measure of reality. As we experience the patterns seen by my eyes, they change their shape with their movements and size with the distance in the visible external object.

The nerve cells are made up of neurons of knowledge. There are ten thousand million nerve cells in the human brain. The abundance of interconnection makes each neuron to the Cartesian soul. Neurons communicate with each other by sending bursts of brief electrical pulses along their fibres. The pulses vary in the frequency of their bursts, which can be up to a thousand impulses in a second. The neurons present arguments to the brain based on the specific features that they detect, arguments on which the brain constructs its hypothesis of perception. To explain things through observation and sensory experience as a reliable source of knowledge is through observing events and gain knowledge by inductive inference and must be the only means by which I can discover truth.

For anything to exist is to be perceived. The sensory nerves of the eye and the skin of the ears finishing around the pineal gland in the brain has to be connected to the soul. Perhaps the most extraordinary map in the brain is the visual one, which has a different scale of emphasises, a different component of colour, shape, and movements, and this is enough to contact the soul. Each time the eyes shift their gaze, a new torrent of information pours through this window of the soul. Only I who have memories can have experiences. Stimulating the visual cortex makes me see flashes of light or swirling coloured forms in the visual field. The stimulation of the temporal lobe and the hippocampus I would suddenly experience an existence plucked from the previous life and would suddenly be transported into the past and would feel myself eavesdropping on a familiar scene.

Gazing into the space, I see spectacles of moving and sparkling tiny particles floating everywhere. It could be energy?

The matter of reality is only temporary in the physical world. The truth of reality is perhaps when we are consciously aware of the possibility in the invisible world of infinity. The capacity to learn is the triumph of evolution that transcendence steps into the development of human life. It is the predictive power of learning and memory that gives me such immense survival value.

I am baffled by the unknown and ever wish to decipher the secret of the mysterious unknown that affect me in such uncanny ways when I stalk light beyond its physical appearance. My experience encountering lights during my spiritual journey has led me to invoke, understand, focus, and attune to light and energy. 'Which was the true Light that enlightens every man who comes into the world' (John 1: 9). So Jesus said to them, 'For a little while longer the light is with you. Walk while you have the light, lest darkness overcome you, because he who walks in darkness does not know where he is going' (John 12: 35). All mankind has a small measure of light that shine in darkness within them. Jesus is the true Light who enlightens every human. The light is in us all; we must believe its pleadings with us to be true, and believe the Light to be the Son of God: 'Believe in the light that you may become the children of light' (John 12: 36). Embody the light and put it into action.

Light, energy, and crystals are always in me, and I connect my higher consciousness to my inner world or the spirit world by stalking lights through my subtle energy. Through that, I discover a whole hierarchy of the higher frequencies of light in the many-tiered areas of aura and white light. The more deeply I study matter, the more proofs shall I find of intelligence working through the whole process of continual unfoldment. Most of the time, I behold the various kinds of colours and lights during meditation. This is not the goal, but I will have to merge the mind in that which is the source for these lights and colours. Reality appears as a virtuality that becomes an actuality in the existential condition. Light is a particularly important factor in my life because it acts as a bridge between matter and, beyond my perception, the ineffable.

It furnishes me with clues, giving vent to the unknown, enabling me to decode the paradoxes regarding the higher spheres and life after life that so mystify me. Perhaps I could already start preparing for this right away, now. It would mean trying to stalk light as far as I can reach beyond its perceptual existential condition. Now, rather than identify myself with my aura, I will identify myself with the light of intelligence.

Imagine that the physical substance of my body, subtle body, and aura is just an infrastructure to sustain an altogether different, non-physical, kind of light. Each time a light rises up from me, a light descends upon me. When the substance of light has grown in me, then it may be the substance of the divine light, which yearns for me, is attracted by my light, and it descends towards me.

Envision myself as being of a luminous mind. Entertain luminous thoughts. This requires me to purify emotions from resentment.

It is not good enough to envision light. I need to cleanse my psyche from its defilement owing to concupiscence, resentment, guilt, and negative thoughts and emotions from within and from others.

During deep meditation or on the Word of God, my third eye or the spiritual eye or the eye of intuition becomes visible as a bright star of white light surrounded by a sphere of indigo light which is encircled by a brilliant halo of golden light. Behold, the light from which all creation emerges, penetrates the darkness behind closed eyes, yet my consciousness and through the third eye transcend even the manifested light and enters a state of bliss beyond all form, yet infinitely more real, tangible and joyous than any sensory perception.

The capacity for joy and true affinity with the divine is accentuated in light radiance that creates a personal label and be known by the colour that is able to emit.

(Joo Lian Carter).

Crystals

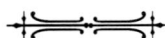

*T*he energetic application of crystals, specifically the quartz crystal, is capable of transmuting the sun's energy into utilisable power by capturing and transforming the rays of the sun. The quartz crystal is considered the strongest power object of all in treating illnesses, energising, and gaining access to higher dimensions of consciousness or higher self. The Atlantis inhabitants had discovered how to tap into the energetic properties of crystals by growing crystals of specific qualities and sizes for particular uses. They also recognised that the source of the disease lay in the higher body where they focus when performing healing with crystals. The pranic forces carried by sunlight is significant to all living cells and the subtle energy and the therapeutic use of the colours produced by sunlight passing through crystalline prisms as well as higher octave colour rays have healing properties.

Crystals used as healing devices can perform laser surgery and can be used to diagnose as well as for the treatment of diseases especially through manipulation of subtle energy to treat the higher body or the subtle body back to wholeness.

Crystalline structure will respond in precise and unique ways to a wide spectrum of energies, including light, heat, sound, electricity, pressure, microwaves, gamma rays, bioelectricity, and even the energies of consciousness, that is, thought forms. Quartz crystals may be useful for rebalancing and cleansing blocked chakras and have special energy properties that have healing effects even without the presence of healers.

Natural quartz crystals have the same transformational properties of the certain aspects of the human energy system. The application of gem elixir is another form of interacting with the crystalline structures of the body, which means that we are light beings surrounded by energy fields and constant energy exchange with the atmospheres we live in. We absorb sunlight and radiate out in the form of heat and wave current or light vibration that can have an effect around us. Crystals, minerals, and stones have the same kind of radiating properties; therefore, has the healing quality that the infrared radiation is absorbed via the skin for healing purposes. We can transcend to perceive the light vibration through our pineal gland.

The pineal gland and the spinal cord are intimately involved in the kundalini process. Therefore, ingesting a gem elixir enhances the practice of meditation, and enables the individual in attaining greater spiritual enlightenment.

The pineal gland is like a crystal situated in the centre of the brain which is a crystalline structure that is important to our psychic receptivity. Because the right brain has a unique crystalline connection to the pineal gland, the right hemisphere seems to be attuned to the higher dimensional realms of consciousness. During sleep, the right hemisphere of the brain dominates and is the landscape of dreams as well as a storehouse of individual image.

The pineal gland receives information from the soul and subtle bodies, particularly the astral body. The subtle body acts like a filter for teachings from the soul and the higher self. Information travels from the pineal gland to the right hemisphere of the brain when it is required to alert the conscious mind to higher information, in the form of dreams through the right brain. Then the left brain analyzes it to see if the information can be grasped which often occurs with clear dreams that offer messages.

Sometimes, our own unexpressed inner feelings and inadequacies are crystallized in the symbolic patterns of the right hemispheric body language can manifest physical illness. This may also relate to particular chakras that have energy blockage that are a reflection of emotional dysfunction which then impeded information flow to connect the higher self to the physical personality.

Chakras

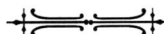

*T*he chakras which are a subtle perpetual system may also relate to the manifestation of diseases. The chakras are also associated with kundalini as a developmental process of daily meditation. To release stress mentally and physically, the energies that are released by the kundalini process flow through the body and up the subtle passages within the spinal cord while progressively activating the roots of the chakras that link with nerve plexuses along the spinal cord. Not only are stresses released, but once the brain and body become more efficient at handling stress, the kundalini eliminates stress rapidly from the body and mind as they occur and also prevent the accumulation of new stress.

From an energy point of view, every choice that enhance our spirit's strengthens our energy field, and the stronger our energy field, the fewer our connections to negative people and experiences.

The chakras are the power centre of the human energy system or life force like the tree of life. There are seven chakras in our energy system. Spiritually, physically, and psychologically our energy is all one and the same force power from the energy field.

Each chakras is related to various aspects of consciousness especially the emotions, which affect the flow of energy through these centres. Each of the seven major chakras has its particular spiritual and emotional specialised energy transformers, which take in subtle energy and direct it to the major glands, nerve centres, and organs of the body. When the subtle energy in the various chakras is blocked, and the mechanism become unbalanced causing chronic stress this can negatively affect the physical body. Under activity of the chakras affect the lack of subtle energy flow and may manifest as cancerous lesion in the deprived chakra in the associated organs. We are all here to experience life through seven sacraments of truth. As spiritual adults, we accept responsibility for co-creating our lives through our power of divine challenge and the sacred contract that we are here to fulfil. We experience the creative strengths of our thoughts and emotion in our physical bodies supported by our seven sacred energy centres to transform us into conscious spiritual adults. Once we are conscious of the truth, we can no longer live an ordinary life. We can be our own inner physicians through our own power energy centres and from the pure divine light force. As we begin to pay more attention and get a better understanding of the functions of the chakras and their relationship to the development and expression of human consciousness, much will be opened to the whole concept, which will change the way in which human illness is conceptualised and treated by the healers and physicians of the future.

To replace that false conviction with truth, spend some time each morning and evening with the following meditative exercise. Before we begin, understand that there are seven chakras that are the energy centres in the etheric body, each representing different levels of consciousness. In the treatment, there are areas that need to be focused and meditated on and the corresponding idea for several minutes on the chakras. It is to transmute the energy of the lower mind to a higher frequency focusing on the appropriate chakras.

When we meditate, whether for health, wealth, or success, we take time to quieten the mind, let go of the appearance of the outer world, and meditate on the lights and colours of the different chakras, wholeness, and completeness of our divine self.

The kundalini energy is the energy developed through gradual enlightening from regular practice of meditation over a period of time. Kundalini energy opens up the chakras from the base chakra to the crown chakra. To allow energy flow through a chakra, it has to be unblocked. Through our lives, we build up subtle stresses that block the chakras, which can be opened up by the effect of the kundalini force accompanied with the gradual realisation of the spiritual and emotional lessons required for the correct functioning of that chakra. The sacral chakra energy is the most active at the time of the first initiation and has to be transported to the throat chakra, thereby transforming the physical creative act into creative process of producing the good, the beautiful, and the true. All the seven chakras correspond and function with each other and each play an important role for our well-being, but perhaps we should pay more attention to the sixth and seventh chakras associated with issues of spiritual seeking. Once we have opened up heart chakra, the energy of love and joy can flow, then the higher chakras, the brow and the crown chakras, come within easier reach for personal and spiritual transformation through the attainment of higher consciousness. Through a surge of interest in meditation, prayer, and quest for greater spiritual direction, more and more people attune themselves to the development of intuition, inner vision, and spiritual awareness. The awakening of the kundalini force and its energy is associated with the endocrine glands which secret hormones that have resonating harmonic frequency of red. Each time we have an initiatory breakthrough, the kundalini opens to the next new frequency. The awakening of the kundalini truly permits the flow of more energy that can make us feel incredibly vitalised and alive than we have previously had access to. Right after the opening of the kundalini, the sacral chakra opens and connects to the third eye and becomes a highly visual state of everything we see and feel. This synchronisation of the right and left hemisphere of the brain, and at this point, of the opening of the kundalini activates awareness throughout the body which is the powerful life force moving through us.

First Chakra (Root Chakra)

The first chakra is known as the root (base) or kundalini chakra which is the foundation of the seven chakras. The element is fire and this life force has a fiery beautiful translucent quality. It contains the colour of rainbow and is reflected in the denser or lower vibration aspects of being. The colour of red is associated with the base chakra. The secondary colour is mauve and brown. The root centre reflects the degree to which we feel grounded in our day-to-day activities. A strong root chakra aids to keep us grounded in life and to enhance the ability to have easy access to higher levels of awareness.

The amount of energy flow of the root chakra is a reflection of one's ability to link with the earth and function effectively based on how well we are able to make daily decision based on our acute needs. The first chakra from a physical level is associated with the sacrum, the rectum, the anus, the urethra, and the spine in general.

Acknowledging any sense of responsibility for each other is simultaneously an act of spiritual awakening.

Psychologically, the first chakra is linked to the adrenal glands the body's major source of adrenaline in time of stress, the basic survival instincts (fight or flight). When too much energy is focused in the root chakra, the individual may develop a tendency to react defensively to most situations.

Crystal system is trigonal; the ray is red, energetic nature—energising and corresponds to the base chakra, which is related to the kundalini energies.

The gemstones are bloodstones, amethysts, garnets, smoky quartz, ruby, rose quartz, onyx, tiger's eye, alexandrite, agates, and carnelians. The aroma is patchouli and cedar wood calms the root chakra whilst lavender, hyacinth, and musk will stimulate it. The trigonal system contains crystals that continually give off energy at a subtle energetic level in a spinning motion, which is of neither a positive nor negative nature, but of a balanced nature. They help to prepare the multilevel energy systems of the body for spiritual work. Each gem possesses unique spiritual, energetic, and healing properties, which may help us in our search for balance and wholeness.

Power of Relationships—Second Chakra (Sacral Chakra)

The second chakra power is situated at the spleen region associated with the gonads and reproductive organs urinary bladder, the appendix, the lumbar vertebrae, large intestines, and small intestines. It represents water element connected for absorption, and it sense is taste. The colour of orange is associated with the sacral chakra, and the secondary colour is gold and amber.

This is our need for the physical safety. Second chakra moves us into the world of money, morality, creativity, expression of sensual emotion, and sexuality, partnership, and empowerment of the other. Everything about our life is involved in our relationship to this energy called power, which, however, expresses this energy in physical form. At this point of our evolution, we can recognise that external or physical power is necessary for health. Health is a direct consequence of the spiritual and therapeutic principles we absorb into our daily life. Personal power is fundamental to material success and spiritual balance.

Woman suffering from cervical and uterine cancer and for man, sexual dysfunction, prostitutes, and low back pain may have blockages or other types of imbalance within the gonad or sacral centre. Other illness resulting from dysfunction of the sacral chakra includes irritable bowel syndromes, colitis, bladder cancer, diseases of the small and large intestine.

Gemstones are garnets, diamonds, and fluorites. Colour of the ray is cobalt blue, its energetic nature is fundamental and earth nature, and corresponds to the sacral chakra. The crystal may be used in meditation or other states of consciousness of an earth plane nature. The cubic system from crystals has an energy pattern that can help in the repair of damaged cellular structures from the DNA molecular level up to the bones of the skeletal system. Other crystals are citrine, topaz, moonstone, jasper, and amber. Aroma of geranium and rosemary stimulate the sacral chakra, whilst amber and musk calm it.

Third Chakra—Personal Power
(Solar Chakra)

The third chakra is the solar plexus chakra, which represents the element of air, and indeed is like an inner fire, burning energies of chemical oxidation through the digestion of food and it has a sense of sight. The colour of yellow is associated with the solar plexus chakra. Its secondary colours are gold and rose. The solar plexus centre is also a seat of aggression, anger, and other emotions that is connected to the individual personal power and feelings in controlling over our lives. It is also an energy centre of the body, which contributes to the outward vitality of the persona, adrenals, stomach, pancreas, upper intestines, gallbladder, liver, and the middle spine.

Self-responsibility, fear of rejection, self-esteem, and an over sensitivity to criticism are issues attributed to illness. The sacred truth of the solar plexus chakra is honouring oneself. The spiritual energies of endurance and majesty have one spiritual goal to help us mature in our self-understanding, self-responsibility, and the relationship we have with ourselves. The spiritual quality is self-respect and self-esteem.

Gemstones are topaz, emeralds, aquamarines, and apatite. The crystals correspond particularly to the solar plexus chakra. The ray is green, and the energetic nature is for growth and vitality.

The crystals are both hexagonal that can be used for healing the endocrine glands, for balancing the energy of all the chakras and subtle bodies, communicating and storing information, and associate with service. Other crystals for this chakra are yellow topaz, malachite, yellow citrine, apatite, rose quartz, and kunzite.

Ylang-ylang and bergamot stimulate whilst rose calm the solar plexus.

The Power Of Love—Fourth Chakra (Heart Chakra)

The heart is the fourth chakra, which is the centre of human energy system.

The element of the fourth chakra is earth and the sense touch. Green is the colour of the heart chakra. Subsidiary colours are rose and rose amethyst.

The gemstones are zircon and chalcopyrite belonging to the tetragonal system, which has ray of pink colour with energy balancing nature that corresponds to the heart chakra. Other crystals are emerald, amber, rose tourmalines, and jade.

The tetragonal class can be useful for attunement to higher dimensions by channelling vibrations into the earth.

Sandalwood and rose aroma calm the heart chakra whilst honey suckle and pine stimulate it Perhaps the most critical chakra imbalance is one that affects the heart chakra as this is the centre associated with the issues of self-love and love towards others. The three higher and three lower chakras are linked by the heart chakra, which is also the centre of human existence from which we are able to express love that we are incarnated to this earth plane to learn the expression of love. It is necessary that we learn to love others but also ourselves.

Love and personal attention are deeply healing and protecting and makes all things bright and new. Above everything in life, give to all who seek help the fullest measure of love.

The heart chakra is so significant and is that an open-heart chakra is integral to an individual's ability to love yourself and others. Love is the life expression of God. The highest form of spiritual love is unconditional love towards others. How we live our life, runs off the most powerful energy of our hearts. It is in our hearts that we are conscious of our spiritual needs and embodies the spiritual lesson that teaches us how to act out of love and compassion.

The power of love energy comes in stages from the fourth chakra. Each of this stage connects in love's intensity and forms—forgiveness, compassion, generosity, kindness, caring for you, and others and the desire to serve people. Love helps you heal others and yourself. Some people experience difficulties in developing the inner potential of the heart chakra, the inner heart centre that can lead to heart disease.

The heart chakra also provides nutritive energy to the bronchial tubes, lungs, and breasts and the circulatory system. If the energy is imbalanced, it can also lead to coronary artery disease stroke and heart attacks. The amount of subtle energy flow through the heart chakra is the reflection of the importance of love in an individual's life.

Being able to love yourself means having the courage to detect and to listen to the heart's emotional messages and spiritual directives, and then you can love others in the same way. Yet for many people loving one often act out in material way through rewarding yourself to satisfy the physical pleasure to express self-appreciation. While this type of reward is pleasurable, it can obstruct your contact with the deeper emotional stimulation of the heart that occurs when you need to access a relationship or troubled circumstances that affect your health. For example, the heart most frequently guides you for healing and is that of the way you were brought up. Within each of us is contained, the stunted emotional patterns of our childhood, patterns of painful memories, of negative attitudes, and of dysfunctional self-image. Unconsciously, we may continue to function within these patterns as adults which lead to negative insecure self-image that may become the source of dysfunctions such as obesity, anorexia, alcoholism, and other addictions as well as obsessive fear of failure. These behaviours can destroy our emotional relationships, our personal and professional lives, and physical, psychological, and spiritual well-being.

The heart chakra is also considered to be an important centre of nurturance.

The breasts are also situated at the level of the heart chakra which is fully dedicated to nurturance of another being. If a child is given too much loving attention to the point of preventing its ability to become independent, the insufficient balance in heart centre result in abnormal stimulation of the bronchial tree, cutting off the inflow of oxygen.

The lungs take in oxygen and being associated with the heart where the heart pumps blood to the lungs, where oxygen and prana are taken in and distributed to the rest of the body's organs. In the digestive system, more nutrients are added to the blood stream, where circulation can distribute them to the physical body.

The Power of Will—Fifth Chakra (Throat Chakra)

The fifth chakra or throat centre embodies the challenges of surrendering our own willpower and spirit to the will of God. When opening the throat chakra, meditate on the colour of blue, and it is used for clairaudience to hear from the spirit when it is developed. The subsidiary colours are turquoise and silver. The element of the throat chakra is ether and its sense hearing.

The types of disease that may manifest in the physical structure due to blockage of energy flow are degenerative disease like hypothyroidism (underactive thyroid). Overabundant energy flow can cause inflammation to the thyroid and carcinoma of the thyroid. Other diseases connected to the—abnormal throat chakra are laryngitis, parathyroid gland tumours, and cancer of the larynx.

At the physical emotional level, dysfunction in the throat centre may reflect difficulties in communication who have difficulty in self-expression and may be seen here as a problem in exerting the will to communicate one's true inner feelings and unable to consciously recognise his or her own needs.

Gemstones are topaz, peridot, and alexandrite, belong to the orthorhombic system, have a unique aspect of encircling and encompassing energy pattern, and its ray is orange in colour. This crystal corresponds to the throat chakra. The crystal can be used to magnify consciousness and help individual isolate problems and contain them until they can be worked out at various level of experience. Other crystals are aquamarine, turquoise, and sapphire.

Patchouli and white mask aroma stimulates the throat chakra whilst hyacinth and lavender calm it. This crystal corresponds to the throat chakra.

The Power of the Mind—Sixth Chakra (Brow Chakra)

The sixth chakra is the brow chakra and it is also referred to as the 'third eye'. It involves our mental and reasoning abilities and our psychological skill at evaluating our beliefs and attitudes. The third eye chakra is the seat of intuition and the subtle organ involved in clairvoyance. The element is radium and the colour associated is indigo. Indigo is the colour to meditate on. The subsidiary colours are mauve and turquoise. During deep meditation, the third eye or the spiritual eye becomes visible as a bright star white light surrounded by a sphere of indigo light which is encircled by a brilliant halo of golden light.

Disease caused by dysfunction of the sixth chakra may cause an individual not to want to see something which is important to his or her soul growth which leads to energy blockages and can cause sinus problems, cataracts, and major endocrine imbalance. The gemstones are jade, azurite, moonstone and malachite; they are crystals of monoclinic system and have a unique constant pulsating action. This action assists to serve as an impetus to action and growth as well as to the expansion and contraction of consciousness. This blue-violet ray crystal corresponds to the third eye chakra. Such crystals when held up to the third eye chakra can be assisted in perceiving self and others on a multidimensional level of spirit. Other crystals are amethyst and purple apatite. Rose geranium and violet stimulate the brow chakra whilst hyacinth and white musk calms it.

Crown Chakra—the Power of Spiritual Connecter

The seventh chakra is the power of our spiritual connector. It is connected to the soul and the higher self and also be easily connected to your brow chakra which keeps you in touch with resonance.

The seventh chakra or the crown chakra is closely linked with the pineal gland. The colour associated is violet with gold and white as subsidiary colours. The element is earth.

It must first bring about a balancing of the body, the mind, and the spirit for the crown chakra to be fully awakened. To enter into the highest state of consciousness, the crown chakra has to be opened which represents the beginning stage of ascension into state of spiritual perfection. The energy of the crown chakra influences the central nervous system, the skin, and the muscular system. Abnormalities in energy flow of the crown chakra may manifest as various types of cerebral dysfunction and psychosis.

While our energy system is animated by our spirit, the crown chakra is directly aligned to seek an intimate relationship with the divine. It contains the energy that generates inspirational and prophetic thoughts, devotion, transcendent ideas, and dimension of life and mystical connections. It enables us to gain an internal awareness through meditation and prayer. Faith in the presence of the divine and in all that faith represents inner guidance, insight into healing, and quality of trust that shadows human fears; devotion.

Turquoise and rhodonite are crystals of the triclinic system and possesses aspects of completion within their make-up in that they form a triad which assist to balance the yin and yang energy within a person. This crystal has yellow and corresponds to the crown chakra which is the highest energetic level and help to balance personalities and attitudes that are unbalanced and also allow individuals to attune to higher spiritual dimensions. Other crystals are white jade, diamond, snowy quartz, celestite, and white tourmaline. The aroma to enhance stimulation is bergamot with amber and rosemary.

Pain and Suffering

$\mathcal{P}$ain is very important because it alerts us to something that is wrong in the same way the spirit of God alerts us, to activate thoughts, words, and deeds that are not of God, by making us feel guilty. It is very important that our spirit is sensitive to God's Holy Spirit of truth. Therefore, we listen to the gentle spirit of God. We must not in any way fail to respond to the prompting of the spirit. Paul said, 'That every one of you should know how to possess or control his own body in purity and honor' (1 Thess. 4: 4). Many struggles through life spiritually immature or lost and in pain physically, emotionally, and psychologically because they wrestle against the issues of pain and life in ignorance and indulge to broken laws, then Cry out to God 'Why' or if there is a God of mercy, how can He allow evil and pain continue? 'For God has not called us to uncleanness, but to holiness' (1 Thess. 4: 7). Well, God loves us, and He does not want to see us struggling in pain, but mankind was created with the mind to free will. Therefore, if we continue to bring evil upon ourselves and the world, choosing to live in our attitude against His will and our purpose, then God would be entirely justified to condemn us on the unholy mess we have made of His creation. However, the Father still loves us by sacrificing His only son Jesus Christ to come to fulfill His law and to save us from our sins and to show us the way back to eternity and peace to the Father's kingdom. 'For the wages of sin are death; but the gift of God is eternal life through Jesus Christ our Lord' (Rom. 6: 23). Jesus, a pure and innocent man, lived like us through pain, persecution, and sorrow. He was crucified on the cross for our sins, and yet he did not complain; instead, he asked God to forgive us so that we can inherit eternal life through his grace in faith and truth. 'It is finished!' (John 19: 30). Jesus accomplished his mission, so it's up to us to have faith and trust him to understand and live God's law (the Ten Commandments) to accomplish our mission too through Jesus. Pain is

God's megaphone and when one begins to find God that's when the pain starts. Jesus took our burden of pain on the cross to redeem us from all our sins, and on the third day, his resurrection conquered death so that we can have eternal life. It is very important that our spirit is sensitive to God's Holy Spirit of truth so that we listen to the gentle spirit of God. We must not in any way fail to respond to the promptings of the Holy Spirit as your compass.

'By endurance on your part you will acquire your soul' (Luke 21: 19).

'Yes, though I walk through the valley of the shadow of death, I will hear and fear no evil, for you are with me; your rod and your staff they comfort me' (Ps. 23: 4). As a person seeks the Lord and obeys to progress, the rod and staff is painful discipline to the hungry soul, bitter, this is sweet. 'The sufferings of this present time are not worthy to be compared with the glory that will be god revealed in us' (Rom. 8: 18).

It is through patience, forgiveness, faith, trust, hope, humility, long suffering, and pain that we can destroy the sinful nature within us that the Lord deems us ready to enter supernatural tribulation.

'This is how we are purified from sin, through suffering in the body in this life, into the fiery furnace that burns away the dross' (2 Pet. 20: 2).

Suffering is a part of the law. Even those who are victims of suffering, though we may not like it, suffer because we have broken the law and if we did not suffer, we would not learn. If we understand the function of pain, struggle, hardship, and difficulty, they all play a very important role in the evolution of the human spirit. If we are to gain our aims and goals, we must be tried and tested. Isaiah 53: 10-11 says, 'It was the LORD's will to crush him and cause him to suffer. After he has suffered, he will see the light of life and be satisfied.' If we have not suffered, we would not have understood the most important lessons of our life and also can our soul be strengthen. No pain, no gain in achieving success, clear vision and inspired ambition. When all the sorrows, struggle, pain, and obstacles have been conquered, the soul have been tried and tested, it rises stronger and more purified, deepened in intensity and more highly evolved.

The experience of suffering is intermittent according to circumstances and stage of our experience is part of the evolution. Suffering is what the heart and mind and soul feel within. Suffering is important and essential to the evolution of character after all we live in this world of which is not perfect. Therefore, to attain development, we have to evolve all the time, and evolution means the gradual perfecting of that which was imperfect and must be a painful process. Because we are evolving complex beings, we will always be struggling towards the light. The greatest progress was made at the time when all seemed dark and difficult. The realisation comes in the hour of bitterness.

If there were no pain and if there were never any heartache or any anguish, the soul would hardly be aware its innate capabilities. We have to suffer and endure ill health, some crisis that will touch us. It is only darkness that we will find light, only in ignorance that we will gain knowledge. With knowledge, we should be living in the light and never fear what the future will bring. Cessation of pain and suffering from its source brings pleasure. We are all involved in a process susceptible to suffering because of the influence of causes and conditions beyond our control. Crisis or challenges arouse people to wake up to respond to the threaten environment in order to bring back peace with solutions. It will also require radical transformation or a paradigm shift of consciousness to gain a strong foundation in our connection that comes in prayer for supernatural intervention to allow our spiritual being to come to fullness to face and cope with difficult challenges.

Jesus said, 'Come to me, all you who labour and are heavy burdened, and I will give you rest. Take my yoke upon you, and learn from me; for I am meek and lowly in heart, and you will find rest for your souls. For my yoke is easy, and my burden is light' (Matt. 11: 28-30).

Sometimes, to vow the virtue of gratitude, we have to give up something in order to gain and to progress in life, to become more and more engaged with God and walk with Him to show us His peaceful way of life. When we reflect on honest virtues in the midst of suffering and trial, avoid sin, and consult the Lord to bless us with the Holy Spirit in our prayer requests for all the tools, we need to accomplish His will.

'Be concerned about nothing, but in everything by prayer and supplication with thanksgiving, let your requests be made known to God. And the peace of God, which passes all understanding, will keep your hearts and minds through Christ Jesus' (Phil. 4: 6-7).

Saved by Grace

Be faithful and do not be afraid,
When you walk through the gate,
I will be there to meet you
To show you what is new.

Fear not for I have redeem thee.
From the Holy Spirit, that you will see,
Be strong and courageous in your act,
Your heart will lead you to perfect.

You are made to grow and glow.
Just go with your love and light flow,
You never know you can win,
Unless you take risk but not sin.

If you win, there is a prize.
If you lose, you will be wise.
Live great heartedly in your lifetime and be free.
In your world of blossom, to fruit like a cherry tree.

To live in your awareness that Christ is there.
All pain and anxiety will be easy to bare.
The fear of God in obedience, leads you to His truth
and wisdom.
Through your wisdom, you gain the joy of peace and
freedom.

Joo Lian Carter

Fear

'The LORD is on my side: I will not fear' (Ps. 118: 6).

'Moses told the people, 'Fear not stand still firm, confident, undismayed and see the salvation of the Lord which He will work for you today. For Egyptians you have seen today you shall never see again' (Exod. 14: 13).

'The lord said to Moses. "Why do you cry to me? Tell the people of Israel to go forward!"' (Exod. 14: 15). When we encounter danger, naturally we respond with fear, which is not a bad thing. But when fear controls your behaviour, it robs you from your confidence and can prevent you from progressing to positive things. Fear is the root of anxiety and if we don't deal with it, unfortunately, it can cause damaging effects in our lives.

Fear of failure, fear of unknown, fear of harm or death, fear of not being in God's will. We all have our own fears, afraid of intimacy and losing control. Because of fear of being replaced by someone, it may affect your attitude to become jealous. You project how you feel and if you feel fearful, you manifest a negative atmosphere that can be a bad influence in your relationship with yourself and others. Some of us miss out on opportunities and experiences because of fear. 'If you will repent at my reproof, behold, I will pour out my spirit on you; I will make my words known to you. But whoever listens to me and heeds what I say, shall dwell safely; and he shall be at peace from the fear of evil' (Pro. 1: 23-33).

Fearing the Lord is the beginning of wisdom, which enables us to make decisions without having fear in life. The key is to identify the cause and overcome the symptoms of fear. A lot of us walk around not knowing who we are and not knowing who He is. We are joint heir with Christ, and we are more than conquerors. When we know who we are as sons and daughter, we know that we are heirs with Him. We have the same power we can walk in identity as more than conquerors. 'For you have not received the spirit of bondage again to fear; but you have received the Spirit of adoption, by which we cry, Abba, Father' (Rom. 8: 15).

But He said to them, 'Why are you fearful, o you of little faith? Then He arose and rebuked the winds and the sea and there was a great calm.' (Matt. 8: 26). Do not worry or be anxious because it will only lead you to fear. Stay loving and positive because fear from the yesterday's regrets and fear of tomorrow destroy your today's happiness. Your past resentment and the dread of future keep you in bondage to change and move forward to a new dimension of life. If you fear tomorrow, you are already frustrated and manifest the frustration in attempt to be unhappy. Being frustrated and apprehensive is a negative feeling which stirs up fear that prevents you from moving forward with hope and belief in yourself and others. 'So never be anxious about the next day, for the next day will have its own anxieties. Sufficient for each day is its own badness' (Matt. 6: 34).

Trust and believe in yourself to develop that hope and faith in God to receive in the name of Jesus to be blessed with His saving grace. Forgiving and letting go the resentful past will release you to love and be loved, to feel in your heart from within that passionate feeling to love, grow, and live a healthier well-being physically, mentally, and spiritually and to create a better relationship with yourself, with others, and with God. God's Word is the righteous way of doing and being right. When God blesses you, he blesses you in full package.

'Keep on, then seeking first the kingdom and His righteousness, and all these other things will be added to you.' (Matt. 6: 33).

Never allow room for fear within us because fear is a negative influence which destroys our lives. It clouds our reason, and it impairs our judgment; it prevents us from seeing challenging situations clearly. Attaining a clear and balanced mind and emotion connecting to our true self, we allow our latent divinity lodged within us to rise to the surface, and then there is nothing that we are incapable of solving or conquering anything. We have so much power lodged within our potential self that is the added strength, courage, and wisdom that we call on when we are experiencing crises or emergency. But that power is there for us to express, and it can be tapped all the time from the higher source. It can give us health to master diseases, direction in time of uncertainty, guidance when we are confused, strength when we are faced with weakness, vision when we are blind, and wisdom when we cannot understand the process of nature and attributed to us and powers that were beyond the natural. Allow God to maintain our lives, he opens door for us to give us full opportunities. What we put in, it comes out of us. 'Now the Lord of peace himself gives you peace always by all means. The Lord be with you all' (2 Thess. 3: 16).

> *Fear attracts darkness and negativity that destroy souls, fortunately love and light is the only source that can penetrate and dissolve darkness to sustain lives. Yet darkness cannot penetrate or dissolve light. (Joo Lian Carter)*

We are living in the light era of supernatural, and as part of the source, we share in the processes of evolution, and we possess the power which shaped the whole universe and gave it direction and purpose that posses the power that is responsible for every facet of life. Instead of living in fear, practice the word of God and that will produce power in our lives, so why must we fear if we have that power, we should live in the light of love, hope, and faith of knowledge based on the confidence that we are infinite spirits and nothing can hurt us forever, and the eternity which God has planned for us. He wants us to go forward in the armour of love and light into the unknown, he is so fed up with us in bondage and wants us to be bold and step forward with courage.

'There is no fear in love; but perfect love casts out fear, because fear is the dread of punishment. He who fears has not been made perfect in love' (1 John 4: 18).

Sometimes, we have to surrender and get out of our minds and check it with our hearts and get advice from God and allow Him to lead us into victory. Until then, we have no time to lick our wounds. This is no time to put us straight to the wheel; let's see what God can do for us by allowing Him to come into our lives in a glorified way. This is the time to invest in missions with love. God rules His kingdom through love. Satan rules his kingdom through fear, before you know it silently takes over your life and takes away all that light force in you while you are soaked in fear. Fear means to run or to take flight. So when you are in to fear, you always run away from something that you should be confronting fear with courage.

When someone is taking control and manipulating your life to cause you fear, you need to confront the person. Losing your empowerment can make you apprehensive', therefore, you feel fearful and lose your confidence. You need to be confident and be valuable to move on in the direction God wants us to move on. Very often we are the by-product of our own obstacles. We create our own fear and especially fear of the unknown. How can we fear of something we don't know? The only thing we have to fear is fear itself, but it is wise to fear God so that we obey his word to guide us to become confidence and courageous. 'Therefore do not cast away your confidence, which has a great recompense of reward' (Heb. 10: 35).

'For God has not given us a spirit of fear, but of power and of love and of a sound mind' (2 Tim. 1: 7).

When the storm of life comes our way and puts us in the valley, we tend to solve our problems on our own. Often, we don't know how to stop and ask the Lord to help. Don't be afraid; see God as big and our problems as small. Allow God to be your salvation, seek His power, and communicate through prayer and ask Him to counsel and direct you out of the deep valley. You will receive His Holy Spirit through faith as you scale the mountain to victory or mountaintop view to see the truth that he wants us to conquer and achieve that destiny He planned for us to our advantage that we deserve. Know your God is your strength and power to conquer your valleys. Accept His Holy spirit as your invincible army to shine light in your path and lamp to your feet. 'Now the God of hope fill you with all joy and peace in believing, that you may abound in hope, through the power of the Holy Spirit' (Rom.15: 13).

'And we are his witnesses of these things; and so is the Holy Spirit, whom God has given to those who obey him' (Act 5: 32).

The spirit of God yearns for our attentions; therefore, if we are obedient to him, He will bless us with the Holy Spirit. Jesus said, 'My sheep know my voice. Jesus said it is better for you that I go away; how much more blessing for those who does not see me and believe in me.' The lowest level of connection is physical and last only short term. The highest level of connection is on the soul or spiritual level which is everlasting. Paul has never met Jesus, yet he knew Jesus more than Peter because Paul chose to know Jesus deeply by the spirit seeing and hearing through the Holy Spirit. The promise of the Father is the Baptism to receive the promise of the Holy Spirit which we now see and hear. The day you receive the power of the Holy Spirit, there is seeing and hearing that the natural man cannot perceive. Your perception becomes sharper and you will know deception because your enemy comes in silence from your back. But God comes in peace and a glorified entrance. Pray in the spirit and communicate with God so that we can have a deep conversation that no one understands him and worships the Lord. We depend on God until our last breath. Don't wait till your last breath to give your heart to the living God and ask Jesus to come into your heart and follow him the rest of your life. May the intimate friendship of the Holy Spirit be with you, and you will be intimate partnership with Him to share your secret. 'For it seemed good to the Holy Spirit, and to us, to lay upon you no greater burden than these necessary things:' (Act 15: 28).

'And when there had been much discussion, Peter rose up and said to them, Men and brothers, you know that a good while ago God made a choice from among us that the Gentiles might hear the word of the gospel by my mouth and believe. And God, who knows the hearts, bore witness to them, giving them the Holy Spirit even as he did to us; and put no difference between us and them, purifying their hearts by faith' (Act 15: 7-9).

Only a believer can receive the Holy Spirit when we are in fellowship with God, He is with us, he is mercy and faithful to us as well as we have to be faithful to Him to work miracles in our lives with the help of His Holy Spirit in the name of Jesus. He is the way and he is our saviour and protects us from deception that is trying to pull people away from God. Follow our heart and keep going forward with faith and hope, don't panic, not to get into fear because bad news introduces fear, so read the good news and listen to what God has to say than what the world say. Do not get caught up in the negativities. We don't have to struggle over and over with the recurring and constant fear that leads to worry and anxiety that we might have tried to convince ourselves is just us. The price to pay is to try and find love and well-being by looking at things as lessons, teachings, opportunities, and challenges to develop our spiritual test or do we look at life as problems? Through our choice and interpretation of the situation, we decide to have fear or love in our lives. It is in our choice and interpretation whether we experience peace or conflict. It is in our interpretation of life whether we will have separation consciousness or oneness consciousness.

'Therefore do not take thought and worry about tomorrow; for tomorrow will have its own concerns. Every day has enough trouble of its own' (Matt. 6: 34). Fear has many controlling motives in our life. For example, fear of hunger and being destitute forces most of us go out to work to earn our living. The emotion of fear can cause you to do something for survival or stop you from doing anything. Without experiencing the sensation of fear, we will never understand many things in life and in nature. Judgement often stems from fear. When we are in fear, we are not influenced by your higher self, and you are prompted to ignore the truth. You become judgmental, prejudiced, and filled with ego. Instead, open ourselves to the light of love in its purest form and tolerance.

'But we are not of those who draw back to perdition, but of those who believe to the saving of the soul' (Heb. 10: 39).

'And let us not be weary in well doing; for in due season we will reap, if we do not faint' (Gal. 6: 9). For me, I don't care how long it takes and how much it cause, I am going forward with no turning back because there is no such thing as failure if I go all the way through with God. Even though it is hard, continue to press through, and be all that He wants me to be. Do that he wants you to do so that one can have all that He wants us to posses? I had fear, confusion, and turmoil, but now I am so peaceful I have joy, I enjoy each day of my life no matter where I am even at solitude, and I am never alone. 'Now the righteous shall live by faith; but if any man draws back, my soul will have no pleasure in him' (Heb. 10: 38).

Walk by faith and not by sight and feed on the Word of God to sustain you in every endeavour. There is no such thing as failure if you endure till the end. 'For you need endurance in order to do God's will, so that after you may receive the promise' (Heb. 10: 36). Confusion, anxiety, and worry—these torment and insecurity leads to fear which prevent us from living life abundantly. To overcome fear, is to focus on the spiritual life where we are able to do things that God requires us to do it as long as we don't run away from it. He will give us strength and show us to pursue the work we need to do and get rid of fear. Fear is the master spirit that the enemy use to control people. God wants us to believe and keep having that faith in Him and when we have faith, faith often seems ridiculous by the way or the natural looks impossible, faith always opens the door for God to work with us and do something in our lives. We need to pray for ourselves and others who do not know how to pray for themselves who are lost and does not know their needs. Every time we pray for someone, it opens the door for god to work on the person who does not know how to open the door for them. We open our doors for God to work in our lives. There is only one attitude to fight fear just say out loud I will not fear as many times until you are as bold and courageous as a lion to conquer fear. Learn how to listen to God to give us protection and light that can penetrate darkness or fear. If God be for us who can be against us that could possibly make any difference at all. Fear not, for God is with us and He loves us.

'Do not be anxious about anything, but in everything, by prayer and petition, with thanksgiving, present your request to God. And the peace of God, which transcends all understanding, will guard your hearts and your minds in Christ Jesus.' (Phil. 4: 6-7).

We can still feel afraid and yet still not be afraid. Do not allow fear to rule us because we do not have to fear.

From the time of birth, the fear of separation from the unknown reality sets in and as you live life, the only definite end result of life is death so that is our definite fear until we realise that we are infinite beings. Sometimes, fear may overtake your control of living that you welcome death. If there is no matter or form to deteriorate or degenerate, there is no death. Therefore, your souls (spirit) have no form and no time but infinite and eternal. The body is subject to the constraints of time and space. When the infinite soul leaves the body, we call it death, separation, transition, or connect to eternal light of God which is something to look forward instead of fear of the dark. Once you realised that death is not the end, fear and separateness disappear, then you merge with the infinite and feel the relief and comfort that this realisation brings. Your recognition and perception go beyond space and time, possibilities, and will be able to connect with the higher energy of the infinite universal mind. Then there is no need to fear death because no matter who you are, there is life after life.

'If God is for us, who can be against us' (Rom. 8: 31)

> *If you choose to live consciously and righteously with purpose and understanding your true essence now to eternity, there is no need to fear death because no matter what you are, there is life after life.*
>
> *(Joo Lian Carter)*

The Power of Choice

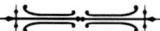

'*But* thanks to God, who always causes us to triumph in Christ, and makes evident the fragrance of the knowledge of God everywhere' (2 Cor. 2: 14).

Jesus answered, 'My sheep listen to my voice; I know them, and they follow me. I give them eternal life and they shall never parish; no one can snatch them out of my hand' (John 10: 27-28).

We have the freedom to choose the life we live because life is a lot to do with choice. We are living in a chaotic world of fear, insecurity, doubt, and stress. So what can we do to change those circumstances? Which direction do we choose at the cross road is your decision to make.

'Casting down all our own decisions, and every barrier that is raised up against the wisdom from God, and bringing into captivity every thought to the obedience of Christ' (2 Cor. 10: 5). It is the power of choice through faith in making the right decision that allows us to live a righteous and abundant life. The need to change and make the right choice requires faith and endurance with persistence and consistence in order to overcome the resistance of change. Falling down, doesn't make us a failure, but if we give up and stay down, we will never get to your destiny. We don't have to accept the current situations to control our lives that we are not satisfy with, but we have the freedom of choice to step out or rise up to the unwanted situations by reaching out appropriately for the truth of the Word of God to set us free of our present situation into the promise of His future. Then Jesus said to him, 'I am the way, the truth, and the life; no man comes to the Father, but by me' (John 14: 6). God gave us a free will to choose, and He hopes that you will choose Him and trust in Jesus Christ. God loves us so much that he chose to offer His only begotten son to redeem us from our sins, which is the only way to His kingdom. When you have chosen all ways and they are not working for you, why not choose God's way through Jesus Christ to lead you to eternal life.

The Word of God is full of promises, but we need to go in to posses that promise so that we might inherit the promises that God has for us. He loves us and desires everyone to be saved to be in His Kingdom some day, and He will see that every individual has a chance to be faced with the real truth of His plan and His purpose. Because he made us free moral human beings, we are able to will and to choose between good and evil, between life and death and either to accept or reject eternal life on God's terms.

Do not just settle for a hopeless get by life; do not just settle for an existence in bondage of our past. Today, we can make choices that will change your future. We may have a bad start in life, but there is a bright future and a triumphant finish in life that awaits us. Overcome the adversity of our past, the abuse of our lives, and adopt the power of choosing life from the knowledge of truth that can set us free to change our lives. The choice we make today, affects our future. Be wise to choose the passion of life today and live God's Word. 'For he shall give his angels charge over you, to keep you in all your ways' (Ps. 91: 11).

Change and Transformation

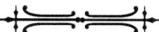

In reply, Jesus Christ declared, 'I tell you the truth; except a man be born again, he cannot see the kingdom of God' (John 3: 3).

Changing to transform is an unpleasant thing when we realise what we are and at what state we are in. It takes effort and time with least resistance to make it happen. First of all, identify what is essential for you and the need to change and make a list to start the process or you may even seek mentor, support, take a course, and read books. Our thoughts control our way of living and to change our way of living, we have to change the way of thinking. Change happens when we change our minds and old habits of thinking, feeling, and acting differently, aligning to the vibration of truth and possibilities.

'Strip yourselves of your former nature that control your conduct, which corrupts itself through lusts and desires that spring from delusion; And be renewed in the spirit of your mind; And put on the newly created nature [of Christ], which is created in God's image of true righteousness and holiness' ((Eph. 4: 22-24).

We are not going to grow if we continue to coast in our comfort zone, instead, it will lead us to discomfort in the long term. It is important to change on the inside, which will then change the outside to transform you to a higher level and stay in control. We are continuously growing as long as we are not afraid of changing according to the positive vibration. When things go in our way, we cannot see the need for change until something hit us with pain, struggle, and feeling hopeless with fear causing life depression. These unpleasant experiences drive us to search for a different and fulfilling life. The only way is to plan to change and transform ourselves to a new level of life from reactive responsive orientation to a creative orientation.

When we feel the need to change or when change is imposed on us, this imposition do not provide real foundation for any lasting change because the underlining structure has as its path of least resistance eventually fall back to the familiar old ones or habits when the level of awareness of oneself is very limited. The key is even when we have values, in the end we all have to face the questions of what is the truth, what is our real nature, what are our values, and what do we really care about? Only by authentic soul searching can we know the truth where, who we are, our values, and our purposes.

In the journey of self-discovery because there is no substitute for knowing, what truly matters to us is the purpose. So to build on truth and the truth about our nature, we really care about is the soul urge and is the deepest longing of human nature to reunite with its life source, which is deeper than our psychological make-up and self-conscious thoughts and intuitive perception. The path of least resistance which leads these two forces to reunite.

Everyone has his own unique value, any moment has a kind of potential and yet can exist through an act of our own creation from nothing to something that matters to us.

The word changing means transitive or to transform from a mechanical being to a real balanced being of knowledge and understanding to make any wise decision. When something is greater than 'I' the magnetic centre attracts us to do something to transform, the third level of consciousness in self, remembering is when we wake up and start self-observation through verification for the possibility of our higher development. To be transformed, we have to be alive. We don't change our mental attitude, but we change from a mechanical being into an awakened being. Learn to apprehend more quickly to discover our inner selves so that we can adapt wisely to the outer world.

How can we change our attitudes to serve our own life, mentally, physically, and spiritually?

We will understand that getting attached to old unconscious ways and bad habits is not the right path. No matter what, getting attached is the wrong path. If we can see our attachment, we will understand that being conscious what is happening now, spiritually, mentally, and physically is the right path for change and transformation. We are responsible for ourselves and our lives no matter what happened in the past without blaming anybody. When we have let go of the past and be willing to fully live in the now, we are willing to change and grow with confidence. In the process of change, it can make us feel apprehensive. The feeling of insecurity that change will bring and having to let go of the past and associate with making choices and facing the consequences that bring fear and unwillingness to effect change. Without change, there is no transformation for growth. Change is like deliberately choosing to close the accustomed door and not look back so that we can see and enter the ones which open for us.

We develop habits good or bad, short term or long term, we become accustomed and controlled by those habits, individual false personality, and the external material world, so we are not prepared to come out of that comfort zone. Until there is struggling and suffering, there is change. It does not have to be that way. Sometimes pain is valuable because it sets people to try anything and make comprehensive lifestyle change. Suddenly, we wake up and realise that we need a change and say no more of that and what do we do? We realise from our mind fears and destructive energy that do not support our health and well-being at every turn. So to break through the fear of change is to make choices that connect to the endless cycle of mentally wanting change, and emotionally fearing change by uniting power of the mind and the heart. We make choices to change to accommodate our unhappiness. Once we make conscious need emotionally, we want to change those parts. We all go through phases of difficult and resisting change as well as peace. Learn to accept and go with the flow rather than try to stop change from occurring. Learn to change through love and forgiveness and let go the unpleasant past to live in the present moment to make conscious change.

Very often, we decide to change and it is best to focus more on the positive than on the negative life challenges. In the law of attraction, you get what you vibrate as well as things will turn round as soon as you change your thinking. Being persistent in your positive thinking and action now, will determine your future. We are the product of our environment so being in the right place, right time, and with the right people will best develop us towards our goal.

Crises make us focus on here and now. When confronted with emergencies or struggling with pain, the shock to the system wakes us up in our invisible world (inner self). Perhaps the present will always have more to offer us than our past and crises emerge to make us value our lives in the moment.

To change or transform oneself, which is your inner world that you alone can only know by self-observation and consciousness is critical. I think you will agree that it is the inner world that you really live all the time and feel and suffer. In this inner world, we have first to open up to let light in so that we can see inside us clearer. It is through self-observation that this light is acquired. It is also important to grasp the reality which is the impressions that we are living in two different worlds.

To transform the new impressions of life is to transform oneself with different perception and remain motivated and remembering oneself of this new way. These require conscious work and effort, and through the understanding of the work, take life as work and then you are in the state of self—remembering and effecting change with good progress.

This state of consciousness leads to the transforming of impressions and your life no longer acts on you in the old way, instead, you begin to think and to understand in a new way, and this is the beginning of your own transformation. Transformation happens when our ordinary perspective shifts, and we attain a new understanding of which we really are our values, purposes, and our relationship with the divine.

We are all responsible for our own soul and actions. Our actions are coordinated from beyond us. First, we have to feed our souls and then we will be guided from the inner will and strength to effect change and transformation. Following our souls is the key to reality and transformation.

We don't have to wait. Remember that when we lift up our consciousness and one with Christ vibration within, we are transforming, helping ourselves, and the world. Change is daunting and waiting for that feeling of safety to come along before one makes a move only cause more insecurity because the only way to achieve that feeling of security is to bravely enter into the process of change and come out feeling soulful and alive again. So start living now and clear out and clean up and expand our consciousness, knowing that we can make a difference right now.

'So then because you are lukewarm, and neither cold nor hot, I will spew you out of my mouth' (Rev. 3: 16).

We are all human beings with souls in this planet no matter who we are and what religion we belong to, no one is more spiritually advanced than another. The only difference is that some have awakened to their true identity. Some of us are asleep, some are awake, and hopefully millions are just now coming out of the deep sleep. During the awakening process, as we work to eliminate false beliefs, negative appearances, and error patterns, we will experience a rise in consciousness.

As we develop a greater awareness, understanding, and knowledge of the Christ within, our outer world will change accordingly. When the total dominion comes, we will be more advanced than our neighbours in our spiritual evolvement, the greater the desire to serve, the higher our rise in consciousness and the more we will express unconditional love towards one and all. An awakened one has no false pride or spiritual arrogance.

I will say here that no lesson in my entire spiritual life is more important than learning to undo the negative ego thought system and to replace it with the Christ consciousness thought system. For example, 'Is the glass of water half empty or half full? 'It is not in the glass of water, it is in our minds. We do not just see with our physical eyes, in truth we see with our minds. Most people think that outside things, people, or events cause them to think or feel what they do. This illusionary thought system of the negative ego show us that life is nothing more than our extending and projecting our thoughts onto the world and that we are seeing our own performance.

The Power to Change Others
Is by Changing Oneself

The talents, skills, ideas, and pure potential all combine to make you who you are. Each of this components bring together unique and wonderful ways to allow your individual expression.

Your weaknesses, strength, and consciousness are the opportunities for growth and expansion. When you act from the wisdom in your heart, you place yourself in the perfect situations to help this growth and evolution process. When you change to see things differently, your action affects others to see a difference in you enabling them in your presence to change too.

Your active involvement in change without resistance allows others to participate in the process you present. Without this willingness this interaction cannot occur. Never underestimate your power and love you supply to the world around you.

You contribute marvellous energy to the people and things in life. Without your energy and effort, they would not have the same qualities. Like a tapestry of grand design, each thread comprises the final picture.

The Process of Born Again
(Saved by Grace)

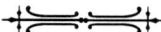

' *T*hen Jesus answered and said to him, 'truly, truly, I say to you that unless a man is born again; of water and of the Spirit, he cannot enter into the Kingdom of God' (John 3: 3, 5).

We become transformed once the knowledge and the truth is revealed from within. God is interested in your character, which is the eternal part of you. Because He is perfect, we can also learn how to be perfect, by practicing the word, not just by hearing it. Obedience and practice makes perfect through Jesus we can be perfect like him. 'By that will, we are sanctified through the offering of the body of Jesus Christ once for all' (Heb. 10: 10).

'For by one offering he has forever totally cleansed and perfected those who are sanctified and made holy' (Heb. 10: 14).

When you are born again, you died with Christ, you live in Christ, you are raised with Christ, you are hidden in Christ, and you are glorified in Christ. 'Being born again, not of corruptible seed but of incorruptible, by the word of God that lives and lasts forever' (1 Pet. 1: 23).

'Therefore go and teach all nations, baptizing them in the name of the Father, and of the Son, and of the Holy Spirit; teaching them to observe all the things that I have commanded you; and behold, I am with you always, even to the end of the world. Amen' (Matt. 28: 19-20).

If we trust God and Jesus Christ, we are in obedience to his command and choose to be baptised in the name of the Father and the Son and the Holy Spirit. It is a public announcement that you believe in Jesus as our saviour and our Lord and choose to accept him and follow him. Confess with your mouth that you follow Jesus Christ that he died on the cross and saved us from our sins by his blood, and on the second day, he was buried and resurrected on the third day. 'Therefore if any man is in Christ, he is a new creature; old things have passed away; behold, all things have become new' (2 Cor. 5: 17).

Baptism is for believers because baptism makes a statement that by my faith in the Lord Jesus Christ that my sins have been forgiven, and I am born again. It means that I have died to my old life and become a new person, and I choose to walk and to follow the Lord Jesus Christ living the Word of God. 'And have purposed to put on the new man, who is renewed in knowledge after the image of him who created him' (Col. 3: 10).

When you realise the spiritual needs, you start seeking reality and eternal truth, which provide a refuge for your physical being and the spiritual nature slowly taking place until you are no longer bound, and all the shackles have fallen off. Thus transformation takes place and you begin to taste the air of freedom and realise what it is to live spiritually and mentally in an environment where there is no fear.

You begin to know and to understand that no matter what, you are not alone or abundant and reassured, that your life is worthwhile once again to serve your true purpose. As your spiritual life progresses, you develop a higher level of perception that enable you to receive impressions and vibrations, which are beyond your five perceptions of senses. Because you are body, mind, and spirit, you must become supernatural minded and you must understand that you have already experienced the supernatural. 'Now to him who is able to do exceeding abundantly above all that we ask or think, according to the power that works within us' ((Eph. 3: 20).

When you got born again, you became a new species in Christ that has never existed before. Accept the supernatural in every area in your life. 'That he would grant you, according to the riches of his glory, to be strengthened with might by his Spirit in the inner man' ((Eph. 3: 16).

Born again means to become consciously aware of your true higher inner self, to be spiritually in touch with your own soul and enter into a new invisible world of supernatural filled with the Holy Spirit, new perception and completely new relation to the universe with all new possibilities in Christ and Christ in you.

My spiritual awareness and journey is a paradigm shift through change and transformation. The evolving soul, also known as the psychic being, is the spark of the divine. It is called the evolving soul because it is progressing through many births in its journey through time. It seeks to gain the essence of our experience for its own growth, or to put it another way, as we grow, so does our evolving soul to progress our spirits.

'Purified your souls by obeying the truth through the Spirit to unfeigned love of the brothers, see that you love one another fervently with a pure heart' (1 Pet.1: 22).

The soul makes its own progress through many lifetimes until it has learn all lessons and reach its destiny.

The process of transformation exactly implies the transmutation of matter from opacity to radiance. There are two stages to this transformation process. First, the body must become translucent from an opaque body and he must acquire the capacity of being penetrated by the light or being filled by the Holy Spirit and Christ consciousness. He must lose his solidity become invisible, unrecognised, and only be seen by another's light. This will require a long period of time in this state to attain the possibility of radiance and enabling him to know his true self and to acquire permanent consciousness of his own. The second stage is connected to the planetary world which is the development of the atmosphere. You have the ability to pivot under any and all conditions with a disciplined mind engaging in good thoughts.

Christ says to Nicodemus, 'Unless a man is born again, he cannot see the kingdom of God' (John 3: 3)

Change leads to transformation which means the changing of a thing into something different. As I have mentioned before, to transform one is also the idea of rebirth, of a man being born again, accepting Jesus and following self-repentance and baptized with the Holy Spirit. To transform the impressions of life is to transform one and only an entirely new way of thinking can affect this. Life is constantly causing us to react to it. To change one's life is not to change outer circumstances, but to change one's reaction. At the beginning of transforming, one has to be detached from the material world. To understand the process of personal and spiritual growth and can work effectively with the process, instead of resisting it.

The more we change, the more our world changes. Our personality controls us to doubt ourselves, which is the greatest fear on earth. We are so afraid to even look into ourselves because we fear what we might find inside us nothing but the truth that we cannot face with. I was like every human being afraid to confront with our inner self our true essence. One day in contemplative meditation, the thoughts that flowed through my mind, spoke of the higher soul.

'When Jesus said, "I am the Way" it was not his personality speaking. It was the Higher Soul, the Christ Consciousness, that which I am. And Jesus said unto him, I am the way, the truth, and the life: no man cometh unto the Farther, but by me.' (John 14: 6).

I began to contemplate on my physical organism and the interpenetrating energy field of my light body, and then my attention turned to my conscious mind and then to my feeling nature and memory bank, which works with the law of use and effect in lower vibration consciousness. Higher and deeper in the inner journey, I found my soul and my spirit's idea of itself in expression made manifest, the mind that was in Christ Jesus, the super consciousness of my individualised being.

'And to know the love of Christ, which passes knowledge, that you might be filled with all the fullness of God' ((Eph. 3: 19).

We are in the end time, and Christ returns is in the minds and hearts of men and women throughout the world, the planet itself will be lifted up into a new dimension of wholeness.

But just an intellectual awareness of the individualised hierarchy of our being will be of little benefit. We must feel the truth, we must know the truth, and we must be the truth. That is why the first signpost on the spiritual path is working on us to realise our highest potentials within us is the truth that sets us free.

What made me change is the absence of meaning and purpose in life that woke me up to recognise the crises. Fear and loneliness sets in making me feel as if I am losing touch with a sense of self and hope. I then become more aware and inquisitive about myself readjusting my life in ways that removed mental and emotional blockages. Regaining my empowerment and development of my inner self, I feel a connection that is more real to me each day that is making me stronger and growing physically, mentally, and spiritually. Through the suffering I went through, my spirit begins to come into its own. As a result, I am able to unfold my healing gift and know what others feel when they need to be healed. It is the awareness and the realisation that touched my soul. Touching of my soul helps my body and mind to achieve wholeness that brings health, certainty, confidence, inner well-being, and awareness so that I am at peace with myself and with everybody else I encounter. Each individual must seek a personal and responsible spiritual life.

The power of meditation, prayer, and the conscious connection with the divine becomes the healing energy through faith of the New Age.

To be real, we have to be transparent so that light can shine in. To be what we are, to give us a way to understand, observe what is inside ourselves from the agitation or do not react from irritants. The philosophy of our time is so self-centred. We can only reflect light out only when we allow light to shine in from a higher level or higher state of consciousness. Everything look better, brighter, and whole or oneness if we allow the light of consciousness and receive Jesus into our life.

'That if you confess with your mouth that Jesus is Lord, and believe in your heart that God raised him from the dead, you have been saved. For with the heart, man believes to righteousness; and with the mouth, man confesses to salvation' (Rom.10: 9-10). 'I have been crucified with Christ. It is no longer I who live, but Christ who lives in me.' And the life, which I now live in the flesh, I live by faith in the Son of God, who loved me and gave himself for me' (Gal. 2: 20).

The spiritual side of what happens to us when we receive Christ our saviour is that we are transformed. Christ in us is the new creation that we are, and actually with the outflow of the glory of God read by the people on this earth we are living epistles; the living Word of God that we develop the powers within us. It is much more than our tickets to heaven; we become a new person on the inside that God put something in our spirit so that from within we want to do good things to serve Him. We feel the need to practice and purify the inner life or spiritual life with the guidance of Jesus Christ. When we come to know who we are in relation to God, we begin to move with faith in the direction towards Him living holy in obedience, leading to righteousness the Word of God. 'It is the spirit who gives life; the flesh profits nothing. The words that I speak to you are spirit, and they are life-giving' (John 6: 63).

Then we align our will with His will, we just have to go out and meet in the direction of destiny through our knowing, then destiny moves in your direction. Every step we climb to reach our destiny we are tested and blessed. When we have crucified ourselves on the inward cross of self-denial, Christ in us totally controls our thoughts, words, and deeds, and we are under the complete control of the Holy Spirit, and there are no laws, and we walk in love and in obedience as prompted. 'And after you have suffered a little while, the God of all grace (Who imparts all blessing and favour) will Himself complete and make you what you ought to be' (1 Pet. 5: 10).

Prayer to Accept Jesus

Lord Jesus, I believe that you are the Son of God and that you love me, and you died upon the cross for my sins, and on the third day, God the Father raised you from the dead. I confess you to be my Saviour and Lord of my life. I am now born again, a new creation, old things have passed away, behold all things have become new. Amen.

Essence

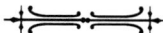

*E*ssence is your true nature, a basic reality in the universe. Essence creates our consciousness, feelings, minds, physical body, and matter. By expressing your essence, your uniqueness reveals. Essence is the substance of unconditional love that cannot be bought, won, or lost because it is always available. We are all born with essence, a gift of life to serve our purpose. You develop your essence, to progress your soul and spirit which is the truth in you. This is why it's essential to develop and nurture your essence to become more and more conscious to come under higher influences of dimension of reality. It is the consciousness, open mind, open heart, and faith that we embrace the dimensions of possibilities and realities. It is through discipline and endurance that you see change and transform within you. This enables the spiritual being to grow in self-mastery, balance your karma, and to become one with your higher self and return to the spiritual dimension of reality in Christ, lead by the Holy Spirit, master of your destiny to fulfil God's plan.

As you live through life, the personality develops and surrounds your essence not allowing it to grow. From education, intentional influences of other people your personality starts to grow at the same time making attempt to conceal the real self to be free from agitation.

The growth of essence depends on the work on oneself. To begin with, it is very important that we identify the deference between the essence and the personality. Personality is active which very often obstructs essence to grow because of its passiveness.

The truth sets you free from unrighteousness. 'Having then been set free from sin, you became the slaves of righteousness' (Rom. 6: 18). Self-remembering enables a person to shed the outer skin of personality to feel and act freely from his essence or to be himself. This way he may separate himself from the pretences and imitations which have enslaved him since childhood and return to his own essential nature, which is accompanied by a sense of freedom and liberation to become a free being in order to develop the essence. Primarily, the essence has to grow to maintain the true nature, leading to self-consciousness and development so that developed essence is the master of personality. During moments of self-realisation or remembering, consciousness is when you have attuned to your soul leading to perceptions of higher possibilities and ideas, greater world and forces, terrible and painful perception taken in a holy way, will nourish and enrich essence. Your purpose and destiny is to attain from control of righteousness that binds you to the service of God in union with Christ, and at the end, is eternal life.

Life after Life

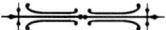

'To those who by perseverance in good works, seek for glory, honor, and immortality, He will give eternal life' (Rom. 2: 7).

> *A man without love, faith, hope, and Christ consciousness accompanying his soul cannot understand the unification of death but fear definitely that one day he is going to die. If he has a conscious soul and spirit, death would be a different meaning to him with more possibilities of an eternal life.*
>
> *(Joo Lian Carter)*

'What you sow is not made alive unless first it dies.' (1 Cor. 15: 36).

'We shall not all fall asleep in death but we shall all be changed. Death is your victory or death is your sting, but thanks to God, for he gives us the victory through our Lord Jesus Christ' (1 Cor. 1: 55-57).

'That if you confess with your mouth that Jesus is Lord, and believe in your heart that God raised him from the dead, you have been saved' (Rom. 10: 9). There is life after death. But that life lies in a future resurrection. Our greatest hope in life is the hope of having eternal life is through rebirth, which is imparted during and throughout our lifetime if we grow in grace by faith, have knowledge of our Lord, repented, believed, and been baptized to receive the Holy Spirit. Eternal life is a new life imparted from God's great gift. That is why we must be born again by a resurrection from the dead through Jesus Christ. Those who are living at that time at the second coming of Christ, they shall be changed into immortal spirit beings and live forever.

If life is only a dream that we imagine our self and dream is reality, how could there be death? But a transition of life to the invisible reality that is much greater, possibly more important and eternal.

The moment we enter into time is the moment of our birth. The point where we leave time is the moment of death. We come here as a speck of cosmic consciousness to have unique experience to evolve our souls. The structure of the self is the etheric body. Before embodiment, we select the womb and the parents.

'God so loved the world that he gave his only begotten Son [to every man], so that whoever believes in him shall not perish, but have eternal life' (John 3: 16). 'Most truly I say to you, He that hears my word and believes him that sent me has everlasting life, and he does not come into judgment but has passed over from death to life. The hour is coming and now is, when the dead shall hear the voice of the Son of God and they that hear shall live' (John 5: 24-25).

'While we do not look at the things that are seen, but at the things that are not seen. For the things that are seen are temporary, but the things that are not seen are eternal' (2 Cor. 4: 18). All mortal man lives in fear of death, but not much man devotes himself seeking the truth about him and eternity. Instead, he seeks and learns about almost everything worldly to be temporarily successful. Flesh is matter and it is mortal. All living matter with a temporary existence is mortal matter. Spirit, however, is immortal. We are also told that you don't seek for what you already have. Immortality is something we don't naturally possess, we must seek for it.

> *Life is like a book with contents, the journey is the different chapters in a book and time is the book ends of life on earth.*
>
> *(Joo Lian Carter)*
>
> *Money can buy you a clock but cannot buy time or love, so why not spent every moment here and now as quality time for love.*
>
> *(Joo Lian Carter)*

'Truly I say to you, there is some standing here, who shall not taste death, until they see the Son of man coming in his kingdom' (Matt. 16: 28).

Transcendence

Transcendence means the power to be born anew, to make a fresh start, to begin with a clean start, to turn over a new life, to enter into a state of grace, and to have a second chance. The past is over to create a new life and realignment of all dimensions to yourself with the very source of your new life with new possibilities. Re-establish a new relationship to your natural goodness, what is highest in you is given a new life.

Transcendence evokes the power to begin from scratch beyond the realm, where previous causal actions are in play. In your new state of being, each moment is alive with fresh possibilities, which may never have seemed possible before. You will be motivated by vision, energised by aspiration, rooted in current reality, being forged by each creative act, and then leading to a transcendence of the civilization as a whole.

Ideas and evolution create great shifts in human civilization. Each individual can be the predominant creative force in his own life by making purposeful effort. Everything in life you have to be responsible to earn it; through earning, you produce creative result and learn lessons through the process of intellectual and emotional experiences and gain the connection, and it opens up your vision and desire to produce result and reward. The vision that is most powerful is the vision that is worthy of you that is what is highest and deepest in you your true self or potential self. It is important to master the fruit of your endeavours and be able to receive and acknowledge the result. There is no failure if you endure till the end. Completion urges you to move forward to a new creation of possibility and from one life to another.

'But he who endures to the end shall be saved' (Matt. 24: 13).

In reality, if you understand death clearly, there is no need to be afraid, because death is a process of pass over and a transcendent into another realm.

In this life, we die three times. First, the conception living in the womb of a mother for three trimesters, and after nine months, living in the womb, you die or being born into time and doing time in this world.

The second is being born again by receiving Jesus into your heart. When you seek God through Jesus, you repent, die your old self to give yourself to God through Christ and until you let go your old sinful, selfish, wilful self to decrease the pride in you, until you become humble yourself and fear God to repent of your sins and allow God to change you to take you to the next ascended level. Then you will start to shift to the right direction, living a righteous life, by changing your mindset and open your heart until your heart is tender to God to live his will, wisdom, and peace.

The third is when your body withered away, your flesh returns to the earth, where your spirit leaves the body to another dimension where your spirit is yielded to God.

Jesus says, 'If you seek to save your life, you will lose it; when you lose your life for my sake, you will find it.' If you desire to save your life for not conquering life challenges or struggle from having any pain, save yourself from going through change and transformation from being righteous, you are going to lose your life. But when you would just let go and move in the direction of God's will in His presence and peace and through Jesus, who died to save us from our sins. Through his death on the cross, I might continue to live my life in him so that I can have eternal life. Death is a door way for the spirit (soul) to transcend from one realm or dimension to the next.

From the time of birth, the fear of separation from the unknown reality sets in, and as you live life, the only definite end result of life on earth is death, which is our definite fear until we realise that we are infinite spirit being. Sometimes, fear may overtake your control of living that you welcome death. If there is no matter or form to deteriorate or degenerate, there is no death. Therefore, your souls (spirit) have no form and no time, but infinite and eternal. The body is subject to the constraints of time and space. When the infinite spirit leaves the body we call it death, separation, transition, or connect to eternal light of God which is something to look forward instead of fear of the dark. Once you realised that death is not the end, there is life after life, fear, and separateness disappear, then you merge with the infinite and feel the relief and comfort that this realisation brings. Your recognition and perception go beyond space and time possibilities and be able to connect with the higher energy of the infinite universal mind. Then there is no need to fear death because no matter who you are, there is life after life, depending on how you have accomplished your God-given purpose and destiny. There is nothing in the world lasting like our sacred souls because God made it. Do not change your life for the lives of this world, but by the grace of God and not by worldly wisdom. Only God who gives you life, can destroy your soul.

'Then shall the dust return to the earth as it was, and the spirit shall return to God who gave it' (Eccles. 12: 7).

Death is a transformation or transcendence from one stage of life to another immortal spirit (soul). When a person has become so laden with disease that is incurable and become so uncomfortable for the spirit that no further lessons can be learned, then gradually the spirit withdraws and leaves the body as the silver cord joining the physical and spirit body gets severed and the spirit drifts off. At that moment of separation, the light energy (life force) is extinguished from the head. It takes three days for all the physical activities to cease and the spirit and soul to become free of its embodiment. There are three bodies.

The flesh body is a denser body in which the spirit can learn the hard lessons of life. The etheric body or magnetic body is less dense than physical body, vibrates at finer and higher frequency and a subtle counter part of the physical made by us which is the personality. The third body is the spirit body which is the immortal soul. Death is not a tragedy to those who die; it is only a tragedy to those who are left behind. To go from darkness is not something over which you should grieve. When a person passes away from the earth plane, he will no longer suffer all the illnesses of the body.

> *If you live consciously and righteously with purpose and understanding of your true essence now to eternity, there is no need to fear death because no matter what you are, there is life after life.*
>
> *(Joo Lian Carter)*

'When he had opened the fifth seal, I saw under the altar the souls of those who had been slain for the word of God, and for the testimony that they held' (Rev. 6: 9).

'Verily, verily, I say unto you. The hour is coming, and now is, when the dead shall hear the voice of the son of God: and they that hear shall live' (John 5: 25).

'Let him know, that he which converted the sinner from the error of his way shall save a soul from death' (James 5: 20).

Jesus Christ set a high estimate upon human life when he left his Father's throne and came into this sin-cursed world to suffer and die that he might redeem us from death.

Death merely releases us from the prison of the flesh and we are liberated just as much as a bird when we open the cage and set it free. We have in essence all the gifts, attributes, and qualities of the spirit within us, latent and unexpressed except perhaps in matters of small degree. If we allow our spirit to express itself, to radiate it loses all things like fear and doubt because the spirit dwells in an atmosphere of confidence.

The soul that needs healing is due to man's ignorance of his true relationship with himself and God.

The light of the soul or the life force is a flame in the depths of our conscious love or consciousness that can never be extinguished, and it can be fanned into all-consuming fire of power and mastery.

Let the light of the soul shine in the heart and is reflected in the mind.

If we will renew our mind, change the vibration of our energy field, and lift up our consciousness to behold the grandeur and majesty of our soul, we can let the light of the soul shine in the heart and is reflected in the mind. 'As in Adam, all are dead, even so in Christ, shall all be made alive. But each man is in his own rank and order, and in Christ, the first fruits; then the anointed at his coming. Then comes the end, when he delivers the kingdom to God, the Father; when he has put down all rule and all authority and power. He must reign, until he has put all enemies under his feet. The last enemy that will be destroyed is death' (1 Cor. 15: 22-26)

In the competitive world, we are more likely to be attracted in the direction of deception, desires, and materialism, which can corrupt your good manners, morals, and integrity. Yet you are expected to be polite and friendly with friends and people you meet. You have to be careful and be wise when you socialize with people without being influenced by their evil ways, conversation, and conduct. It is through individual choice, weather to win the approval and favour of God or of men? When you are in fellowship with God, this doesn't mean that you do not have the right attitude to the people you associate with. It is just that you will not socialise with them because it would be painful and harmful to you. Instead, your righteousness and faith might eventually influence them, like Jesus influence mankind as our counsellor and Saviour.

Mountaintop Consciousness

I live upon an exceeding high mountain.
To quench my thirst I go to the fountain.

I must devote in writing the book of inspiration where
it stands.
I must devote to the culture of flowers and fruits
from the land.

It is very hard for me to give up the view from its
supreme height.
I scale the mountain with conscious might.

I will enjoy my many years of repose and grandeur.
As far as my dreams will take me, I will endure.

I must devote the remainder of my life to helping the needy.
There is nothing like serving humanity.

For many years to come as my strength began to decline.
I'll feel the ascent so tedious for my feeble body and mind

But my spirit transcend to reach the mountaintop
consciousness,
Living in heaven on earth in righteousness and in Oneness

Joo Lian Carter.

Consciousness

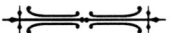

To be conscious means thinking the reality of the condition. Life put us to sleep and that programmed us to think. We desire and imagine all other thing. Being of lazy nature, well servers live well, does not serve me well but the truth and light serve my purpose. It is a process of thinking about better ideas and to combine the ideas and effort together to attain the final goal of eternity.

Consciousness at different levels of body, mind, and spirit:

Meditation can help to expand the state of consciousness because it silences you from the external world and gives you time to listen and connect to your inner world of true nature and to develop the high sense perception. Through my experience of expanded consciousness, it felt like there is no boundaries but my sense of perception reach for the infinite reality which I could not comprehend before. Altered state of consciousness is experienced during seeing or channelling that can lead to deeper understanding of high sense perception that connect to the deepest part of our higher self, the divine spark within. It is the communication within our attitude, how we act and react that result in our vision, not communicating in our vision of the world. Not what your dream is but what dream state you are in.

Pondering is answering questions from essence in a practical and intellectual manner. When we ponder, we use our mind and emotion.

Contemplating is contact with thought forms.

No statement can be understood without the effort of conscious assimilation; this brings realisation, which is felt and sensed.

Reasoning is the logical function from the thinking centre, which is composed of definite organs—concentration, pondering, meditation, and contemplation.

Humans have a higher type of instinctive reason than animals. Associative reason, which functions according to verbal associations, which we practically know nothing, can be acquired by voluntary conscious work and intentional effort. The reason of ordinary man is the reason of knowledge and understanding.

At the stage of consciousness, there are different levels of consciousness through inner change and development within each individual. Being awake is being conscious. We are not awake because we imagining that we are awake. We cannot be present right here right now being aware at this moment. Consciousness is a material thing which is measurable, achievable, and expanding your awareness of thing not specific but in general.

To become conscious of my own existence and my relation to the surrounding universe means the moment I am conscious of my existence, I know what I am and what I am not to know the difference between my essence and personality as well as what is in me and my outside me.

The Different State of Consciousness

In our day-to-day life, we all experience consciousness in three different states

1. The awakening state is when we experience awareness and the objects of our consciousness originate from the physical reality around us.

2. The dream state in which we experience awareness, but the objects of our consciousness have some internal origin.

3. The deep sleep state, there is no awareness.

4. During meditation, there is profound awareness of nothing, but transcends consciousness, which is pure self-awareness. During that pure self-awareness, one can see pure white lights together with other spectrum of colourful lights and that is untellable, lighting the very light beyond all signs, but can be describe as in a state of peace and bliss

Since we are manifested with an infinite consciousness from the divine spark, at this stage, we are experiencing the divine of our own being or oneness with God. This consciousness shows the cosmos to consist entirely immaterial, spiritual, and entirely alive; it shows that there is no death, that everyone and everything has eternal life and that the universe is God and that God is the universe.

An experience of higher dimensionality is achieved by an integration of experiences and level of consciousness. After certain experiences of deep meditation on the plane of three-dimensional consciousnesses, we can transcend a totally different reality where all opposites are unified into an organic whole. The human world as we see it is based on self-consciousness, which we acquired at the age of about three and developed our percepts, recepts, and concepts as we experience. Self-observation and self-remembering means to become more aware of most of the things that I resisted and are hidden away.

Slow to apprehend means stupid and when you realise that you are stupid, you become wiser and earn to apprehend more quickly.

Personality develops and grows like fresh water pearl. True personality is like the pearl of wisdom, and it is so important because it harbours many truths. There are pure pearls and cloudy pearls a bit like the mind. The purification takes place once the mind has got rid of the clouds. The shackles will fall away and the mind will be free from impurities.

Cosmic Consciousness

A recept is made up of many percepts; a concept of many recepts and percepts and an intuition is made of many concepts and percepts in conjunction with other sensation elements connected to and influenced from the emotional nature. It is the result of all this blending that cosmic consciousness is acquired. Like other forms of consciousness, including the development of all the different psychic faculties, cosmic consciousness is capable of growth and it may have different degrees and forms. A person acquiring cosmic consciousness does not mean that he is therefore omniscient. Although he has reached a higher level there can be different degrees of consciousness.

Consciousness is I believe being able to shape and direct matter is the primary concept of reality. The planets and stars, you and I, and the animals and plants in this universe were created through consciousness and natural law. As we are made in the image of God, therefore we are all fragments from the cosmic consciousness and evolution, and we are all little pieces of same consciousness that has deliberately fragmented itself through initiating consciousness so that we are all individual beings for its own evolution and its own growth. So you could say the universe is oneness with God or may I call it cosmic consciousness, the concept of psychic and spirit phenomena rest upon a cosmology.

Spiritual insights are thoughts that come into minds of human beings from a number of sources outside of the ordinary intellect. A person can encounter both the physical cosmos and the energy field around via the subconscious mind through meditation, prayer, and other consciousness techniques.

The three levels of mind are the subconscious mind or the instinctive mind, the conscious mind or the rational mind, and the superconscious mind or the spiritual intuitive mind.

Higher consciousness is required for psychic activity.

Coherent light laser highly focused can decode hologram.

Incoherent-light bulb is light waves travelling characteristically.

Coherent thought activity (increase brain wave coherence) may be associated with other psychic events. The key principle is that coherent consciousness may display properties that go beyond ordinary waking consciousness.

We as human consciousness evolve towards higher potential a greater acceptance of the principle of vibrational medicine and the hidden holographic universe. The revolution in consciousness and healing assist us in understanding the concept of humans as multidimensional beings and in comprehending the evolution of consciousness through states of illness and health. So it is up to us to apply our human potential and wake up to our consciousness towards developing a new hope and approach of healing the body, mind, and also spirit, our true nature our spiritual higher self.

Superconsciousness is soul that exists beyond body and mind. It is the soul that gives birth to the mind and the body. The soul can be viewed without dimension through consciousness, time, and space. When we expand the ordinary mind, until it impinges on the superconscious mind, we are able to feel God's presence. Our spirit is the conscious force that is life itself. We incarnate to the physical world to evolve our souls and taking ideas from spirit within and interpreting those ideas as form and experience in the material world. Time and age exists in the physical world but in the spiritual world, it is timeless. When it comes to evolve the soul there is no age and no limits, therefore, you can progress to another dimensions. But in time, the lower vibration of soul in the dense physical body became conscious of only the third-dimensional world.

From the love of God in action, we descended into province of Karma and came under the law of cause and effect. This is why there was a sense of separation as the higher soul remained one with the spirit as the Christ consciousness, while the lower soul dropped further into darkness of the mortal ego. Now we understand why we must regain our Christ awareness, the soul consciousness that we had in the beginning. In the ordinary way, we are not conscious of our existence; energy does not flow through the system and what then happen to our souls? Do we have to admit that the ordinary man has not yet found a soul or it has to be created? Or a man's soul is the totality of the moments of self-consciousness during his life?

Spiritual Healing

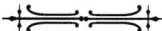

There are more and more turning to the power of spirit for healing. Health is wholeness of body, mind, and spirit. There are many forms of spiritual healing. Self spiritual awareness and personal evolution healing, vibrational healing, healing through chakras power system, meditative and yoga healing, spiritual healing from medium's body who is imbued with healing energy from the spirit world.

The word spiritual originates from the Latin spiritus meaning 'breath of life'. Healing can be defined as regaining balance of mind, body, and spirit. A principle of the spiritual approach to health care is that while hardship happens to everyone, it is possible to grow through it and become more emotionally strong and resilient leading to maturity. When experiencing heartfelt or challenging psychological situations, spiritual awareness empower us to understand and act in a positive way calmly, in the place of anxiety and hope in a place of despair. I have experienced this myself that in times of stress, suffering, physical and mental illness, loss, dying and bereavement, spirituality comes into focus, therefore, it is important that the health care encourage this awareness. Because pursuing spiritual life is a sacred realm of human experience concerned with people finding meaning and purpose in their lives, as well as the sense of belonging, of community.

Spiritual healing can compliment conventional medicine by treating the whole person—mind, body, and spirit and spiritual healers act as a conduit for healing energy, channelling this healing energy from a spiritual source to someone who needs it. The healing energy from this source can be experienced by all. During channelling, the healing energy is usually transferred to the patient through the healer's hands. The healing does not come from the healer, but through him. The healer will place a hand on the person being treated to channel the energy from the higher source. The benefits of healing can be felt on many levels, including mental, physical, and emotional levels with profound effects.

Everyone has a healing mechanism that flows as an energy force around the body, mind, and spirit to keep them in perfect health. Living a hectic life, plays havoc with this balance and very often, stress, poor diet, a negative attitude, and other adverse factors can block our healing mechanism of the energy flow needed to repair or to restore the energy balance to heal the illness.

What is Spiritual Healing?

Before praying, a short time should be engaged in quietness and in meditation. This creates the connection of spirit to spirit or spiritual vibration upon which the prayer operates. At the close of prayer, apply the same process. This allows the higher vibrations to be contacted and to be absorbed by those who pray and by those who receive the healing power of prayer at a distance. Similarly, it can also be raised by thought operate. Love breathes a powerful healing prayer where all healing is transmitted. The love ray or light first connect with the spirit and endeavours to rise to help others. The channelling of healing energy from its spiritual source to someone who needs it is called spiritual healing.

Developing Spiritual Life

1. First, build the spiritual life based on the foundation of unconditional love and His word given to us by Our Farther. In the vibration of love, through faith, it connects us to everyone to receive the support and understanding from each other to drive us to sustain our spiritual lives.
2. Building spiritual strengths through daily prayer or meditation.
3. Regular attendance and participation in church or your preferred spiritually based organisation can inspire and facilitate spiritual growth and the practice of spiritual healing.
4. Regular reading of the Bible and inspirational literature can provide spiritual knowledge and wisdom leading to truth. It is

good to read at least once per day, either upon awakening, during your lunch break, or before retiring.

5. Regular practice of meditation is very important to achieve psychophysical and spiritual goals. It enhances self-awareness, to reach a higher level of consciousness, to achieve stronger centeredness, relaxations, and to get peace in mind and soul.

6. Regular practice of prayer or spiritual affirmations. All conceivable support and all spiritual help will be extended to those who without fear of human judgment work for the advancement of the truth and light. Fear and negativity keeps the entity close.

7. Put off the old nature that was not safe and start acting like Christ. The bridge to get there is to change your thinking into a spiritual attitude. It is your thinking that allows you to behave and to live a spiritual life.

8. It is fundamental that you do not allow spiritual deception that prohibits you from seeing your true spiritual condition. If you have a hunger for God's Word, are walking in the light, a desire to walk daily in the power of the Holy Spirit, and have a passion to win souls for Jesus Christ, you are true Christians.

'Put on the created nature of Christ, this is created in God's image of true righteousness and holiness' (Eph. 4: 24).

God gives all the credit for all the success that we ever have. Apart from Him, we can do nothing. But neither is God going to do everything for us without us joining Him with a faithful effort.

Leaning on the Holy Spirit, allows you to think right and choose your thinking you need to do it so carefully because what you think is what you become. You can think as much as you want, but God knows what is in your mind and He sees what goes behind closed doors, and he knows your feelings in your heart. Every day, keeping our thoughts right is a battle. Start thinking about what you are thinking about until you think you can defeat the enemy. When your mind is set victoriously, keep it set that way with confidence and courage to walk forward in oneness and righteousness. When you are operating in the mind of Christ, you have dominion over darkness. 'If then you are raised with Christ, seek those things that are above, where Christ sits on the right hand of God. 'Set your affection on things above, not on things on the earth' (Col. 3: 1-2).

You still have the choice to go with your mind and your flesh or your mind and your spirit or in wholeness. But once you really made your mind up, you can do anything. Especially anything God tells you to do you will do it with your heart and soul successfully if you endure and not give up. A quality decision is not one that you make in the height of emotions. It's easy to start on a diet when you are full, but only the people who have made their mind up will stay on the diet to get past the hunger pains that will come for what? You can learn how to be compatible with somebody that you are incompatible with. Once you made your mind up, you can overcome any kind of broken past, any kind of bondage, and any kind of addiction if you just get with God and say, well, this is what happened to me, but God is on my side. All things are possible, but nothing is impossible when the power of God is on your side. 'And do not be conformed to this world; but be transformed by the renewing of your mind, that you may prove what is the good, acceptable, and perfect will of God' (Rom. 12: 2).

'I would have fainted and lost heart if I had not believed to see the goodness of the LORD in the land of the living' (Ps. 27: 1).

Hopelessness is terrible; it is the absolutely most worst horrible place that you can be. I have seen eyes of hopeless women and children in many places of the world who are so hungry and poor that they cannot feed their children.

Prayer

God please give me the strength that I need and provide thoughts to lead me. With your hands to heal and to sustain me and you're blessing upon me, Amen.

Spiritual Values

$\mathcal{J}$t is through the value of our spirit that we communicate with God. If we love Him we wait on Him and soak in His presence to hear His words that convict us, teaches us, encourage us and guide us with his love.

It is explained in (1 Cor. 2: 10-12) that God has revealed them to us by his Spirit, for the Spirit searches all things, yes, the deep things of God. For what man knows the things of a man, except the spirit of a man that is within him? Even so, no man knows the things of God, except by the Spirit of God revealing them to him. Now we have not received the spirit of the world, but the spirit who is from of God; so that we might know the things that are freely given to us from God.'

Then we begin to view everything in a bigger picture from the spiritual perspective, life is a process or journey of discovery and development, during which personal maturity may importantly be gained through adversity. To deny this by being only concerned with the relief of suffering through the removal of symptoms is to risk impoverishing the experience of all involved, careers and professional colleagues as well as patients. There is a distinction to be made between curing symptoms and helping a person to heal through natural processes to become whole again. The first is interventionist while the latter is more restorative in approach. Developing some form of spiritual awareness and acknowledging what may be called 'spiritual' values allows a values-base to sit beside an evidence-base in daily practice, so restoring a necessary and healthy balance to the practice of mental and physical illness.
'It pleased the Father that all fullness should dwell in him; to reconcile by him, all things to himself; by him, whether they are things on earth, or things in heaven' (Col. 1: 19-20).

Many have discovered another principle of spiritual care that of reciprocity, according to which giver and receiver both benefit from their interaction. There is a high incidence of marital breakdown, drug dependency, alcoholism, depression, and suicide among mental health professionals. Other careers are affected by similar stresses. It is hopeful that time invested in learning about spiritual care giving has beneficial consequences, including spiritual growth, new insights, new interpretations of personal situations, a new vigour in professional practice, and protection from burnout.

The different perspectives of professional and lay caregivers come together through the unifying and healing values of spirituality, which offer common ground for constructive discussion when suffering persists despite everyone's best efforts. Importantly, too, spirituality offers a silent space in which to come compassionately together and share in grieving when little else can be done. It allows for bewilderment, fear, guilt, anger, and other painful feelings gradually to settle and, by fostering mutual respect, it promotes healing powers of forgiveness and love. Spirituality is therefore worth contemplating and discussing as a deep human concern, whether or not it is part of a specific faith tradition, especially in the context of mental health care, where emotional pain and grief are encountered so frequently. There is a growing consensus that mental health and spiritual health are closely related. Even where there are differences of experiences, opinion, and belief, common ground and similarities emerge as more important.

Further qualitative and quantitative research is obviously going to be helpful. But it is abundantly clear that the religious and spiritual lives of patients do matter and that everyone benefits, careers included when these are properly evaluated and respected. Continuing professional development for health care professionals must include the spiritual dimension. Fostering good relations with health careers by including them, for example, in ward rounds and team meetings can only be of benefit. This is trend-setting practice. Let us hope, with a degree of expectation, that many involved with the care of the mentally ill will come to recognise and fully value the spiritual dimension.

Spiritualities

*U*ntil the process of spiritual awakening and transformation takes place, the individual character is not altered. Their habits, traits, and idiosyncrasies and characteristics remains just as they were. The most significant eternal relationship is the connection to our own individual spirit or the true self. We are all spiritual beings, so when this connection has been made, you will realise that it is the most realistic and lasting power you have in your life. As much as we long to know our divine self, the reality and richness within, but do we know how? We all have to find our way of spiritual truth and spiritual perfecting and through the intellectual way is one of them. There is other way that is open to everyone the possibility of seeking their own spiritual development by their own efforts through devotion to a teacher or guru by intellectual search by withdrawal from the world but that there is also the fourth way of service and shared effort and committed to change and inner self-transformation.

Although the path to spiritual maturity is the same as the path to our own empowerment, spirituality and religion each has its own way being one way in which humans can experience spirituality and connecting with the divine to reach God. Religion is not identical with spirituality; rather religion is the form spirituality takes in civilization.

We are living in a time of sore distress when many souls are grievously troubled, when many hearts are filled with despair, when physically we are loaded with burden, with diseases, and mentally disturbed with confusion. Millions who do not know where to turn and lost hope, who cry out for some light to come to them. We must remember that so long as the power of the divine spirit is there for us, we must yearn and claim and demand the liberty of the spirit, of the mind, and of the body. This is how our new world will come into fulfilment. More and more individuals will gradually wake up to be more conscious to develop his inner self and come into his own, and his spirit will shine triumphant in his life everywhere.

Everybody has got to become spiritually developed because every soul has to find reality, which is the truth that brings us freedom of spirit and liberty of soul. No matter who we are, with an open heart, we can bring spirituality into our life by simply asking and we will receive it. By participating and by accepting the how of living rather than the why of understanding allow us being present with it. Every responsibility and action we take is like sowing the seed that will sprout. The quality depends on your awareness of sowing good seeds on well-prepared soil. Do not procrastinate, act now, and try to accomplish to do because life is short and time is precious, we do not know whether we will be alive tomorrow.

When you become aware within you, every day, look deep into your mind and process your thoughts as though you are weeding out the unhealthy seed to allow room for the healthy seed to grow into good quality productive harvest. Every day seeds are coming in the mind. They will take root and if you allow them to stay there long, they will be harder for you to root them out, but if you can throw the seed before it germinates it will be helpful.

Usually, when we are on spiritual path, we do not see our blind spots. The inner work is to uncover our denial and open our hearts to allow divine to shine in. We must heal our shame, guilt, and blame and begin the process of open dialogue. We are more than matter and we are mind and spirit, and there are vibrations that belong to the mental and spiritual life. There are vibrations that belong to the super physical life, which is beyond the earthly world. We can register the vibrations of this life in which we live, and the vibrations of that larger life which one day will be our eternal habitat. Always hold on to the spiritual truths, for this will endure and the riches of the spirit, once we have obtained them, can never be taken away from us. These are our eternal possessions.

Life goes on beyond this world. Spirituality is connected to immaterial reality; an inner path allowing you to discover the essence of your being or your true values within by which you live. Spiritual practices, including meditation, prayer, and contemplation are intended to develop an individual's inner life. Living a spiritual life often lead to an experience of connectedness with a larger reality, yielding a more comprehensive, wholesome self and open doors to God and perceive everything and people in life in a bigger picture with more possibilities.

Specific Benefits of Developing Your Spirituality

There are a number of benefits to spirituality. Through my own spiritual life, that is benefiting from a deep spirituality, as it applies to healing emotional and physical problems. Spirituality is a realisation and an awareness of the inner reality of your spirit being, the true self—the soul within. Being spiritual creates a channel in your being that opens you to the spirit and aspires you to realise God, light, truth, wisdom, freedom, and immortality is inevitable, a divine life to serve life purposes. Spiritual knowledge and experience is a journey to realise your spiritual force, a permanent and integral absorption into the being that has the power to alter the conditions of your life. Realising spiritual qualities transcend you into oneness with others and life, acquiring inner silence, connecting with your evolving soul, feeling divine love and attaining enlightenment. They each can be known, experienced, or realised on an ascending scale.

Soul Light

Sweet star, of pure brightness,
That for a transient day
Shed over our souls such lightness,
And then withdrew the ray.

Emanating with immortal lustre.,
Sparkling brightly now,
Amid the gems that cluster,
The third eye focuses brightly from the brow!

We close our bright brown eyes,
Where all the hopes are sleeping
While our souls purify,
We sleep soundly without waking.

We glance towards the skies,
And while our hearts are breaking,
That bid us dry the tears from our eyes,
That bright star in the heavenly is breathtaking.

From a distant magical pattern,
With our pure spirit's love,
And those clear rays are laden,
Like angels flying above.

Joo Lian Carter

The Soul

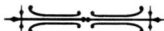

'God proceeded to form the man out of dust from the ground, and to blow into his nostrils the breath of life, and the man came to be a living soul.' (Gen. 2: 7)

'This is why the father loves me because I surrender my soul in order that I may receive it again' (John 10: 17).

We Have Evolved in Technology, but Have We Evolved Our Souls?

Right within us is the light, there in our souls where God speaks to us from within. We listen to God for guidance with our spirit's ears not our natural ears. When we do not pay attention to this silent inner voice, we allow the natural ears to take over focusing on the external world, therefore, our ability to hear God is lost. We are guided by the love and light of God if we are lacking of wisdom we should ask God, trusting Him in every decision we make by the circumstances and by our senses or emotions. By nature, God is love, light, and perfect; by nature we inherit that characteristic from Him. Because of our original sin, we have to be saved and be made perfect through Jesus Christ. 'Just as the Father knows I and I know the Father; and I surrender my soul in behalf of the sheep' (John 10: 15).

Grace is a teaching process of repentance, living in righteousness and purity, bringing salvation, perfection, and seeing God. Salvation and justification come by faith that purifies your heart and soul through His grace. But you must first be purified in this life; to understand the true promises of Jesus, the real hope that can release the power of God to purify your heart and soul. It is important to purify your spiritual channels, increase your energy of light frequency, and uplift your soul. There is no beginning and end to a soul-spirit, but some souls are more evolved than the other. All souls-spirit come from the God's light and that becomes the individual energy current and that consciousness is you that was formed. The soul is the vehicle of the spirit. The ever-moving power of the moving spirit controls, purifies, and transmutes the invisible elements that attract them by their material correspondence. It passes from the earthly life along with physical death, and its use is ended. We communicate with our spirit world through consciousness.

The purpose of a soul when incarnated into the physical world is to evolve, to heal, and to balance the karma to grow our spirit. There are souls who remain in the non-physical realm and continue to develop their souls in advanced level of light as spirit guides or teachers or masters. Everything serves our true purpose of incarnation and human experience and learning is to serve the health of the soul. The energy of the soul supports the physical well-being. The soul light is shaped by consciousness. Changing the frequency of your consciousness changes life experiences.

'For what benefit is it to a man, if he should gain the whole world, but lose his own soul? Or what will a man give in exchange for his soul' (Matt. 16: 26).

Only through responsible choices that shape the light that flows through you, you create the reality within you, and consciously invoke growing, and consciously invoke wisdom from your higher self, the empowerment within you, to challenge negative emotions or to overcome temptations to prevent sin. Therefore, to cultivate and to nourish the needs of your soul and to challenge and to release the wants of your personality, you have to make responsible conscious choices. It is the 'simulacrum' of the body and is often mistaken for the immortal part, the enfranchised spirit.

Soul Communication Healing

The light of the soul shines in the heart and is reflected in the mind to heal. Each individual interacts within the body, mind, and soul energy through communicating in harmony, which is part of the continual healthy learning and wholesome healing process to a different energy vibration level. This is why soul communication is extremely valuable for healing and soul growth. It assists in identifying issues that need healing. It is the vehicle for making a connection with the issue to assist healing. Soul communication is used to receive information for healing and to direct the healing process and accelerates healing with profound benefits. During deep meditation, the third eye or spiritual eye or intuition becomes visible within the central part of the forehead (the sixth chakra). Intuitively, this ability of the soul communication can be helpful and used for healing. With this ability, you can see energy and even spiritual blockages. This happens in several ways. One way is to identify the body's accumulated energy blockages or where energy is deficient. Ill health in most cases is due to energy blockage progressing to disharmony in well-being, resulting in manifestation of diseases in the body and mind affecting the spirit. Identifying the source of energy imbalance and the cause is the start of the healing process. Intuitively, the root cause of the health issues can be identified by the intuitive sufferer or healer which then effective self-healing through soul mind and body energy balancing process.

When you see an area in the body with an excess of energy, you know to direct the healing blessing there. If you intend to use one hand near, one hand far, your third eye images allow you to know the proper placement of your hands. People with a very high-developed third eye, can see in much more detail. When you use your third eye, it is important to remember you are receiving images, an image of the blockages and image of past life experience. Everything is an image, so it is important to interpret what you receive. You can be a very powerful healer without third eye capabilities. It is an aid to supplement the healing process. This is a very helpful ability. Those who have this ability are very blessed, and it helps them to accelerate the healing process for themselves and others. It is also amazing to see what is happening during the healing process. This will enhance one's understanding of soul, mind, body, and medicine as self-healing techniques.

When you receive information from the soul language, it is important to understand and then translation is a vital part of the process and accuracy is very important. One way is your physical response. If you feel comfortable throughout your whole body, then this is the sign the translation is accurate. If you have pressure on the crown chakra, this also is an indication the translation is accurate. If it promotes love, peace, and harmony it is also an indication. Accuracy is extremely important to identify health issues. The accuracy of your translation will increase with practice.

Sacred Contract

Our souls made a sacred contract,
A fountain and a shrine intact,
And all the flowers are perfect.
We are here together, love,
Mountains and sea surrounding us,
Trees wreathed with fruits outburst.

Our hearts that have understanding,
Seeking knowledge that is outstanding.
As well as truth that is inspiring.
From day to day, it carries us along,
We graciously and constantly perform,
Filling the place with love and songs.

Patiently and faithfully lay the foundations,
For what it's worth with good intentions,
To attain the spiritual vibration,
We practice the lessons of wisdom.
And the precepts of religion,
To enter the gate of God's kingdom.

We endure and pray every night,
To receive blessings from the divine light,
Until all things are lovely and bright.
He guides us with love to His divine plan
We serve humanity with united hands,
To be together in His promised land.

Joo Lian Carter

My Dreams of Reality

Jesus said, 'It shall come to pass afterward, that I will pour out my spirit upon all mankind; and your sons and your daughters shall prophesy, your old men shall dream dreams, your young men shall see visions' (Joel 2: 28).

Vast majority of people spend an average of one-third of their lives asleep, where the body and mind reprocess and while the spirit is most active in the spirit world. The most common way to receive God's message is through your dreams. Dreams give us insight and understanding even when our conscious mind cannot perceive them. Dreams can also hold message to the future. In reality, God is Spirit, therefore, we communicate with Him in spirit. He speaks to us in dreams; in the presence of His peace that comes in knowing that you are truly being guided by Him. This does not necessary means that every dream is prophetic. Most dreams are a God-designed process, where the brain reprocesses information in highly symbolic language. Something happens in the dream-state, which allows us to make better decisions. Yet, for the believer, we can renew our minds through reading His Word and through worship in the spirit.

I would like to share one of my dreams that I encountered which I think is spiritual and inspiring. Not what my dream is, but what dream state I was in.

The inspiration that I received in this dream has guided me to interpret this dream as soul rising. To elaborate it is not about winning the race with each other. It is about purifying the souls to perfection and to the highest level. Normally, people do not think about soul rising but instead in a racing car competition, the car is to drive forward as fast as the vehicle can take him to the goal post. In the physical world, we take things literally, but in the mystical inner world of the psychic mind and spirit, the soul is the vehicle of infinite life that evolves.

This is something to compare and to challenge? This is how the dream goes. To be successful in the race, the goal is how high the vehicle can rise vertically, not how fast forward it can achieve horizontally. The symbol of the cross represents a single moment in a person's life. The point of intersection of the vertical with the horizontal is now or present. But this only becomes now in its full meaning if a person is conscious. If he is not conscious in time, being hurried on from past to future, identified with everything, now and present moment does not exist in his life, therefore, purpose of live has not been fulfilled.

There were three vehicles involved in the race.

The first vehicle was controlled by a sensual unconscious man or not aware of his spiritual self, which means only the most external sides of his centres are working, and they absorb his energies. The man alive only in those parts of him turned towards the outer senses, towards life. So he was controlled by the car that can only move forward, therefore, was not successful in the race to raise him. Wake up and be watchful, and strengthen the things that remain, which are ready to die. 'For I have not found your works perfect before God' (Rev. 3: 2).

The second vehicle is a matured scientific man wearing a white coat, and the creation he came up from, his vehicle, was very impressive, innovative, and it got people's attention and applause straight away, looking like a hi-technology laboratory. When the race starts, the vehicle does visibly rise but could not sustain the power, and it then crashes and gets pushed aside together with the egoistic inventive driver who then becomes insignificant and does not achieve his height with God or attain his totality of the moments of self-consciousness during his life. 'For the day of the LORD of hosts shall be upon everyone who is proud and lofty, and upon everyone who is lifted up; all shall be brought low' (Isa. 2: 12).

To win the race, the two men from the first and second require to develop their magnetic centres, with an inner wish to understand more he is a man with far more inner senses than outer senses. But the inner senses require to be developed through his self-observation which is not ordinarily used. He has to be reached by his inner senses to be raise to his true self.

The third vehicle was controlled by a little boy with me trying to help him from the external world to achieve his goal. He was only about six years old but very awake and innocent still maintaining his true essence, inquisitive, putting his innocent mind, heart, and soul, finding his way around the vehicle like searching for the truth from inside on how to lift the vehicle from his own inner world to get where he wants to be and not worry about the vehicle or the race. 'He will guide the meek in what is right and he will teach the humble his way' (Ps. 25: 9). 'Blessed are the meek, for they shall inherit the earth' (Matt. 5: 5). Although his vehicle did not move, but, finally, he found that magical button under his seat pressed it at the last second of the race and he was raised up a few inches in his secured seat but very high in his inner world that he can imagine in his true essence or true spiritual self. Thoughts from essence are thoughts from the most simple and the true side of us. But the quality of thought from essence is of a far higher order than that from personality. 'Let no man despise your youth; but be an example for the believers in word, in conduct, in love, in spirit, in faith, and in purity' (Tim. 4: 12).

Although the little boy's vehicle did not impress or move in the material world, but he was able to connect that he has not won the race but his soul was raised nearer to God. The law of evolution brings each and every soul to the point where it must return to God. 'When the dust returns to the earth just as it happened to be and the spirit itself returns to the true God who gave it' (Eccles. 12: 7).

Our purpose in life here is to find God and how to return to Him that spark of love and light to be oneness. One of the key is realisation and is awareness and connects within to your higher self and then the answer will be revealed to you in your own time. There are three bodies that make up life—the mental body, the physical body, and the higher spiritual bodies, which are constructed on principle of the ray of creation. It is an organism and all organisms obey the law of creation.

The law of three is the Christian tenet of the Trinity that comes between God and the world. The connection of God or the Absolute and the process of creation can only be understood through the Trinity or Primal Triad of Three Forces and the derivation of subsequent trial.

Everyone and everything has a soul that sparks of spirits from the Creator. We are all being controlled by the power of our own soul and spirit. Soul power including soul secrets, soul healing, soul wisdom, soul knowledge, and soul practices which transforms humanity, nature, animal, and environment. The soul has the power to heal, rejuvenate and to lift and transform life. In the soul light era, the evolution of humanity will be created by soul power. There is a cascade of consciousness that comprehends all that we are when we are in touch with our souls. As we become more intimate with our soul, we will experience true love, compassion, and healing. The invisible infinite soul is the only reality compare to everything else is impermanent.

One of the ways to connect within is to meditate every morning, night, and whenever there is a little spare time during the day. Meditate before food and sleep and feed your soul with God-communion. Filled with the Holy Spirit inspiration found by deeply divine meditative mind, he is able to perform happily all the duties of the day and also with the free will we can choose the material will or the divine will? How can we serve God to manifest His Kingdom? First, we must establish righteousness to serve our purpose, transform and restore the imbalance of every soul and the planet to create that promise land and His Kingdom. We must repent our sin and receive the Holy Spirit through Jesus. You must pray, then, this way: 'Our Father in the heavens let your name be sanctified.' (Matt. 6: 9)

'Let your kingdom come. Let your will take place as in heaven, also upon earth' (Matt. 6: 10).

The past and the future are the same like the bud of the lily that blooms today and fades tomorrow, that it shall be sweet and beautiful in its season.

(Joo Lian Carter)

Destiny

My destiny is in my own hands,
So where I am now progressing to ascent,
How I live my life
Determine how I am qualified.

To be even with God,
Or to adore the odds,
It is all up to me
To accomplish my destiny.

No matter what the circumstances may be,
I value my effort and purpose that matters to me.
Do not make circumstances my victim,
Just think, feel, and act from love within.

In my orientation of creation,
The truth reveals in the expression.
I live to my highest potential,
To accomplish my most profound essentials.

I have to attain my spirituality,
My heart is open to new experience and reality.
My character shapes my destiny.
Just act with good will, love, and morality.

(Joo Lian Carter)

Purifying the Inner Life and Truth

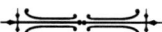

$\mathcal{W}$e are constantly seeking and wanting to know the truth and when you have found it in the Word of God, how you live the truth is the faith you develop towards that truth. The truth sets you free to fulfill your purpose and experience abundant life in this world to determine your qualification for a position after life to reconcile with God. If you are wise and faithful, trust in Jesus to direct you in your journey. But it is essential that the works of loving obedient faith is necessary for him to direct you to ever realizing restoration to life, justification, purification, and salvation. When you are ready, God will work through you to fulfill your life with righteousness in his peace and joy.

Purification promotes humility and effort, which enable you to apply the truth in your life to become more spiritual and holy. With God's help, you become less selfish and more generous towards humanity. Besides purification, you need regeneration that reminds you of what God has already done so that you find strength and joy to continue your spiritual journey. In Christ, you are a new creation, and this truth will be life to you to overcome discouragement and transgression. 'For whoever calls upon the name of the Lord shall be saved' (Rom. 10: 13). 'And take the helmet of salvation and the sword of the Spirit, which is the word of God' (Eph. 6: 17).

The most important thing in the universe is God's truth, without Bible truth, no one ever becomes a Christian, and no Christian ever grows or have the knowledge to purity or sanctity.

'Every man who has this hope in him purifies himself, even as He (Jesus) is pure' (1 John 3: 3). The hope of seeing Jesus appear in your heart is the hope that saves and purifies you—the total internal change through Christ. But you must have the hope for the power of God to be released to purify you. 'He who practices righteousness is righteous even as he is righteous' (John 3: 7). Jesus said 'My food is for me to do the will of Him that sent me and to finish his work.' (John 4: 34). The Word of God is the food for our souls.

'God is Spirit and those who worship Him must worship in spirit and truth' (John 4: 24).

Pilate asked Jesus, 'Are you the king?' Jesus answered 'You yourself are saying that I am the king. For this I have been born into the world and should bear witness to the truth. Everyone that is on the side of the truth listens to my voice' (John 18: 37).

> *The pearls of wisdom harbor many truth, pure pearl and cloudy pearl, a bit like the mind once the mind has got rid of the clouds, the purification takes place, the shackles will fall away, and the truth reveals.*
>
> *(Joo Lian Carter)*

I was lately confirmed of these desires during my spiritual journey that I begin to question for the truth. Questioning and searching for the truth is essential for human consciousness. When we become conscious of our own inner world of spirit self, the truth reveals. 'Remember the former things, those of long ago; I am God, and there is no other; I am God, and there is none like me. I make known the end from the beginning, from ancient times, what is still to come. I say, 'My purpose will stand, and I will do all that I please.' From the east, I summon a bird of prey; from a far-off land, a man to fulfill my purpose. What I have said, that I will bring about; what I have planned, that I will do' (Isa. 46: 9-11). You need to wake up and act on the truth in your life while it is available because God will powerfully fulfill His prophesy and purpose. 'Behold, the days come, says the Lord GOD, that I will send a famine in the land, not a famine of bread, nor a thirst for water, but of hearing the words of the LORD; And they shall wander from sea to sea and from the north to the east; they shall run to and fro to seek the word of the LORD, and shall not find it (Amos 8: 11-12). 'Blessed is he that reads, and those who hear the words of this prophecy, and keep those things which are written in it; for the time is at hand' (Rev. 1: 3).

There is no right or wrong, the truth is seldom heard. The truth of the Word will lead you the righteous way. Call for our Father in the name of Jesus. If you call upon Him, He can deliver and will deliver or show you your personal needs family needs, national needs, and global needs. God loves you He is gracious to you, He gives you hope and peace in the name of Jesus.

'For I myself well know the thoughts that I am thinking towards you, is the utterance of God, thoughts of peace and not of calamity, to give you a future and a hope. And you will certainly call me and come and pray to me, and I will listen to you; and you will actually seek me and find me, for you will search for me with all your heart' (Jer. 29: 11-13).

Those who seek truth will always carry his star
in his heart.

(Joo Lian Carter)

God's word is the truth. Having faith in God is the highest truth. Do we need a spiritual middleman which is religion? God did not tell us to follow religion; He said to follow Him and His word.

We understand the laws because we make them up, but do we understand God's laws or the truth? If you don't understand God's laws, the only way is to study His word, then you will be blessed with His grace to lead you to the truth to set you free.

In answer, Jesus said to him, 'Most truly I say to you, unless you are born again you cannot enter the Kingdom of God.' (John 3: 3).

Jesus answered Nicodemus, 'Most truly I say to you, unless anyone is born from water and spirit, he cannot enter into the kingdom of God.' (John 3: 5).

The spirit of Jesus is in you learn how to abide in Him and know the reality that the Holy Spirit is inside you. A sanctified person has respected the anointing of the Holy Spirit and received the anointing needs to be cultivated and reap from it many more fold. Just ask the Holy Spirit of God always to bless and be in obedience.

Christ in speaking of rebirth to Nicodemus, 'Except a man be born of water and the spirit, he cannot enter into the kingdom of God.' The truth is a person who knows his true self (spirit) through Jesus Christ leads us to the truth that is God. In the end is His word that really is the key to the truth and reality.

The living truth makes a man alive in himself with spiritual truth. It is the knowledge that refers to reaching the higher level of inner evolution. How a man must know, think, feel, understand, and do to reach his inner truth about himself and the kind of person he is and how he can change into a ready and willing being to be taught so that his mind is receptive to receive God's word of truth. The commandments were written on tables of stone. It must be understood that truth about a higher evolution and must rest upon a firm basis for those incapable of seeing any deeper meaning. A man on the higher level cannot be understood by a man on a lower level. We cannot reach a higher level unless we possess the knowledge called truth that can lead us to it.

The truth about God's purpose is that human form is only temporary, and we are designed that we transform from mortal to immortal and from temporary life to eternal life. This transition is something that God has given us a mind with a free will to choose through His grace to learn and to grow to perfection and to live a godly life of righteousness. Apart from living according to our own will choosing to obey God's will and to become a part of His family. 'Jesus promises the holy spirit to all believers; He who has my commands, and obeys them, it is he who loves me; and he who loves me shall be loved by my Father, and I will love him and will show myself to him' (John 14: 21).

Jesus died on the cross for us to give us new life. Three days after his crucifixion, he rose from the dead. He is alive; he wants to come into your life. Jesus himself said, 'I am the resurrection and the light, he that believe in me, though he was dead shall he live.' Almost two thousand years since he rose from the dead, he still lives today as the greatest and most powerful influence in the world. All powerful statesmen have come and gone, rulers, scholars, scientists, theologians have come and gone, but Jesus still lives today, and he is the most unique person who has ever lived. His birth and his life were unique; the Bible tells us that he was born of a Virgin Mary. His life was categorised by the supernatural, he lived a holy life without sin and performed great miracle that anyone has ever lived. His message was unique; he offers love, hope, forgiveness, and new way of life to all who receive him as savoir and Lord.

Wherever his messages have gone, there have been new life, new hope, and new purpose for living. His death on the cross was unique. Two thousand years ago, the God of the universe sent his only son Jesus Christ to be sacrificed for the sin of all men. He died for you, and his resurrection was unique, and three days after his death, the most amazing event in history took place. Jesus rose from the dead. His birth, life, death, and resurrection, all prove who Jesus exactly is, who he claimed to be the son of God, the saviour for all mankind. This same Jesus Christ is alive today, He wants to come into your life, forgive your sins, and give you the power to live an abundant life. Listen to his words. 'Come on to me all you laden and heavy laden and I will give you rest. I am the way the truth and the life no man come to the father but by me.'

The Bible says we all have sin and come short with the glory of God. It also says for the wages of sin is death, of the gift of blood is eternal life through Jesus Christ, our lord. When Jesus died, he paid the penalty for your sin. Right now, he stands ready to come into your life. 'Behold, I stand at the door and knock if anyone hears and open the door I will come into him.' with experiences of love and forgiveness and receive eternal life, you must receive him as God's scarifies for your sin and invite him to come in to your life by faith.' If this is the desire of your heart, you can pray a prayer of faith and Jesus Christ will come into your life.

This is a suggestive prayer: Lord Jesus, I surrender and believe that you are the son of the living God and God the son. I thank you for dying on the cross for my sin. I am sorry for my sins and I ask you to forgive me. I need you to come into my heart. I open the door of my life and receive you as my savoir and Lord. I accept you and give myself to you right now and promise to follow you all the days of my life. Take control of my life and make me the person you want me to be. Amen.

If this prayer expresses the desire of your heart, pray this prayer right now where you are, pray this prayer silently. Invite Jesus into your life, and you can be sure that he came in because he promised that he would if only you would ask me. You can also be sure that your sins are forgiven that you are a child of God and have eternal life. If you want to experience a full and abundant life with Jesus Christ, talk with him every day in prayer. Discover his wonderful plan for your life by reading his scriptures and meet with others who love and follow him. Finally, remember always, his wonderful promises. 'I will never leave you or forsake you I am with you always even I unto the end of the world.'

A great man is always willing to be little or humble, and his strength grows out of his weakness. The truth is what I have experience in this lifetime that my physical self is a temporary temple to accommodate my evolving spirit (soul). Until I reach a point that I will listen to God and begin to receive true knowledge of Him, then God will begin to share His spirit with me in order to give me the ability to begin seeing Him that's the truth. Such seeing is something spiritual not through human eyes but seeing in the mind of the spirit.

Every moment of our life can be represented in the cross, in this vertical line, is cut across by the horizontal line of time. The point of intersection of the vertical line with the horizontal line is living consciously now and up. To continue on the horizontal line is the unconscious future. So which direction do we take our journey? Do you pick up the cross and follow the Christ consciousness in the light or deny the cross and continue along the horizontal line in the dark?

The truth is we are spiritual beings and lying within the richness will be just what it contains with your own nature and what is important is not what happens materially, but what happens to you spiritually, to your nature and your eternal nature no more no less. That is the lesson to be learnt in the earthly life. If you learn it, you are wise and have found your true self, and having found your divine self, you will have found the great divine spirit. It is just the simple truth about our own nature and yet it is not possessed by many.

For every person, when you are beginning the spiritual life because you wish to be saved, you aim towards light, and finally, on account of the truth and good that you love for the sake of oneness in presence of God, loves truth and good and turn away from darkness. All the way through we are safe by grace through faith, and it's not done in a moment and the process is dependent on our continuing faith in the Lord Jesus. Purifying or repentance is to show you are repenting. Is there anything in my life that Jesus doesn't like? Then live the will of God, you will be saved by the grace. Go on believing in Jesus Christ, be baptized, and believe in saving grace in the biblical way out of the God generous heart who loves to give.

When one is purified from life impurities, pursuing a spiritual life living God's Word and sees everything as a form of love and light, and then he is being sanctified and enlightened. We are rational people so if we fill our lives with knowledge and wisdom, then we begin to understand the work of God. With this understanding, we understand His Word which is the truth. Because the Lord is in the Word and the Word is divine truth, and divine truth is light.

'Most truly, I say to you, He that hears my word and believes him that sent me has everlasting life, and he does not come into judgment but has passed over from death to life. The hour is coming and now is when the dead shall hear the voice of the Son of God and they that hear shall live.' (John 5: 24-25).

For when one have reached spiritual maturity and sanctified, he is like an oak tree growing from its acorn. He is well connected with his inner divine truth and has affection for righteousness, holiness, and has developed a true faith in God and Jesus Christ. His spirit connected to God with hope of resurrection (Luke 23: 46) and Jesus called with a loud voice and said 'Father, into your hands I entrust my spirit.' When he had said this, he expired.

'When he had said this, he expired. Therefore we were buried with him by baptism into death; so as Christ was raised up from the dead by the glory of the Father, even so we also should walk in newness of life. For if we have become united with him in the likeness of his death, we will certainly also be united in the likeness of his resurrection; that our old man has been crucified with him, that our body of sin might be destroyed, so that we would not serve sin any longer' (Rom 6: 4-6).

The New World

We come and go to this earth plane,
But the world will always remain,
There are lessons and work to be done,
We are here to learn and still have fun,
Great work requires willing hands, hearts, and minds,
To discover the prize of truth, we set out to find,
The most that we can do,
Is to make our passage through.

If we help one another to awaken,
Then we will not be forsaken.
For our being to grow in stature,
We set out to life adventure,
The quality of our spirit is determined,
By the way, we live and have been examined,
To abide the natural law of cause and effect,
Might be the way we can be perfect.

We need courage and patience for evolution,
We encourage peace and not revolution,
The truth is we have made more progress,
Unless we are grateful the world will be a mess.
Nothing stands in our free will to choose.
Perhaps we will be more concerned with truth.
With our creative knowledge and wisdom we bring to bear,
To create a peaceful world with abundance to share.

If we were to see the misery, struggle, and pain.
We desire to transform the world so that it should not
happen again.

Joo Lian Carter

Future and the New World

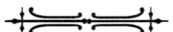

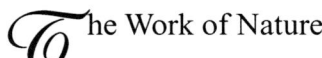he Work of Nature

'For no other foundation can any man lay than what has been already laid, which is Jesus Christ' (1 Cor. 3: 11).

We are responsible in building ourselves up to have a sound foundation in this world and that is laying the foundation of Jesus in our lives.

First of all we must be grateful and respect the Creator of our planet. He graciously have plan for our destiny before he created us so that we can walk our way with Him through His word to accomplish His great plan for mutual purpose.

It comes as a point in human history, development, and realisation that it is absolutely essential for the attainment of world peace and higher spiritual consciousness. We have the capacity to understand and to realise the importance and inevitable of the revolutionary world that we must transform and evolve with the law of nature in the new age and the dawning of a new era.

'Coming to him the Living Stone, rejected indeed by men, but chosen by God, and precious; you also, as living stones, are built up as a spiritual house, a holy priesthood, to offer up spiritual sacrifices, acceptable to God through Jesus Christ' (1 Pet. 2: 4-5).

All the struggle in life into which man is born to the world of want and materialism, a love of controlling over others and from a love of possessing the goods of others, and all the delights of man's own life becomes driven by what he desires and want, that rules a man's life so the loves and delights of these evils belong to man's own life and weak foundation.

Being grateful, respecting, loving, and nurturing the Mother Earth, this is as important as respecting, loving, and nurturing oneself and others. The law of nature will never change for us but will always evolve from its own existence. It is our duty to appreciate what the earth can provide us for our survival. Therefore, the least we can do is to enjoy and to return with intelligent treatment and obey its natural law for our long-term survival. In whatever state the planet is in, we are encountering various consequences partly from the effect we may have caused. It is now that we are all experiencing the prominent situations in our lives that the natural disaster is affecting us more now than ever. We are faced with inevitable destruction more now from imbalanced ecology threatening all lives with earthquakes, tsunami and floods, extreme weathers, drought and impure water from contamination, wars, new variant virus and diseases, our demand from the natural resources to cope with higher technology and life changes and more.

Is this a sign for the nature to round up her great circle, and making conditions a new era?

As we lose sight of our natural purpose, life and the natural resources is been tempered and demised in accord with the cycles of nature we think and believe that more inventions may correct the disaster and violations against nature and humans. All these consequences cause imbalances which result in war, social disintegration, and natural catastrophe.

We are evolving towards a period of human history as the new age vibration begins to affect more and more people. For twenty years of life, where I was brought up in a poor family that I experienced in the East to the extent of forty years life in the West have allowed me to understand the way of living in the two different world. In the world of community living in the east with less advantage yet contented compared with in a world of western civilization of discontentment.

Fortunately, we are evolving towards a time as the new dawn vibration begins to influence more and more people to realise the change in world affairs and cosmic energy and callings by stirring the spiritual awakening of thousands of unconscious minds. Through this callings, awakenings, and awareness, we will begin to embrace the energy of light, love, and healing vibration that may eventually be able to transform the planet earth into a place of greater peace and balance.

A science of spiritual evolution could be introduced based upon the God's Word through the teachings and ethics of Jesus Christ, for a more conscious, purposeful, fulfilling, and harmonious life here and after.

This will make them known just as people are recognized by the higher education curriculums from which they have graduated.

As I am writing this, I myself is feeling rejuvenated, and I am delighted and have faith in this new prospect of living in abundance with love and light. There is no death! Man is the arbiter of his own destiny. When there is darkness in your days, look up into the invisible world and live abundantly with hope and faith in the Holy Spirit because the spirit is eternal.

As individuals, we all have a free will to be our own eternal spiritual master led by Christ to create our own heaven on earth and later a transition to a greater eternal life and heaven. Instead of feeling doomed and gloomed, the new dawn of enlightenment and new dimensional possibilities are there to be realised and awakened by the individuals. It is up to individual responsibility and commitment to live abundantly in God's will and follows His word to guide us. As I mentioned earlier in the book, fearing darkness in your present will not progress you to a brighter future, but fearing God is to keep us in obedience to Him to walk in the light.

'Let all the earth fear the Lord, let all the inhabitants of the world stand in awe of Him' (Ps. 33: 8).

We have to let go of any negative past to embrace and live righteously for humanity in the light of sharing and caring. Also, be preparing to receive instructions from the super naturals that have demonstrated in the word and found truth to show us the way.

Power of Peace

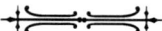

'If you have peace, no matter what you may lack, life is beautiful' (Matt.5: 9).

Everyone seeks for peace, but what is peace? You have to understand what peace means to you; otherwise, you won't know what it is when you have found it. When you make peace with God, He is on your side and you can be victorious in peace of mind. The peace that is found in the midst of a storm is true peace of God. You will find peace as a gift from God when you have pleased Him. The pursuing of righteousness and the spirit enable you to attain peace and sense of wholeness. Take responsibility for who you are and what God wants. not what you want, then you will have peace. When God wants you to do something, it is not easy, but you can depend on Him to give and show you peace and joy, even in the midst of a difficult task serving Him. The world we live in, desperately need hope, peace, and love.

Every person has the responsibility to live a life for a purpose that serves God. The physical laws, that give order to our world, affect our learning and experience, but it is most important to learn the spiritual laws that regulate human happiness and wholeness. When we stop playing God ourselves, instead, turn to the magnificent God's spiritual law which reveals a way of life that will enable all mankind to learn how to love and serve Him and have His divine blessing. This law and His word also teach us how to truly love one another, therefore, attaining an unprecedented depth of peace and joy. 'Glory to God in the highest, and on earth peace among men with whom He is pleased, men who are of goodwill; Peace is the gift of God' (Luke 2: 14).

The world peace depends on every individual to create his or her own true natural peace from within, then capable to influence the peace vibration around us and the world. Do not just pray for peace but become that natural peace that resides deep within and can be found when you allow your true self to emerge into the surface of your life to the real feeling of peace to everyone and everything around you. Let go of your fears and your doubts and that of others by forgiving. Most of the time in order to make peace, we have to give and take with love. Be extreme in what you focus your attention upon right now and question the messages and reflections. If it is loving, critical, or in any way invokes hatred, fear, or anger release it and return to peace. Create your own pictures of reality and fill them with peace and love. Walk in joy and harmony and know that is well. You can put your energy to this by contemplating peace and tapping into higher desire for peace at any moment. The natural part of your existence is a loving life which is so beautiful that you have to accept to love yourself for what you have within is what you can then give out. When you have built an innate love, wisdom, and power foundation, your true self from within you become the privileged and conscious being of your wondrous world. Where there is no freedom and spiritual awareness, there is no peace. Christ said that 'In me you shall have perfect peace.'

'Therefore being justified by faith, we have peace with God through our Lord Jesus Christ' (Rom. 5: 1).

In 2009, on 17 December at around 6 a.m. following completion of reading the book of Revelation I had a personal encounter with Jesus. My life and I was radically and permanently changed for the better and more peaceful. I have made a public confession that I am a faithful believer of Jesus and born again. 'Whoever therefore shall confess me before men, I will confess him before my Father who is in heaven. 'But whoever denies me before men, I will also deny him before my Father who is in heaven' (Matt. 10: 32-33). 'The disciple is not above his master, but everyone who is perfect will be like his master' (Luke 6: 40).

Our visions and hopes for a free and peaceful world can only manifest from our higher spiritual selves, the invisible world to drive the visible world by attaining a free, hopeful, and compassionate heart. This vision is possible when individual is renewed from his own consciousness to thrive on righteousness. We are here to live with each other, help one another through storms and tribulation to learn lessons and to progress in life. The key is to be wise, work skilfully, effectively with creativities, and compassionately with others, as part of interwoven systems of connectivity that bind us together for a sound foundation to relieve suffering. When I look back on the processes of history, I learn that the nations are renewed from the bottom or foundation not from the top and from within and without with the help of God's grace.

Every human being has a unique quality to influence or contribute in his own thoughtful way and in his own time and peace to the society. Everything I know in my experience and observation that has given me the knowledge that the real wisdom of human life is the experiences of a conscious mind and living in peace. It's not just to pursue peace, but share it. In the state of economic crisis, we are all affected globally, and we must awaken ourselves to reality of what's happening today in our government, social revolution, and living conditions.

'How do we build the foundation? By hearing and doing the word through storms' (Matt. 7: 24-27). The search for peace has become a global obsession because we are constantly living on edge that leads to illness physically, mentally, emotionally, and spiritually. To find peace, you have to take responsibility to seek within your own spirit that can give you peace of mind and then only can you create peace in your environment. Peace starts from an individual attainment to share with each other in harmony. Jesus is the prince of peace, reconcile with him to attain his peace in you.

Our progression in life is like a magnificent tree that grows from good soil up through the trunk into the branches to the foliage and the blossoms that bear fruits; this is when we have reached our goal when the fruits are ready for harvesting. A nation is as great, and only as great, the quality of the life of people.

In this current society, the masses of humanity have been exploited by greed that excuses itself as the operation of impersonal market forces. What meets their eyes everywhere is the destruction of moral foundations vital to humanity's future, through gross self-indulgence masquerading as freedom of speech. When you seek and attain peace, which is the result of having attained righteousness, quietness, confident, trust and hope, the peace of Christ will rule your heart, your thoughts, your words, and your deeds.

'Delight yourself in the LORD, and he shall give you the desires of your heart' (Ps. 37: 4).

Hope for New Age Children

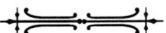

' *A*llow the little children to come to me, and do not forbid them, for of such is the kingdom of heaven' (Matt. 19: 14).

As parents, we must be approachable for our children, whereby they are not afraid to come to us to confide in their problems, feelings, and needs. Today most working parents have no time for their children, and they don't even know their children are crying out for love and attention. Children desperately need somebody to love and care for them when they feel insecure and being available to give them advises when they are lost and feeling despair. I see different level of distress in them the vacancy in their eyes and has no desire to live because there is no hope within them. There is a new generation of light children and we have to share their mind and desire. As parents, we have a definite responsibility to assist our children in fully awakening and understanding their mission and purpose. Given the opportunity of a different school, where our natural love of understanding the world around us and our desire to make a difference are continually nurtured. Parents should support them to become more aware of how they make sense of things, how they construct their world, allow their children continue to pursue their innate curiosities about why things happen the way they do. They learn through taking responsibility in their doing rather than being controlled and told what to do.

Our generation have been a horrendous job of raising kids. We need to reconcile our generation with the next generation of our own children; they are the reason for the new beginning of the light era so that we do not raise another generation of self-absorbed and in bondage with the material desire. I see so many children feeling lost, unloved, and hopeless and need healing. As parents, we have been too wrapped up in our own problems losing sight and attention for our children who desperately need love and affection and care and support. For them, we must possess that passion to fulfil our mission to touch our children's hearts to enable growth with strength and passion within them. Value them so that they can value themselves, love them so that they feel the love even to be able to love them self and give them the security of safety and hope to live like angels.

Forgive our children who have no idea how to live to cope with the condition we are now in. We must nurture and honour our children with the mother's blessing and the security of hope for their future.

Our children need us to heal them and teach them how to love, how to give, how to share, and how to live a passionate life. Parents will learn more for by listening to their children and then able to give them the right attention, quality time, and involvement. Children in many ways learn whatever that suit who they are as unique people will seek out the adults who have life experiences they value who represent role models they respect, who can mentor them.

In this light era, Indigo children are being born with a more highly developed spiritual power than earlier generations. These beautiful children of the new age who are beginning to grace our planet with their special spiritual and talent presence shall come of age in the next century. They bring a special gift to the world a level of love and remembrance. Where there is love, sharing, and understanding, there will be harmony, peace, and happiness. If we recognised all these values, it will lead to establishing sharing and goodwill, which will induce cooperation and this is what the world need right now. The combination of the civilised and cultural and the inner spiritual way of life has to be recognized so that we can enter into the future new world community living system with an open mind and racial unity.

Equal education and jobs opportunities open to every human race. New world community living has to be accepted, appreciated, and become way of life. There must be appreciation given to people who seek to work under the light for better human and planetary conditions.

They are the new age generation of teachers for the planet, and they are our future. They are the future leaders if we allow them to help, they will lead us to the beautiful new world that awaits us. They are the rainbows bridging between what is today and what can be in the future based on the spirit of goodwill, intelligence, and understanding of the needs of humanity. Parenting children is becoming a much more significant role in the life of the world than in the past. This is because of the connection with a greater number of children born with essences capable of developing new forms of consciousness like the indigo and crystal children. They are much evolved beings of light who have come in joyful service to humanity.

Education for Children

$\mathcal{N}$early all so-called civilized people set to work to cram the minds of their children, at the first indication of any degree of intelligence, with a religious bias such as they themselves have inherited or have been taught. Then the intellect must be shaped, forced, and driven into accepted moulds, and the human being is considered ready to be turned out into the world to fight the battle which everyone, in one way or another, must fight all along the way of human life to begin to test the value of the ideas and principles with which the soul has been furnished to meet all the exigencies incident to the pilgrimage from birth to the final exit from this state of being. It has taken uncounted ages to produce the perfected types of physical humanity we see on earth today.

Thousands of children, too young to choose for themselves, are being fettered in spirit by the chains of old, effete superstitions; their intellects are being stultified by the absorption of narrowing creeds and vulgarising ideas of God and his universe. There are numbers of spiritualists and 'liberal' men and women who expose the tender minds of their children to these same influences for society's sake, knowing though they do, from hard experience, what an effort it costs to free the mind of such serious bias and re-educate it aright. The noblest teaching is that which puts us in relationship with our own inner, unspoken, and unrecognised perceptions. No truth, however, manifested can adjust itself to our soul's needs, save as it finds in us a response through that preparation which comes from a certain degree of previous knowledge.

Many children, too young to choose for themselves, are being restrained in their intellect and spirit by the chains of old superstitions. It is the parents' responsibility to nurture new life that they bring into the world. It is the parent's duty how they act as role model to expose their attitude to the tender minds of their children. The noblest teaching is that which puts us in relationship with our own inner true self, unrealized, unrecognized perceptions, which can be revealed through the freedom of self-quest for truth.

Women

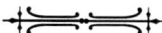

*R*ise up, you women who are at ease; hear my voice, you careless daughters; give ear to my speech' (Isa. 32: 9). 'But sanctify, Christ as Lord in your hearts, and always be ready to give an answer to everyone who asks the reason for the hope that is in you, with gentleness and reverence' (1 Pet. 3: 15). The one who pleases God gets knowledge and wisdom.

When we speak the truth, the truth sets us free to take up the torch to speak and deliver and share the freedom of choice. Threatening people into obedience is not practicing freedom of choice. When a girl is taught from the cradle to be a pleural wife, they are being conditioned to a humble and quietly acceptance. In some cases, women and children are by-products of physical, emotional, and sexual abuse and suffer in silence and despair. We all have a moral obligation to speak out against this. Woman and children have lost their voice suffering and pain they go through.

'For it is better, if it is the will of God, that you suffer for doing good than for doing evil' (1 Pet. 3: 17).

Lifting the veil of deception is eminent because God is challenging us today to rise up especially those who have lost their voice. Women bound in polygamy must leave the place of defilement to restore her own empowerment and by the power of God. 'Woman, we can do it let's rise up together and speak up and be a part of that army to set women free.'

From the slavery of all the past, the redemption of woman is well underway and it is indeed a glorious sign.

In history, no lesson is plainer or more readily demonstrated than the fact that the degeneracy of a religion and the degradation of woman go hand in hand. 'For in this manner, in former times, the holy women who trusted in God adorned themselves, being in submission to their own husband' (1 Pet. 3: 5).

New Age Courage

Let it be the aim of every youth,
To lift this glorious banner as proof,
Soar upward to a surpassing Excellency,
Let them seek to excel in all things high with glee.

Never let them stoop to do evil act,
Nor degrade themselves with their comrades,
Never be envious against evil men,
Neither desire to be with them.

Be just, loving, kind, and fear not.
Serve one another with what we've got,
Serve humanity when you can,
Because that is part of God's plan.

Let all the ends we aim be bright,
For our world thou shall unite,
Let it be the aim of every youth,
Thy God's and Truth's.

Will always be your proof
Whatever dims your sense of truth?
Or stains your purity
Count it as sin to thee.

(Joo Lian Carter)

Serving Humanity

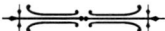

'Feed the flock of God that is among you, serving as an overseer, not by constraint, but willingly; not for filthy lucre [money], but readily' (1 Pet. 5: 6).

'Charge those who are rich in this world not to be high minded, nor to trust in uncertain riches, but in the living God who gives us richly all things to enjoy' (1 Tim. 6: 17-18).

'For who is greater, the one who sits at the table or the one who serves? Is it not the one who sits at the table? But I am among you as one who serves.' (Luke 22: 27).

Greatness consists in the desire to be of service, not for what we receive, but for what we give. Whatever gift or talent we have, we place it at the disposal of mankind to be used to help others and then we have nothing to fear because our divine blessing rest on our work effort and service to others. When we are motivated by our desire to serve others, we develop a caring, giving, sharing, and generous spirit.

As lives has been transformed, advancing all the time, our knowledge progress and ignorance has been chased away and light drives out the darkness, our willing hands, hearts, and minds set out to serve humanity to make our passage through it worthwhile, by helping souls, then we have not failed. The power of the spirit behind an individual can do a great deal because each one of us possesses the infallible monitor within his own being to his own thinking and behaviour; that is his conscience that tells him what is right or wrong. It is through the conscience and the urge of the spiritual needs that we fight the enemy who keeps the human spirit in subjections and keep the soul in bondage. We all have a right to live in freedom which is part of our divine heritage and spiritual growth. Being evolved, the soul shall find the richness of expression in this earth plane to qualify the spirit for the next life. Draw near to God to help us turn our hearts to Christ and embrace the cross in a deeper way.

The way that you have lived your life, determine the quality of your spirit. You are what you make yourself to be by your own conduct by your own actions, thoughts, and by the whole of your life that has moulded your character. When your spirit leaves your physical body, you take with you, your character that determines your eternal possessions of your spiritual qualities and are with those who are on the same spiritual altitude as yourself.

Serving humanity is a biological, social, and spiritual necessity, which improves our health, and it serves a more purposeful life. Serving humanity requires spiritual awareness, knowledge, responsibility, commitment, and selflessness. One has to change from a self-centred person to guide-centred in order to serve others. If we are to live the vision that we share and care in society, all of us must be willing to look into our hearts and rid our minds of the fear that keeps us separate. That is to open our hearts and mind to love. Each time we reach out for each other and compelled to help, that powerful act has profound healing effect. We must re-educate ourselves to the urgency of what we must do to save our souls. We must bring to life the joy of what it means to work for the good of the whole; that is, we must serve the community. Then we will be able to create a society that works for everyone. Then will we be able to make corrections of our past indulgence in materialism and crimes. Then we will understand that we cannot lose because there is no us or them. We must focus on the wholeness of life to increase our growth by doing the inner work to mature our spirits.

To make new world community living and serving humanity possible, perhaps if we desire and speak of it, think in international terms and plan for it, the future world will become possible. Serving humanity is not only a way of service, but also a way of self-development and self-transformation. Anyone who wishes to serve, being able to sacrifice is a necessity. To start with, daily sacrifice doing without things and allow others to get the better of us without a big inward change. People have to be committed in changing themselves to become competent with good will especially if we wish to serve in the world effectively to make a difference.

Unity demands the truth of the Word of God in the spirit. The united system is part of the team effort, teamwork, and team commitment that we all share to assist each other so that nothing is lacking. Engage in good deeds to achieve pressing needs to reap fruitful results. By our love, we know who we are to be fruitful so that lives are blessed; their lives will shine to each other in their faithful relationship. The key to right relationship and loving faithful friendship is our credibility built on our character. Leadership, truth, loyalty, unity, love, care, and response, the right way to each other are the qualities to make a difference in our lives in the community and the world.

Without imposing ourselves on people, we will have to be able to tolerate them completely and accepting them as they are. This is not easy and it requires skills, but we can be shown how to overcome our egos weaknesses and develop our knowledge and skill to become more effective in our action of service.

Especially now we have to understand one another even though we live always through different emotions, which has cause disharmony. It is not easy that we mutually find a way to feel emotions simultaneously then only we can understand one another. In the magical world of mutual understanding, lie the principal charms of love and unity.

There is only one way to succeed in the affairs of life and that is by raising oneself to greater usefulness and service. By doing things better than they have been done before, by bearing greater responsibility, you serve humanity better, and, therefore, merit success. When a person has an inner desire to serve, he requires a solid foundation that lasts, which is determined by the merit process and character, the competency with the skill that he believes in.

We must stay in the centre of the spirit of revelation with prayer, praise, and prophecy, instead of just wisdom. Live out of your Holy Spirit not just out of your natural mind. In every one of your mind are the seeds of life, and you speak it into other people's minds you fertilise them where they are going to bring forth new lives in the salvation. So it's time that we begin to let the Holy Spirit have its way in our lives and receive impartation by faith with greater consciousness. We are going to receive the Lord, who is going to ride in our own mind to motivate and to direct us where he wants us so that we can be victorious in our own will through the presence and message of God to guide us in our thoughts and feelings to unite us to his kingdom in spite of our differences.

The desire to serve God is to serve humanity. When you make yourself available and selfless, He will give you the desire of your heart. He will call you to work through you and give you the privilege of His authority to serve people. Jesus is the divine example on serving humanity faithfully with humility. God is waiting for a willing heart to serve Him. In order to serve Him, you have to serve humanity. 'If I then, your Lord and Master, have washed your feet; you also should wash one another's feet' (John 13: 14). Service is the core value of Christ, and he saves us to be servants. When you put others first to serve them, you glorify the Father with your good works to please Him. We are built to reach out to serve one another. The key to serve others is to make yourself available, have authority by serving under their direction, serve with humility, responsibility and able to give an account of the works you have faithfully done as we are faithful to God and serve with all our heart and glorify Him in Heaven.

Community Living

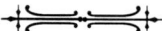

'*But* you are a chosen generation, a royal priesthood, a holy nation, a peculiar people; so that you may show forth the praises of him who has called you out of darkness into his marvellous light; the people of God; who had not obtained mercy but now have obtained mercy.' (1 Pet. 2: 9-10).

'Dearly beloved, I beg you as strangers and pilgrims abstain from fleshly lusts that war against the soul.' (1 Pet. 2: 11)

'And I say to you that you are Peter, and upon this rock I will build my church; and the gates of hell will not prevail against it. And I will give you the keys of the kingdom of heaven; and whatever you bind on earth will be bound in heaven; and whatever you loose on earth will be loosed in heaven.' (Matt. 16: 18-19).

Our purpose of being here is to evolve to live wisely with the free will and love that we inherited as creative beings to serve and to learn from each other and share our knowledge, wisdom, and creativities with compassion to make this world a better place like heaven on earth with more possibilities.

When the world goes through crises, the way of accustomed life has been threatened, people become unsettled and look for reassurance so that they can feel secure of a worthwhile life in the midst of what is happening. Today, we all hope the difficult period that we are living and perhaps the forecast that there will be some degree of destruction and devastation to this planet which will affect nature, therefore, affect lives. Maybe not, but there are reasons to believe that generally with increased population and whether changes will affect vegetation that we are entering a period of healthy food and water shortage. We may fool ourselves or continue to live in a dream world. We all have an obligation towards the healthy condition of the planet that is our Mother Nature.

Ecologically, human, animals, and vegetation depend on other forms to supply the energy it needs. As human beings, we also have to provide energy for higher forms of life. Consciously, we can all contribute our work efforts to increase and store these valuable energies.

Within a community, we need to learn and to encourage cooperation and share work in groups with high purpose to maintain the balance. The advantages of sharing work in groups have to be more effective because each individual can contribute whatever skills, knowledge, and creativity they can provide. We need to have individual consciousness as well as group consciousness with mutual support spiritually, mentally, and physically to achieve group common goal. It will also need the requirement of that harmony, higher energy spiritually, endurance, and strength mentally and physically with good will living in God's Word. We must bring to life the joy of what it means to work for the good of the whole; that is, we must serve God to serve the community. Then we will be able to create a society that works for everyone.

God's zeal is that his kingdom is to be established through Jesus Christ our Lord and blessed with peace, righteousness, and justice.

My desire in agreement with heaven is the desire for two thousand years since Jesus Christ was born to save us to have that ticket to enter the Kingdom of God. What this generation about to do is amazing that government, business, education, health, culture, society, lifestyle will progress in the direction of God's way and the holy practice living in harmony with one another. Also the breeding ground will be raised in the Word of God. We know a lot about grass roots because it's our nature we develop ourselves that way, but we don't know anything about top down. We don't have to know anything if you know your God, have faith in Him, then He will let you know what you need to know by giving it to you or show you the way to do things with conviction. We depend on God on all great things with answers and results because we are not that strong and powerful but some like to think they are. Our wisdom and knowledge come from the reality of truth and all we have to do is trust in God.

'Trust in the Lord with all thine heart; and not unto thine own understanding. In all thy ways acknowledge him, and he shall direct thy paths' (Prov. 3: 5-6).

Spiritually mature people who can see differently in a bigger picture willing to rise up in humanity to be tomorrow's quality people who can take leadership into their hands to move forward the contract in God's plan. We don't really know what he wants yet, but as he reveals bit by bit it is probably it will make it more achievable for us with faith, hope, believe, strength, knowledge, and wisdom. We must be able to connect what God wants not what we want to create heaven on earth leading to His Kingdom. 'Thy Kingdom come thy will be done as it is in heaven.'

In heaven, there is one God in the name of the Lord Jesus Christ, and we are oneness perfect form or condition. No sickness, no divorce, no hunger, no poverty, joyful and abundant life, compassion, kindness, everything is in harmony, and peace. 'You will keep Him in perfect peace, whose mind is stayed on you, because he trusts in you' (Isa. 26: 3).

Prosperity and Success

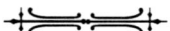

*B*ut as for you, the anointing (the sacred appointment, the unction) which you received from Him abides (permanently) in you; so then you have no need that anyone should instruct you' (1 John 2: 27).

Most people go on through life trying to make ends meet, seeking for success, wanting to be rich and famous, yet not realizing their purpose and goals in life here and after. In order to have a successful smooth journey, they need to have purposeful plan to their destination. They seek earthly success to live and evolve, which is temporary but it is wise to also seek for spiritual maturity for eternal life.

There are several keys that can help you to open doors to success.

1. Choosing the right goal and with purpose and stay in focus throughout the journey to your goal.
2. Obtaining the right education to become knowledgeable or specialized in the field of your goal to apply and function in the right direction.
3. Maintaining good health and self-awareness to give you strength and stability physically, mentally and spiritually to sustain you in your task as you progress in your journey. Good physical health is not just eating the right food but also require regular exercise, sufficient sleep, plenty of fresh air, cleanliness and proper elimination. Mental health requires positive or right thinking and clean living and right attitude. Spiritual health requires quite valuable time to reflect and connect to your potential self by meditating on the word of God to guide you in your life and to mature your spirit for your next life. Most people still cannot live a fulfilled life no matter how successful or how much they posses because they leave God out of the equation.

4. The results of your success depend on your work and effort, which require your passion, resourcefulness to overcome obstacles and persevere to completion to attain your goal.

5. The most important and everlasting success is through God's plan. We are all natural human being and sometimes we cannot perform task that are supernatural unless you are spiritual and allow God to work through you, by his Holy Spirit power of spiritual wisdom to accomplish your God-given destiny at His will and word. 'If any of you lacks wisdom, let him ask God who gives to all men liberally and does not criticize, and it will be given to him' (James 1: 5).

Angelic Living

'*Are* they not all ministering spirits, sent forth to minister to those who will be heirs of salvation?' (Heb. 1: 14).

'Neither can they die anymore, for they are like the angels. And they are the children of God, since they are the children of the resurrection' (Luke 20: 36). 'And it shall come to pass afterward, that I will pour out my spirit upon all mankind; and your sons and your daughters shall prophesy, your old men shall dream dreams, your young men shall see visions' (Joel 2: 28).

During the course of writing this book in May 2010, I encountered spiritual realm while praying and feeling the presence of God, I heard the message 'Angelic Living' three times, then I looked up and I saw a being of exceptional importance and dignity in every look and movements head three quarter looking at me surrounded by bright lights. This has inspired me to research into angels and started to write about angelic living.

And he said to him, 'Truly, truly, I say to you that in the future you shall see heaven open, and the angels of God ascending and descending upon the Son of man' (John 1: 51).

As I am drifting more and more into the energy current of mind and spirit, my consciousness develop a personal spiritual connection with God. I believe in the reality of the afterlife and angels. If we ask for help at time of despair, the guardian angels can come to our aid. Some of us believe that there are angels watching over us and as spirit of love, they come to our aid when we need protection from danger. We all have our own psychic support system, our spirits, and our personal guardian angels that protect us. We are intimately connected with our guardian angel that watch, nurture, and guide us from birth till our pass over. Having confidential connection with our guardian angel is very personal and private, so we can relax and accept their presence and appreciate them as our spirit helpers with the power to keep us nurtured and safe. If our hearts are more open and spirits are strong, the chances of consciously connecting and interacting with our angels are far greater. We can talk to our guardian angels and ask for help directly they are always there to listen and act as our constant companions, messenger from God and eternal bodyguards. Share our joy in accomplishment with our guardian angels and don't' forget to thank them for their assistance.

To live like angels, we have to raise our light beings to a higher and finer frequency of light bathe in our spiritual realm. That is aim for the light of the soul into our lives on earth. To do this, we have to abide to the spiritual laws, and as you progress in your spiritual life and consciousness reaching the cosmic consciousness, we are in the process of reaching a higher vibration that enables us to better understanding towards reality. This then affects your biological system so that you can bring forward higher consciousness, knowledge, wisdom, and spiritual gifts from the spiritual realm of God's nature.

In the invisible world of reality and with God, all things are possible and unlimited. We all have an opportunity for developing higher energy vibration for ascension. When we receive Jesus into our lives, we will be like him and live like Him. Jesus said, 'He that has my command, and does them, he that loves me, the Father will love him and I will manifest myself to him' (John 14: 21).

'For the Son of man will come in the glory of his Father with his angels; and then he will reward every man according to his works. There are some standing here, who shall not taste death, until they see the Son of man coming in his kingdom' (Matt. 16: 27).

Angels

*A*rchangels are God's most powerful angelic force and important messengers in the celestial realm. At any time, we can invoke them for extra help. There are different archangels that are in charge of different aspects of guardianship and protection.

Archangel Michael fights against Satan and rescues the souls of the faithful and brings mankind souls to judgment.

Associated with the fire element, colour is red and his symbol is a fiery sword, the defender of the faith. His divine qualities are protection, faith, will of God perfection, power, and omnipotence of God. He gives service to life in response to our free will call and decrees, protects our consciousness and strengthens our faith, spiritual gift of freedom from doubt and fear and inspiration to leaders.

When we need strength, confidence, self-esteem, courage, protection, and power, we call for Michael, who is regarded as one of the chief archangels, and he is heaven's greatest defender and mightiest warrior against evil.

Light vibration is blue.

Archangel Gabriel rules over the tree of life also known as Angel of the annunciation and of resurrection. Associated with the water element and the colour is sea green. Gabriel is the angel of incarnation, of conception, and birth and of dreams. Gabriel instructs souls for nine months before reincarnation.

Gabriel gives revelation of your life plan and purpose, guidance in your spiritual life, releases joy, happiness, and fulfilment, and helps to establish discipline and order in your life.

Light vibration is white.

Archangel Uriel is a multitasked angel and he is known as angel of repentance, music, poetry, and angel of prophesies. Uriel is associated with the earth element and the colours are white and gold. Uriel also assists in communicating with nature, with material, and earthly matters.

Light vibration is purple and gold.

Archangel Raphael is in charge of healing, science, and knowledge and known to be charming and fun loving. Associated with the air element and the colours are sky blue and gold. He assists in healing of body, mind, soul and spirit. Light vibration is emerald—green.

Raquel is in charge of law and order.

As you would notice, all the archangels' name end with 'el', which means 'Shining Beings' in Hebrew.

Orbs are angels they will lead us and show us what to do for our purpose. They help you in spiritual things to fulfil your mission. All the colours have spiritual meaning. In the future, angels are going to tell you what to do before you go to places and then you will do it. Angels come because of the praise to do miracles and for your purpose they have no testimonies in heaven. (Heb. 1: 6)

Green orbs awesome teacher.

Blue orbs bringing revelation.

Red orbs means get ready for salvation.

Purple orbs get ready for holy experience.

Black is the colour of the bride.

We are born again with white light.

The white light within a righteous person is the Holy Spirit, and there is no darkness, but an inner glowing, like a sun shining out of his body and radiate out of glory and when that falls over people, they will be healed. Demonic realm cannot stand that white light in you because the white light means totally righteous people. The righteous people of God have got an authority that is beyond your own imagination. If you're conscious of your spirit that it be clean, God can give you the works of life and a foundation being lead in the church of morality. Everything is build on morality, but God is holy and he says be thou holy because I am holy be righteous because God looks after the righteous, and its time you begin to ask and can make the difference. God is not going to destroy a righteous nation, he may shake it to wake the idols up to worship Him.

We need the praise, and the praise raise prophecy. Praise, prayer, and prophecy bring in the kingdom. This is the year the kingdom is coming out of you and you need to be in the move into the kingdom that is within this is what you are speaking from within you bring it and proclaim it. Pray for the gift of the discernment and the feeling of the peace of God from all your senses. When we are spiritually mature and are faithful, we believe and receive the Holy Spirit to be in union with God.

Angelic living is a rite of passage for love and light seekers, and seeking to be sanctified. People who receive this alignment have been guided to it at a critical turning point in their personal spiritual growth. Have you ever caught yourself getting the same unhappy results, time after time, in different situations? Things start out great, but somewhere along the way, it falls apart? Then start to understand and seek knowledge of truth from God's grace.

Angels are the extensions of the divine; they represent all that is good, truth, beauty, love, and light. Within each person, there are the angels from the divine to serve you. It is important that you are attuned with the angels who can help in a dimensions that you have not being able to conceive and in turn can express your own loving and creative higher self to express your truth as you were originally created and meant to be.

Angels in disguise to me is angelic living, it is to live life providing act of service to others when they most need help. Invoking the divine by praying for someone is the purest and invisible act of power.

Angelic Healing

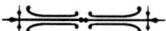

For seeking angelic and spirit guided healing, we have to bear in mind, that they are not substitute for seeking professional medical, psychological, and emotional care when we need it.

The Archangel Raphael looks after our energy level, body, mind, and spirit.

When our energy becomes imbalanced, we become unwell, we then invoke Raphael to heal and reenergise us. Speak to our hearts, not our ego that will make us feel peaceful, self-accepting and self-loving. Especially when we are lacking of faith and feeling disconnected and imbalanced from our loving divine can become a struggle to be healed. To overcome that, we can ask our healer angels by opening our hearts to quieten our minds and raise our vibration, then healing can occur. All illnesses are lessons and experience personally and those around us.

Spirit Guides

The highest purpose of our healer guides is to restore our self-awareness and self-esteem and accept the love and blessing from God. Opening our hearts and mind to our self-worth is the best healing of all. Next is prayer to our guardian angels and Holy Spirit to which they respond promptly. We must open our hearts, find love and compassion for ourselves, and be willing to be healed. Then with cooperation the healers will do their utmost to heal us. 'God help those who help themselves'. Your angels and spirit guides will lead you in the right direction to be healed.

My experience with choosing books to read is a fine example of guidance from the Holy Spirit guides. I believe that if a book is recommended to me or revealed to me when I am searching for a book to read usually the book is very inspiring, therapeutic, and exactly what I was looking for. These spirit guides are overseen by the healing angels. Together they guided me to the mirror to see what I have become and led me to focus on my neck. To my awareness, I was directed to feel round my neck incidentally, I discovered a lump in my right neck. I was then diagnosed of hypothyroidism causing the colloid goitre. I was advised to have the lump remove surgically by my consultant. Through the cause of making the decision whether to have the lump removed surgically, I decided that my faith in the loving divine through gods will is stronger than submitting myself to the surgeon. Life with faith lifted me to deal with my struggle and connected me to my loving divine and the healing forces of the universe. So I was healed and the lump disappeared without surgical intervention.

Divine Health and Wealth Require Discipline

*S*cience backs up the principle of Word of God. We have been created in the image of God through God in me, and all things are possible. The Holy Spirit will help you to accomplish your goal.

Read the Word of God and pray every day. Allow God to build your faith.

Talk to God every day, then you become the person He wants you to be.

Diet

People choose to live the lifestyle they desire, but current social and environmental influences have a lot of effect on our health and quality of life. We are what we feed into our bodies, so our health and wealth depends on knowing who we are, what we need, and not what we want.

The basic is we are all made of spirits in our own body. What we do and what we eat affects the body and the soul. Intake of high calories in our body leads to overweight and, therefore, affect our health and self-esteem affecting our souls.

The food we eat feeds and nourishes our body to satisfy our souls to house our spirit.

The Word of God feeds our soul so that we maintain that power to feed our spirit and body in a supernatural way and see a profound change in life.

As we prosper, even as our soul prosper (John 3: 2).

God have created a kaleidoscope of food and also instructed us how to live long, disease-free, cancer-free, lives by observing certain habits, and lifestyles. If you do what I say and obey me, I will not bring all these disease upon you. Every word of God is important for edification, for correction, how to live our lives.

We have all moved a long way off from these instructions. This is reflected in the fact that despite amazing advances in the standard of living, we are still affected by the diet and lifestyle choices we make. In this twenty-first century, even though we have all the modern technology, we are still a victim of the ten top killer diseases which are due to 99.9 per cent of our diet and lifestyle. Stroke, diet, stress, smoking, alcohol, and infection can be minimized by hygiene, rich in omega 3 like pumpkin seeds antioxidant diet. This is reflected in the fact that despite amazing advances in modern medicine, the top ten killer diseases are still due to diet.

Prevention

Heart diseases can be prevented by cutting down on high-cholesterol diet. Live a life with healthy food, controlling weight, and exercising.

Reducing stress can improve blood pressure and reduce incidence of stroke. Give up smoking and passive smoking can prevent lung cancer.

Chronic Obstructive Pulmonary Disease is caused by smoking and unhealthy environment.

Influenza/pneumonia can be prevented by being vaccinated and can be minimised by protection and stop the spread of the infection.

A diet of sunflower seeds rich in omega 3 and 6 can prevent prostate cancer. Eating high in fibre diet can prevent colon cancer.

Preventing exposure to radiations can prevent lymph cancer.

The prevention of Alzheimer's/dementia is to have a diet of rich in antioxidant, blueberries, nuts, and seeds and fish oils.

Aortic aneurysm is weakness of the main blood arteries. The cause of aortic aneurysm is not known. However, the risk factors can be reduced by eating healthy wholesome food, whole grains, vegetables, and fruits and avoid eating food high in saturated fat. Maintain a healthy weight; seek treatment for high blood pressure and infection.

'Every moving thing that lives shall be food for you; I have given you all things, even as I gave you the green plants. But you shall not eat flesh with its lifeblood, with the blood still in it' (Gen. 9: 3-4). No mushroom or contaminated blood containing germs, bacteria, and viruses, undercooked meat or rare when eaten, puts the eater at risk. Blood-borne diseases are not recommended; due to the life in the flesh is in the blood as our digestive enzymes do not kill all germs. Yes, to wholesome food like herbs, greens, seeds, fruits, and nuts. A cell can reproduce itself before dying. Post Noah period: those born after the flood had a much-reduced life span, tailing off with each subsequent generation. We will feed on the Word of God and stay healthy to live a long life.

Healing Power of Food

Our body is designed to stay alkaline and when we consume acidic foods and drinks, stop exercising and continually have negative emotions our body is overloaded with acids, and this cause extensive disruption to the function of the body. The pH balance, alkaline and acid in our tissues and blood affects our health. Therefore, it is important to maintain the pH balance through our diet, body weight, and emotions and have the knowledge and understanding how to keep it at the proper pH balance for an alkaline lifestyle. Alkaline diet energises and vitalises our well-being. To become alkaline, we simply need to start focusing 80 per cent of our diet on the alkaline foods and try to limit acid foods. Drink plenty of quality clean purified water and refrain from excessive alcohol. Avoid eating sugar because it affect the pH of the blood and cause damage to the body.

I believe alkaline food can be a diet that energises your life to change your inner world. It is important to listen to your body in order to understand your needs to make wise choices to attain wholeness. You have to realise that your emotions can also be a predisposing factor for ill health and diseases. Bad emotions like guilt, stress, deprivation, and all other negative emotions can cause acidifying to the blood than diet. When on an alkaline diet, you can still be social and still have treats; you should and enjoy naughty food without feeling guilty and still enjoyed life. Life is about enjoyment and moderation in both directions is essential to make you feel vibrant.

The power of food can keep you stay healthy and conquer disease. Food is the biological need of every human being. Sometime healing through food comes at a critical time. I was going through a very emotionally trying time, consequently lost a lot of weight. I essentially eat very small amount each time, consequently lost a lot of weight but as long as I was eating the type of food for thoughts, minerals, three portion of fresh fruits, or vegetables a day, to stay healthy. Food not only nourishes your body it also nurtures the spirit while feeding the body.

To offer someone a home-cooked meal is always very welcoming which is a gesture to show that you care and to express the creativity, love and joy it can produce in home cooking. The appreciation from people enjoying the food can be deeply satisfying and nourishing for the body and soul. It lets people know you care. When we cook with love, care, and attention for someone, your care can be a genuine act of healing as well as act of love and service to ourselves and others. Because we are made of the same spiritual light energy, and we are meant to take care and help each other for our physical and spiritual survival depend on one another.

Learn to develop the habit of eating the orangest, greenest, dark purplish food, and all kinds of vegetables, and fruits may prevent you from cancer. Fruits or vegetables rich in carotenoids, including beta carotene and green tea is critical after you give up smoking which may help to prevent lung cancer. Food rich in carotenoids such as beta carotene are tomatoes, broccoli, carrots, squash papaya, pumpkin, sweet potatoes, mango, Brussels sprouts, apricot, peaches, spinach, kale, cantaloupe, and more exotic fruits and vegetables.

One of the exotic super fruit is mangosteen.

What is mangosteen? In 2002, a powerhouse botanical was found to have over forty xanthones offering therapeutic value this fruit stand in its own class of antioxidants. Xanthones can be found in trace amounts in certain vegetables and fruits; however, the pericarp of the super fruit mangosteen is the premier source where these nutrients are found in concentrated amounts.

The Tree of Life

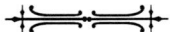

*W*here I live, I am surrounded, nourished, and protected by coconuts and my home-grown fresh organic food. A coconut a day not only keeps my doctor away but could slash my risk of coronary heart diseases by a large percentage.

Just take for example the coconut tree is called 'The Tree Of Life'.

The coconut tree provides food, shelter, fuel, medicine name it, the coconut has it.

Coconut meat can provide coco flour, desiccated coconut, coconut milk, coconut chips, candies, shredded coconut meat, lactic copra, and animal feeds.

No oil can compare with Virgin Coconut Oil (VCO) which provides prevention and cure a wide range of diseases. Virgin coconut oil provides energy quickly and last for many hours. It does not cause obesity instead it reduces obesity. The medium chain fats even though they are saturated, are especially different from the other fatty acids. They have the lowest caloric value gram to gram but still provide the highest energy expedition. Medium chain fatty acids circulate as fatty acids, not as triglycerides, and they are not deposited in the fat depots. It also has a thermogenic effect which raises the body metabolic rate, which induces satiety and makes one stop over eating.

VCO improves digestion and nutrients absorption as well as regulates bowel movements. It boosts immunity to cancer and also an anti-inflammatory in autoimmune and inflammatory disease. It is effective against skin diseases when topically applied and also moisturises the skin relieving itching and chafing. It kills lipid-coated virus, gram-positive organism, fungi, yeasts, and a few protozoa. It is resistant to oxidation and has the longest shelf life of all oils. VCO is the only treatment so far that has shown dramatic effect in reopening the clogged ducts in various internal organs as well as skin and mucus membranes in Sjogren's syndrome sufferers. The pathology is lymphocytic cellular infiltration of tissues. When the sweat, tear, salivary, lachrymal ducts, and mucus glands are blocked, tears, sweat, saliva, and mucus cannot pass through.

Prevention of Kidney Stones

Vegetarians are less likely to have kidney stones than meat eaters. Vegetarian also eat twice as much fibre and excrete less calcium. Cut down on sodium and high protein reduces the amount of calcium in the urine. Eating oxalate-rich like protein foods may help boost urinary oxalate, which can combine with calcium to form stones.

Bukolysis is a medical process of reducing or dissolving urinary stones of the urinary tract system using buko water from seven to nine months old coconuts.

Everything in the universe is made of Chi (energy, information, frequency, and vibration). Quantum medicine and energy healing consciousness is alive in nature and in whole foods. Quantum medicine and energy healing shows up in abundance in many foods and here is another whole food worthy of mentioning.

Hope and Wisdom

Your hope and future depends on your faith,
Change your life and it is not too late,
Trust in the Lord with all your heart,
Because you have His plan to take part.

Fear the Lord and live his word.
Then your prayer will be heard.
It's time to let your light shine,
Before darkness make you blind.

Put your best foot forward,
And avoid acting like coward,
Acknowledge the Lord to keep you on track,
For a life with no regrets.

Wisdom is the key to truth,
The Word will show the proof.
From the physical dimension of the first, second,
and third,
We progress to the spiritual dimension above.

Understanding is the ability to conceptualize the truth,
Like a house built on sound rock with a transparent roof,
Spiritual understanding opens to super nature,
Oneness of truth the higher life of true nature.

By wisdom the Lord created the universe,
By understanding He established heaven for us.
Hope sets you free from the past.
We are saved by grace through faith and hope at last.

Joo Lian Carter

Wisdom

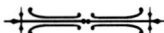

*W*isdom is the principal perception, and God is the source of wisdom. Spiritual wisdom is a God-given ability to understand and to perceive the truth and making decision to impart the will of God's reality through faith.

A natural man in his natural state cannot perceive supernatural wisdom, but a spiritual man in Christ can recognize and understand spiritual wisdom driven by the Holy Spirit.

Natural wisdom is the ability to make the right choice and decision through understanding and use knowledge of truth in a way that causes one to stand out and make a difference. When you embrace wisdom, it promotes you with honour and to have true success.

Wisdom is the principal thing, therefore pursue wisdom, and with all your pursuits, get understanding' (Prov. 4: 7).

How to Be Wise and Prosper?

The wisest thing to do is to diligently seek God's wisdom. He loves you and he wants you to have His wisdom to grow into perfection. 'If any of you lacks wisdom, let him ask God who gives to all men liberally and does not criticize, and it will be given to him' (James 1: 5).

The fear of the LORD is the beginning of knowledge, but fools despise wisdom and instruction' (Prov. 1: 7). When you fear God, it is a healthy respect and obedience for His authority and power to share His wisdom as a gift to you and in return you release that wisdom into your life to live righteously to please Him.

'Through wisdom a house is built [in your heart]; and by understanding it is established' (Prov. 24: 3).

Seek the truth, read the Bible, you will find the truth and the true knowledge and understanding, will make you wise so that you don't waste your life. Wisdom leads you to perfection

The Bible tells you the truth about yourself and tells you what you can be and learns how to be yourself in Christ.

A wise man always knows his truth, God, and the world.

A wise man seeks, finds, and knows God. To live for the future is wise and that depends on how you live wisely in your present.

The Bible shows you the truth about yourself, God, and the world.

'And if a person loves righteousness, her labours have great virtues; for she teaches moderation, and wisdom, and justice, and strength, which are such things as people and have nothing more profitable in life' (Ws. 8: 7).

It came a time when I found myself stranded in the valley of my life struggling and having to cope with life's challenges, made me realise my true purpose and my destiny that I turned to God in faith. The salvation of God's calling, His amazing Grace and love enables me to immerse in His presence in the name of Jesus. I brought myself into repentance and asked for forgiveness to receive Jesus into my heart, which I was born again, and walk with him in truth and in wisdom. My life was transformed; Jesus keeps my heart alive and gave me love, hope and wisdom to climb my mountain to reach the summit of my destiny. 'But by him you (who have matured]) are in Christ Jesus, who by God is made to us wisdom, and righteousness, and sanctification, and redemption' (1 Cor. 1: 30).

'And Jesus increased in wisdom and stature, and in favour with God and men' (Luke 2: 52).

Wisdom and favour can be increased through prayer, requesting for the knowledge of truth that come from God through Jesus. Wisdom is the principle focus in any prayer request. The more they are immersed in God, their wisdom increase, leading to increase righteousness, and then live in holiness and redemption. The words of wisdom through the Holy Spirit enable them to live wisely in truth and abundantly. 'If any of you lacks wisdom, let him ask God who gives to all men liberally and does not criticise, and it will be given to him' (James 1: 5).

People living ungodly; destroy their lives emotionally, physically, and spiritually. 'This wisdom does not descend from above, but is earthly, sensual, and devilish; for where envying and strife exist, there is confusion and every evil work' (James 3: 15-16).

'But the wisdom that is from above is first pure, then peaceable, gentle, and easy to be entreated, full of mercy and good fruits, without partiality, and without hypocrisy' (James 3: 17). They need to submit to fearing the Lord so that He can work through leading them to climb their own mountain righteously with His helping hands and strength, to sustain them to reach their summit of prestige and honour. Wisdom leads to righteousness and purity, which gives them the dominion to practice justice that brings balance and harmony to create peace to abolish bondage and oppression. 'Many shall be purified, and made white, and tried; but the wicked shall do wickedly. And none of the wicked shall understand, but the wise shall understand' (Dan. 12: 10).

Wisdom and maturity are related to each other. Wisdom is the application of knowledge or truth we learn from God's Word. Wisdom plays an important part in our lives of the revelation we have about God. 'Do not work to be rich; cease from your own wisdom' (Prov. 23: 4). 'That you might walk worthy of the Lord, pleasing in all things, being fruitful in every good work, and increasing in the knowledge of God' (Col. 1: 90). 'However we speak wisdom among those who are perfect; yet not the wisdom of this world, or of the rulers of this world who come to nothing' (1 Cor. 2: 6).

'I love those who love me; and those who seek me early and diligently shall find me. Riches and honour are with me; yes, durable riches and righteousness. My fruit is better than gold, yes, than fine gold; and my profit is better than choice silver. I lead in the way of righteousness, in the midst of the paths of judgment; that I may cause those who love me to inherit wealth; and I will fill their treasuries' (Prov. 17-21).

Hope and Future

'We are saved by hope' (Rom. 8: 24). 'Now the God of hope fill you with all joy and peace in believing, that you may abound in hope, through the power of the Holy Spirit' (Rom. 15: 13).

You can find hope in the Word of God by putting Him first and begin to shift from hopelessness into faith, allowing God to work through us and activate the principles that He has provided us in His word. The harvest is white, but there are not enough workers.

'Do you not say that there are still four months to go and then the harvest comes? Look, I say to you, lift up your eyes and look at the fields, for they are already white for harvest' (John 4: 35).

'Wake up and be watchful, and strengthen the things that remain, which are ready to die.' 'For I have not found your works perfect before God' (Rev. 3: 2). Faith and obedience to the truth purify your heart and soul. We must not hide our true self or spirit in our flesh, unveil, and reveal in the Holy Spirit of Jesus to shine from your heart.

Most of us are continuously facing trying times, living in an unpredictable hopeless world. In order to function in our lives, now is the time to fill our future with renewed spirit, soul, and body, we must expand our vision with living hope to fill us with spiritual strength, positive anticipation, and expectation. We have to be in an attitude of hope so we could continue to grow spiritually. We have no future if we aren't growing spiritually. 'But grow in grace and in the knowledge of our Lord and Savoir Jesus Christ. To him be glory both now and forever. Amen.' (2 Pet. 3: 18)

Striving to perfect ourselves in an imperfect world of corruption, disruption, uncertainty, and disharmony is a hopeless battle. Unless we trust God to intervene in our lives to save us with spiritual strength, courage, and hope, it is impossible to solve these hopeless situations as mortal beings. Jesus Christ is our living Hope and his return is our eternal future. Those who are sanctified, holy, and loyal to God, will be transcended as children into the Father's family. To understand the concept of it all, you are required to be spiritually aware to conceive this life's transcendent process and by your faith, the substance of things hoped for, through Jesus and the Holy Spirit to lead you to this potential spiritual transformation.

On the long-term economic solution, we have to really think about changing the system of capitalism, which does not work anymore. The constant effort to accumulate wealth, maximize profits is really the true political economic crisis in too many wars. This movement is causing many people to think in that direction that the system of capitalism does not bring hope and peace. By focusing on resources to employ workers and organise their labour and effort, can be a potential outcome for confidence investors, employers, employees, and abolish corruption in order to stabilise the economy.

'And now, Lord, what do I wait for? My hope is in you' (Ps. 39: 7).

'For I know the thoughts that I think towards you,' says the Lord, 'thoughts of peace, and not of evil, to give you a hopeful future.' (Jer. 29: 11)

We are in the most profound chapter of our lives, but it is not doom and gloom. In fact, we are in an exciting and challenging transition, and there is a hope for a brighter future. 'For with God nothing is impossible' (Luke 1: 3). Take for example, I never thought it would be possible for me to produce this book because I walk with faith in God to lead me with his words and thoughts that inspired me from start to finish through endurance.

'The LORD is the portion of my inheritance and my cup; you maintain my lot' (Ps. 16: 5).

'If we do not deny our sins, he is faithful and just to forgive us our sins, and to cleanse us from all unrighteousness.' (1 John 1: 9)

Just ask God to forgive you because He is glorious, and His glory is rising and His light is shining on the people on earth.

He loves us unconditionally, and he is trustworthy, and I can have special intimate relationship even to tell him all my secrets because he listens and answers my prayers. He brightens our life and allows us to choose and learn to accomplish our purpose in life. He shows us the way with his word and leads us to His great plan and our destiny. He is merciful, gracious, generous, and kind and wants us to be joyful and perfect like Him and his son Jesus Christ. He just wants us to be like His holiness. 'We desire that every one of you show the same diligence in realizing the full assurance of hope to the end; So that you are not slothful but followers of those who through faith and patience inherit the promises of God' (Heb. 6: 11-12).

In favour, He gives us the power to rise to come to past divine favour which we cannot physically accomplish.

'Blessed are the God and Father of our Lord Jesus Christ, who according to his abundant mercy has given us new birth into a lively hope by the resurrection of Jesus Christ from the dead' (1 Pet. 1: 3).

Every day, we feed our body with food, but do not forget to feed our spirit with God's words in order to maintain our spirit, soul, and body into balance through the word of God that he has provided us in the Holy Bible. Learn how to put on our spiritual coat to receive the Holy Spirit that God pours into our lives and soak in His grace to give us the strength that we need the thoughts to lead us and sustain us with His blessings. 'I am the gate. If any man enters in through me, he shall be saved, and shall go in and out, and find pasture. I have come that they might have life and that they might have it more abundantly' (John 10: 9-10).

'Seek and communion with God is giving Him attention with trust and respect in receiving from him to meet your needs that makes life victorious. I sought the LORD, and he heard me, and delivered me from all my fears' (Ps. 34: 4). 'Trust in the LORD with all your heart; and do not depend on your own understanding; in all your ways acknowledge him, and he shall direct your paths' (Prov. 3: 5-6). If you want to walk on a shining path, give attention to the Word of God that leads you to his master plan. Anybody can do it; it's your choice you make. We need to reap the harvest of favour from Him by knowing how to sow love and when to reap the harvest and what we can offer relevantly to ourselves and to the communities of the world, the peace and freedom to stay in harmony and prosper. God will supernaturally supply our needs, ask boldly with faith like the heart of a lion that shine with courage, it is God that gives you the power to prosper.

Learn how to be significant in our prayer to have that sacred relationship with God and Jesus Christ to create that unity and diversity of our life within through our heart and the renewing of our mind to be born again that is where the Holy Spirit lives in you, is more powerful than the spirit of the world. Worshiping in faith and holiness is by knowing who we are and where we belong, to live for a purpose to serve God's Glory in the name of Jesus Christ. The presence of God is most powerful, where we relax in Him to feel love and peace. Hold out your candle and light up the darkness for the lost to see and follow His light of salvation. Our Father created us in His image and graciously gave us a free will to choose to love Him or not. Learning to yield in love is important to establish our true relationship. Money cannot buy love but makes the world go round creating roots of materialism and bondage. When you are facing financial storm, it can affect your life significantly in your living and relationship. Perhaps prayer can help you because God will answer your prayer in His ways to change your life to prosper in many ways. 'Hope does not disappoint us, because God has poured out his love into our hearts by the holy Spirit, whom He has given us' (Rom. 5: 5).

Our sinful thoughts and attitude prevents us from true love, the ability to live and honour one another and God. God is calling us to make right choices to see things from a different perspective, in a realm of holiness, reality and eternity. We are now in the end time, and most of us are living in the now hopelessly with fear and some are living in the now in faith and hope for a brighter future. Which realm would you like to be in? It is our choice. We are judged by our works and efforts performed in respond from our thoughts and actions. Living unconditionally without calculation, but within reasons in righteousness is where healing and salvation begins. Then we can create heaven on earth living like angels. Heaven has a culture on the earth. The Lord is the King of Glory and Culture of Faith. 'He who follows after righteousness and mercy finds life, righteousness, and honour' (Prov. 21: 21).

Revelation is what it's doing right now in our generation. It is the calling for changing our minds to think in the vibration, in the frequency of heaven, and to a much higher, much deeper and much wider perspective change. It is so simple, and it can change education, it can change the government in society, and it can change anything we need change that can change. God actually is saying this is always going to be available since the beginning, but now He has risen up and culminates the mature people who want to inherit it to increase a government of peace.

'To the abundance of the princely rule and to peace there will be no end, upon his kingdom in order to establish it firmly and to sustain it by means of justice and by means of righteousness, from now on and to time indefinite. The very zeal of God of army will do this' (Isa. 9: 7).

God verses people on earth and his spirits filled communities all over the earth expressing and sharing the hearts of the gospel. My challenge to ask today is it that centre place in our hearts? Unquestionably, many of us have given as much as we can, but for further research, the Lord wants to waken us up again to expand to the priority that there should be more churches. Our reasons for existence are to work with God's plan so that we can be a one universal family in His kingdom. Each of us has a unique purpose that the Lord has plan for us so how do we conform to this Almighty plan? We have to obey His Word and live with reality and strengthen our faith in God.

Hope is confidence in our self. Hoping for material can be disappointing, but hope in God, He will not let you down or forsake you if you seek Him.

'So that the God of our Lord Jesus Christ, the Father of glory, may give to you the spirit of wisdom and revelation in the knowledge of him, by having the eyes of your understanding enlightened; so that you may know what is the hope of his calling, and what are the riches of the glory of his inheritance in the saints, (Eph. 1: 17-18). God has a unique plan for each and every one of us to accomplish His great plan. For God to hear us, cry out to Him, trust and confess to Him, then you will begin to feel His presence and understand the truth to fulfil your purpose in your life in wholeness. Together, we will be in oneness with God and Jesus Christ through our faith effort, living the Word of God, to give us supernatural freedom, supernatural peace, and harmony to prosper like heaven on earth. Maybe, if we feel that God has forgotten us, but how could He forget us because He cares for us, even when we don't care. He cares for our destinies, including hopes for us to accomplish His plan, promises and everlasting glory. All these, require supernatural strength and power to work both ways in the name of Jesus Christ. God allows us to go through things so that we can grow in our faith. 'Without faith it is impossible to please God' (Prov. 3: 7).

What glory? The kingdom of heaven is the glory you can enter when alive on the earth and then be there forever as a loyal, true Son of God.

'When Christ, Who is our life, appears [in your heart], then you also will appear with Him in glory' (Col. 3: 4).

'In a moment, in the twinkling of an eye, at the last trumpet; for the trumpet will sound, and the dead will be raised incorruptible, and we shall be changed' (Cor. 15: 5).

'But why do you call me, 'Lord, Lord,' and not do the things which I say?' (Luke 6: 4). Jesus said; 'Not everyone who says to me, 'Lord, Lord,' will enter into the kingdom of heaven; but [only] he who does the will of my Father who is in heaven' (Matt. 7: 21).

At the beginning, writing this book, God showed me the Bible and by the time I finished writing, he showed me the Ten Commandments and said, 'Push to the limit.' I know God is unlimited and to my knowledge, He meant do not give up. 'But he who endures to the end shall be saved' (Matt. 24: 13).

'For this is the love of God, that we keep His commandments. And His commandments are not burdensome' (1 John 5: 3). So you will genuinely love and honour God by living an obedient life based on following the way of the Ten Commandments, just as Jesus did, possessing true relationship with God is to walk with Him, to talk with Him, to really know and worship Him in spirit and truth. 'He who has my commands, and obeys them, it is he who loves me; and he who loves me shall be loved by my Father, and I will love him and will show myself to him' (John 14: 21). When a young man came to Him asking the way to eternal life, Jesus said, 'If you want to enter into life, keep the commandments' (Matt. 19: 16-18). Worship with obedience in spirit and in truth through Jesus, shapes your character to become like Him to please God, to see Him become more real in your life as you truly serve and obey Him. It is not about you; it is about how much God cares for your destiny and planned for your victorious life, to prepare you for when you encounter the time of insecurity and storms.

Live in the realm of responsibility and possibility, and don't run from your tough or suffering time. God will use you to come out with a purpose to live; he will equip you with a vision and the Holy Spirit to guide you through the process of total surrender to Him and Jesus takes you to the limit. 'Through the spirit, a person grows in grace, and in the knowledge of our Lord and Saviour Jesus Christ' (2 Pet. 3: 18). Jesus said; 'man does not live by bread only, but man lives on by every word that proceeds out of the mouth of the Lord' (Luke 4: 4). Living holy involves constantly meditating on the Word of God and always being in the spirit of prayer. 'We know that all things work together for good to those who love God, to those who are the called according to his purpose' (Rom. 8: 28). When you are responsible with the ability, God will extend His responsibility to you. Know your God and your strength and have positive faith in Him, He will develop and prepare you for eternal life through His spirit working within you. If God is for us, who can be against us? (Rom. 8: 31).

He is your invisible army to conquer your problems to attain your goal. This is the time for the courageous to get up and rise to inspire. It is time to create that outer limit vision for you and for the nations. Those who have vision will reach the summit of your own mountain, the best position to view the true value of the purpose, the inheritance that you have been seeking that you are destined to reign in the name of Jesus Christ.

'You have made him (mankind) a little lower than the angels; you have crowned him with glory and honor and set him over the works of your hands; and put everything in subjection under his feet' (Heb. 2: 7-8). All things are possible with God and He gave mankind authority over the earth. You must be trained and progress in godly qualities, live understanding your transcending spirit, and inherit eternal life, sanctified through Jesus, abiding and trust in God's Word and his magnificent plan that he promised to share and give us greater dominion over the universe for our future. Living like angels and have dominions over everything.

'Fear God and keep his commandments for this are the whole duty of man, For God shall bring every work into judgment, with every secret thing, whether it is good, or whether it is evil' (Eccles. 12: 13-14).

'Heaven and earth shall pass away; but God's words shall not pass away' (Mark 13: 31).

'In that day you will know that I am in my Father and you are in me, and I am in you' (John 14: 20).

'For this is the love of God, that we keep His commandments. And His commandments are not burdensome' (1 John 5: 3).

Jesus is the perfect example; therefore, he said that the way was obedience to the law of God the father and surrender to His will. On the last day of Jesus's physical life, he said to love one another as he has loved us, was simply an expression of love. Jesus Christ is the same yesterday, today, and forever.

It's all about 'JESUS CHRIST' lived as man on earth to show us what we can be and brought:
Justice
Eternity
Spirituality
Unity
Sanctification

Cross
Holiness
Revelation
Intercession
Salvation
Transformation

Justice: Jesus came and strengthened the law to bring justice and grace by showing us the way and the word to the Father's Kingdom. His warning, teaching and promises are the Father's expression on love towards us. He died on the cross that we are justified by his blood to redeem our sins 'But so that the world may know that I love the Father, I only do exactly as the Father has instructed me to do' (John 14: 31).

'And when Jesus comes, he will prove the world wrong [reprove all men] concerning sin, and righteousness, and judgment' (John 16: 8).

Every mankind will be judged on his faith, works, and word. When at judgment, the words we heard and ignored will be remembered, and those same words will judge us.

Eternity: The most important thing in the world is the destiny of your soul for all eternity, but as mortal beings, we cannot accomplish that without the gift of the Holy Spirit from God through Jesus. 'For you have given him power over all flesh, that he should give eternal life to as many as you have given him, and this is eternal life that they might know you the only true God, and Jesus Christ, whom you have sent' (John 17:

2-3). The good news that Jesus announced to all was the availability of God's heart and soul purifying grace to free us from bondage of sin and enter the kingdom of heaven while on earth and eternity, becoming a new man, in union with God and Christ. Jesus said. 'Let not your heart be troubled; you trust in God, trust in me also. In my Father's house are many mansions, and if I go and prepare a place for you, I will come again, and take you to myself; so that where I am, there you may be also' (John 14: 1-3).

Spirituality: God is Spirit, therefore, we need to be spiritual to connect and understand His will to live a fruitful life like a living branch. The words that Jesus spoke are spirit and they are life giving. The spirit of grace both reveals your sins and then removes them, just like Jesus said, 'Repent,' and be healed. 'God is a Spirit and those who worship him must worship him in spirit and in truth' (John 4: 24). 'And you shall know the truth; the truth shall make you free' (John 8: 32).

Every believer in the face of the earth has spiritual authority. God's authority is never over people, Christ is our covenant to obey God's word. Jesus said, 'You are clean through the word that I have spoken to you.' 'It is the Spirit who gives life; the flesh profits nothing. The words that I speak to you are spirit, and they are life giving' (John 6: 63). His words that we hear him speak to us impart the life of God, engraft in our hearts. To acquire more of Jesus, you must receive the Holy Spirit. 'The Spirit of truth, which the world cannot accept, because it neither sees him, nor knows him, but you know him because he dwells with you [now], and shall be in you [soon]' (John 14: 17). 'However when the Spirit of truth comes, he will guide you into all truth. For he shall not speak of himself, but he shall only speak what he hears; and he will show you things to come' (John 16: 13).

The Holy Spirit and whom the Father will send in my name, will teach you all things, and bring all things to your remembrance—whatever I have said to you' (John 1: 26).

Unity: 'In that day you will know that I am in my Father, and you are in me, and I am in you' (John 14: 20). Then Jesus said to him, 'I am the way, the truth, and the life; no man comes to the Father, but by me.' (John 14: 6)

'Let not your heart be troubled; you trust in God, trust in me also. I will come again, and take you to myself; so that where I am, there you may be also' (John 14: 1-3). The only way to reconciliation with God is through obedience to the heart and purifying grace of Jesus who reveals all truth and the mysteries of God. Jesus is our light and the life of God to which we must be restored in the righteousness and holiness of God's image, Jesus Christ. 'And all things are from God, who has reconciled us to himself by Jesus Christ, and has given to us the ministry of reconciliation' (2 Cor. 5:18).

Sanctification: Jesus helps us to penetrate the mystery of his teachings. He inspires us to grasp the truth with his sanctifying gifts of wisdom, understanding, knowledge, piety, council, courage, and fear of the Lord. 'He who has my commands, and obeys them, it is he who loves me; and he who loves me shall be loved by my Father, and I will love him and will show myself to him.' (John 14: 21). Jesus prays for his disciples and those who believe in him that the Father protects them from evil and sanctifies them with the name of Jesus, by means of the truth that they may be one as the Father and Son is one that they may share His joy completely.

Cross: Jesus Christ was crucified and died on the cross for our sins. The Word of God portraits the cross and the message of the cross is God's way. The only way to understand the significance of the cross and to have faith in the cross is faith in Christ. Therefore, to benefit from the cross, pick up the cross and crucify your inward cross of self-denial. The cross is as an example to us of the obedience necessary to slay our selfish spirit so that we could be reconciled to God. Jesus said, 'I am the resurrection, and the life, he who believes in me, although he might die, yet he shall live' (John 11: 25). Jesus conquered death for our eternal life.

Holiness: In this present life, the end of sympathetic judgment is holiness and we are saved by grace through faith, the hope of being taught and led by the holiness of God, seeing Him, hearing Him, being delivered from sin, being cleansed, purified, perfected, brought to holiness, and then union with God, entering the kingdom through Jesus Christ. 'Having then been set free from sin, so now yield your body to the slavery of righteousness that results in holiness' (Rom. 6: 18-19). Therefore, it is wise to allow Christ into your life to guide you to become holy to please and to honour God in your actions, every word is of love, is totally virtuous and serves God by serving others with humility to attain everlasting joy and peace.

Revelation: Jesus Christ came to reveal and deliver the good news about God's purpose and his coming kingdom. God allowed Christ to reveal through John, the final vision of the future events. 'The revelation of Jesus Christ, which God gave to him to show to his servants things which must shortly come to pass' (Rev. 1: 1).

Intercession: Jesus is the intercessor for mankind to enter the Kingdom of God, and under the authority of his blood and the Word of God, he intercedes on behalf of born-again believer to receive protection from the Holy Spirit and the Word of God.

Salvation: Jesus is our Saviour, 'But now being made free from sin and having become slaves to God, you have the fruit of holiness, and at the end, everlasting life, for the wages of sin are death; but the gift of God is eternal life through Jesus Christ our Lord' (Rom. 6: 22-23).

Transformation: Christ is our transformer. The impact Jesus has in your life is transformational and transcendental. Jesus said, 'Truly, truly, I say to you that unless a man is born again, he cannot see the Kingdom of God' (John 3: 3).

'To Him is glory in the church by Christ Jesus to all generations, forever and ever' (Eph. 3: 21).

Jesus came and spoke to them, saying, 'All power is given to me in heaven and in earth. Therefore go and teach all nations, baptizing them in the name of the Father, and of the Son, and of the Holy Spirit; teaching them to observe all the things that I have commanded you; and behold, I am with you always, even to the end of the world.' Amen. (Matt. 28: 18-20).

Prayer

Father, thank you, for the victory that you have promised us, the spiritual weapon you have given us as your people. Help us to be on the offensive against the enemy and win the victory you have planned for us in Jesus name. Amen.

God Bless you.

Index

Lightning Source UK Ltd.
Milton Keynes UK
UKOW051453280812

198161UK00002B/3/P